UNIVERSITY OF WALES    BOARD OF CELTIC STUDIES

## SOCIAL SCIENCE MONOGRAPHS

*General Editor:* Harold Carter, Gregynog Professor of Human Geography,
University College of Wales, Aberystwyth

Number 8

# URBAN SOCIAL STRUCTURE

A Multivariate-Structural Analysis of
Cardiff and its Region

by

WAYNE K. D. DAVIES
Professor of Geography, University of Calgary

Cardiff
University of Wales Press
1983

261172

©UNIVERSITY OF WALES, 1983

**British Library Cataloguing in Publication Data**

Davies, Wayne K. D.
Urban social structure: a multivariate-structural analysis of Cardiff and
its region — (Social science monographs    ISSN 0307-0042; 8)
1. Sociology, Urban   2. Multivariate analysis
3. Social structure — Wales — Cardiff Region
I. Title
305'.09429'87      HN398.C/
ISBN 0-7083-0833-3

*Publication of this study has been made possible, in part, by a grant from the Endowment Fund of The University of Calgary.*

*Printed in Wales by South Western Printers Ltd., Caerffili, Mid Glamorgan*

For my mother

# CONTENTS

## LIST OF FIGURES

## LIST OF TABLES

# PREFACE

Social scientists differ from other investigators of the human scene because they attempt to produce precise, quantified statements of human patterns and relationships that are linked to theoretical structures. In the pursuit of such objectives social scientists have frequently adopted the methods and techniques of physical scientists. Inevitably, the application of these methods in the human context has led to criticism. One is the fact that the quantitative, theoretical approach tends to encourage the description of normative patterns. Another is that it does not identify causes but concentrates on observation and description. The consequence is that the approach rarely leads to the improvement of the human condition. In addition, it often ignores the symbolism and meaning of human life. Most exponents of the scientific approach readily accept these criticisms; they recognize they are only dealing with *part* of the human mosaic. Indeed, the complexity of society is such that it is inconceivable that it can be understood by means of a single approach — whether scientific or humanistic. Yet such a conclusion does not deny the utility of the scientific method; it merely recognizes that the scientific approach is only *one* of a series of alternative approaches to the pantheon of human knowledge, and *all* have their particular weaknesses.

Even if one accepts the presence of alternative approaches to the study of society three other damaging problems have to be faced by exponents of the social scientific approach. The first is the realization that its exponents find it difficult to manipulate or control their phenomena in the same way as physical scientists. Secondly, the number of variables to be dealt with is often impossibly large since social scientists do not have a set of variables comparable to those basic temperature, pressure, mass indicators of the physical scientist. Thirdly, the fact that social scientists are dealing with society as it is lived means that there are many other observers of the scene — producing a confusing, overlapping body of information on societal variations. In an attempt to avoid the worst consequences of these three problems researchers of a scientific persuasion have developed systematic approaches that are designed to integrate the results of individual studies by using synthesizing techniques that work directly on the multivariate reality of society. This means that the variations in society can be studied *in situ;* then the results can be integrated to produce generalizations about the character of society that are expressed in terms of theoretical ideas and empirical regularities. Among these synthesizing techniques the families of multivariate procedures known as factor analysis and cluster analysis have proved particularly useful. Not only do they deal simultaneously with many variables, so as to uncover the latent structure or patterns of variation in data sets, but they enable investigators to group phenomena into discrete and identifiable classes. These synthesizing approaches, therefore, complement the analytical methods more familiar to the physical scientist where individual indicators are usually manipulated in bivariate, or two variable situations. As yet the basic sources of variation in urban areas are not clearly understood so the use of bivariate methods alone can be quite limiting.

Hence, one of the useful features of the multivariate approaches has been to define the sources and patterns of variation.

In this study a set of synthesizing multivariate techniques are used within the context of the quantitative approach of the social scientist. In its search for the social differentiation of the case study areas at the urban and regional scale two basic objectives can be defined: one methodological, the other substantive.

**(a)** The methodological objective goes beyond the specifics of the case study. It develops a systematic approach for the investigation of the social differentiation of cities at the urban and regional scale. An important part of this objective is the attempt to establish the *context* and the *limits* of the quantitative methodology employed here. As a result Chapter 1 reviews the alternative approaches to the study of urban character and the history of ideas in the systematic study of social variation. Chapter 2 describes what is called here the Multivariate-Structural approach to urban social differentiation, in which the technical or multivariate stages in any investigation are complemented by the philosophical background represented by the structural approach. Problems associated with the structural approach adopted here (in particular the various meanings associated with the work 'structure') are identified in order to provide the limits for this method.

**(b)** The substantive objective is the application of this methodology to case studies of Welsh urban areas at two scales, an internal or intra-urban analysis of Cardiff and a city-regional study of Cardiff City-Region. These studies are designed to contribute to the general literature on urban social differentiation as well as to increase our understanding of urban differentiation in Wales. The particular problems to be dealt with in the studies, as well as the choice of areas and data, are reviewed in detail in Chapter 3. Here it is shown that the Welsh examples are used to test one of the most general assumptions of the literature on urban social differentiation, namely that there is a standard model of urban social structure in Western cities and city systems. Chapters 4 and 5 deal with the social structure and patterns of Cardiff and Cardiff City-Region respectively. Chapter 6 provides a conclusion for the study and a discussion of the utility of these results for the development of more rigorous theoretical ideas in the study of urban social differentiation. The study is not, therefore, primarily designed as a contribution to urban social *theory*. Its objectives are more closely associated with the development of a systematic body of literature, so as to provide the raw material from which theories can be constructed. This also means it cannot be viewed as a planning study — one designed to improve the 'quality of life' in the area — or one pointing to the serious problems of economy and settlement in the area, along the lines of the reports contained in the recent collection of essays and conference proceedings ''The Valleys Call'' by P. H. Ballard and E. Jones (1975).

It must be admitted that the decision to use Welsh settlements for the study was not taken lightly, given their relative size and location on the periphery of Europe. It may have been more productive to have illustrated the methodological and substantive concerns of this study by dealing with larger or more modern urban centres than the ones studied here, since these will be familiar to most people. Indeed, part of the huge impact of Social Area Analysis (Shevky and Williams 1949; Shevky and Bell 1955) can be attributed to the fact that Shevky's first case study dealt with Los Angeles, the archetypal modern metropolis of the Western world. However, since one of the additional objectives of this study is to demonstrate that a *variety* of urban structures can be found in the Western world, the use of a set of Welsh settlements is not without merit. On *a priori* grounds, the half century of economic stagnation and the high levels of welfare in British society led to the belief that if divergent patterns to the modern North American urban society studied by Shevky and Bell (1955) are to be found, then one of the areas peripheral to the main economic centres of the world was an appropriate place to study. Previous studies (Davies, 1975; Davies, 1977) have shown that Welsh towns displayed somewhat different social structures to the three or four axis pattern that is usually treated as the standard Western structure, so Wales seemed an appropriate place to study — apart from its intrinsic interest to the author.

In addition to this general issue of urban dimensionality, the case studies of Cardiff (Chapter 4) and Cardiff City-Region (Chapter 5) are designed to investigate the extent of technical dependence. The scale issue is studied at an enumeration and ward area scale within Cardiff in Chapter 4, and parallel analyses are reported in Chapter 5 at the regional scale by analyses of the settlements of Cardiff City-Region. From these comparisons the relationships between social and spatial differentiation can be traced and related to the differential resource base of the settlements in the area.

The methodological objectives mean that *the study is designed primarily as a contribution to the literature on urban social differentiation* as reflected in its title. But the substantive results of the case studies obviously provide a lot of information on the 'social topography' of Cardiff and Cardiff City-Region as defined by the small area census derived from the 1971 Census. As such the study provides precise measurements of the regional differentiation of Cardiff and its region and adds a quantitative basis for the identification of sample communities and urban sub-areas that could be used for behavioural investigations. In many ways — particularly in terms of the utility of this study for planning purposes — it is unfortunate that this study is only a cross-sectional analysis. It is restricted to one time period — to the situation described by information from the census in 1971. Yet the decision to limit the study to one time period allowed the analysis to concentrate upon the many methodological issues involved in the development of a systematic literature on urban social differentiation. These issues are, in total, more important than the specific cross-sectional results of the situation found in 1971. However, the decision was also based on the knowledge that small area or census data have only been available from the British census since 1961. But even at that date few census indicators were available and only for quite large enumeration units, as previous work by Giggs (1970) and Herbert (1970) in Wales has shown. These problems — essentially issues of scope and scale — meant that there seemed little value in attempting a comparison through time. Instead, this study concentrates upon the methodological problems in the field, and hopefully, sets the scene for a replication of the work using data from the 1981 census when this is available in late 1983 or 1984. If such a study can be completed, the comparison of 1971 and 1981 data can contribute to an understanding of the *social change* within the area, in addition to the variations in social structures and spatial patterns. Such temporal work would have much more obvious utility for social planning than this cross-sectional analysis — in particular the measurement of the effects of two decades of regional and urban planning policies.

I am grateful to the following authors and publishers for permission to reproduce individual diagrams : Professor B. J. L. Berry, Dr P. H. Rees and the Editor of the *American Journal of Sociology* for Figure 7; and Professor Brian Robson and Oxford University Press for part of Figure 12.

As with all studies of this nature many people helped with various stages in the investigation. Thanks are due to the Country Planning Officers of Mid and South Glamorgan for providing access to the enumeration district data from the 1971 census when it was made available in late 1975, and to Mr Alan Reid and Mr Nick Holmes for helping me find my way through the maze of enumeration district maps and data sets. In addition, I would like to thank Dr John A. Giggs and Dr C. Roy Lewis for reading and commenting on the manuscript. The skill of Jeanne Keech, Gaynor Hamer and Carol Parry in typing the drafts of this study, Marta Styk and Minnie Medwid for drawing the maps and diagrams, and Susan Waters for help in punching the computer cards for the analysis, are also all gratefully acknowledged. Moreover, I must gratefully acknowledge the access allowed to the various facilities of the Department of Geography at The University College of Wales, Aberystwyth, during my sabbatical there. Finally, I must thank the human geographers at U.C.W. for their warm companionship during the writing of this monograph in the Spring of 1980.


WAYNE K. D. DAVIES

CHAPTER 1

# MEASURING THE SOCIAL CHARACTER OF URBAN AREAS:
## AN INTRODUCTION

> The facts which I have used to classify the inhabitants of London could be applied to any city — to Paris or Moscow, New York or Melbourne, Calcutta or Hong Kong . . . but in all of them the intensive method of investigation should go hand in hand with the extensive. Without a full comprehension of unexpected details, general statements are always lifeless and often misleading; without some trustworthy generalizations . . . elaboration is partly thrown away . . .
>
> . . . I have ventured to direct your attention tonight to the working of an instrument designed to be used in the careful examination of our existing social balance. It is, I think, a good instrument, though by no means an exhaustive one. Many such could be constructed. What I hope is that this one may be sufficiently interesting to tempt and rouse the ingenuity of inquirers to the invention of further tests touching other springs and wider vistas; comparing, checking, correcting each by each, till we win firm ground, and reduce the possibilities of error to a minimum . . .
>
> (Charles Booth, Presidential Address, *The Royal Statistical Society Journal* 1893, pp. 590-1).

Any review of the most pressing social or economic problems of the last century would undoubtedly allocate a great deal of time and attention to cities. With the typical myopia that characterizes so much of our contemporary commentary we tend to view our knowledge of cities and their problems as particular to our age. Some obviously *are* different for they are linked to particular modern values and technology; but it is salutary, in an intellectual sense at least, to remember that many of our modern urban problems, and even solutions, are little different in type, if not in detail, to those experienced by other societies. To take one example, Rome at the dawn of the Christian era suffered from overcrowding, sprawling growth, and rapacious landlords (Frederick, 1965). The result was that at least one emperor, Augustus, introduced rent control and height restrictions on buildings, while the creation of traffic-free zones in the centre of towns was established planning practice (Mumford, 1961). But just because so many of the problems and issues of urban life were similar — albeit with a different set of values and technology — this does not, of course, mean that cities can be said to have a similar role or character in history. Rather the opposite is true. Cities, and settlements in general, fulfil many roles and represent a complex, constantly changing social and economic phenomena that are at best imperfectly conceptualized, let alone adequately defined and measured. This study deals with the latter issue; the general problem of providing systematic measurements of *one* of the major facets of urban character, *the differentiation of the social structure of urban areas.* A particular focus of the work is the concern with systematic enquiry. The attempt is made to provide a coherent methodology for measuring urban social differentiation — as well as systematically organizing the substantive results into an interrelated body of generalizations.

As with all measurement or systematically orientated studies — particularly those dealing with human phenomena — it is easy to forget that the analysis only applies to

1

part of the urban phenomena being investigated. The first part of this chapter, therefore, establishes the wider context within which this systematic study is set. It summarizes the range of social variation in urban areas and the difficulties faced by investigators seeking to conceptualize the character of these places. After this general overview the precise objectives of the study and its organization into three parts are described in the second section. These three parts are: firstly, a brief, but critical review of the development of ideas in the study of urban social differentiation; secondly, the description and justification of a particular quantitative method of analysis, called the Multivariate-Structural approach, which extends the currently popular Factorial Ecology method; thirdly, the application of these ideas to two case studies of settlements in Wales at the intra-urban and city-region scales. These studies have three objectives: firstly, illustrating the methodology used in the study; secondly, describing how certain problems in our understanding of the bases of urban social differentiation can be solved; thirdly, contributing to the specific understanding of the differentiation of settlements in the study area. However, it must be emphasized that this study concentrates upon the general characteristics of settlements. Size constraints preclude the addition of Booth's 'intensive' methods of investigation described in the quotation above, namely, the description of the sights, sounds and other details of areas — an approach best dealt with by other methods.

## 1. The Conceptualization of Urban Social Character

The multi-dimensional nature of cities makes it difficult, if not impossible, to conceive of a completely unified and systematic literature on urban social character. Six problems can be identified as accounting for this situation. These can be summarized as: academic specialization, limited conceptualization, homomorphus, alternative roles in society, symbolism, particularism. Naturally these are only problems for those engaged in the systematic approach; in themselves they provide valuable evidence of the varied nature of cities and demonstrate the dangers that exponents of the systematic approach face.

(a) *Academic Specializations and Philosophies.* Despite an enormous literature on the character of urban places, most of it is written by specialists working in a wide variety of different disciplines, whether urban geography, urban history, urban sociology, urban economics, urban planning, etc. One consequence is that the knowledge attained is difficult to integrate. It has been filtered through a quite different set of disciplinary perspectives, temporal, spatial, prescriptive, or others. The stress that these disciplines place upon only one part of the urban character means it is difficult to obtain a balanced and comprehensive view.

These disciplinary variations should be considered to be subservient to philosophical differences in approach. Students of urban character can be found on both sides of what the poet W. B. Yeats called the 'primary-antithetical' divide in his book *A Vision* (1938). The former signified the search for general laws of nature and society, the 'primary' reality that is adopted by scientists, the latter is the search for man as an individualized maker: man the creator of processes of 'imaginative emanation'. To the latter approach we owe the lucid, character summarizing insights of the poet or novelist. For example, Dylan Thomas (1943, p. 1) summarized his home town of Swansea as:

> an ugly, lovely town (or so it was, and is, to me) crawling, sprawling, slummed, unplanned, jerry-villa'd and smug-suburbed by the side of a long and splendid curving shore.

Such a description, full of the adjectival emphasis that is the poet's style, is a clear, if individualistic description of the town that in its 'ugly, lovely' juxtaposition provides an insight into Dylan's ambivalence to the centre. Yet despite the value of this type of description it is difficult to see how it can be used for the development of any systematic body of urban literature; it is an individual, particularistic conception. Such a view should not necessarily be thought of as applying to all urban characterizations from literary sources. For example, this is how Thomas Hardy described the Wessex town he modelled on Dorchester (Dorset) in *The Mayor of Casterbridge*:

> Casterbridge was the complement of the rural life around; not its urban opposite (1886, p. 229).
> Casterbridge was in most respects but the pole, focus or nerve knot of the surrounding country life; differing from the many manufacturing towns which are as foreign bodies set down, like boulders on a plain, in a green world with which they have nothing in common. Casterbridge lived by agriculture at one remove further from the fountain-head than the adjoining villages — no more. The townsfolk understood every fluctuation in the rustic's condition, for it affected their receipts as much as the labourer's . . . (Hardy 1886 p. 233)

Hardy's words provide a brilliantly incisive characterization of the intimate town — hinterland relationships of a country town. In addition, it illuminates the very different processes of urban growth, between what geographers of a scientific disposition call a 'central place' as opposed to a 'basic' or 'export industry dominated' settlement. However, we must be careful; although Hardy may have conceptualized the two processes this is the end of his discussion. The detailed analysis of the way these functional processes operate, and the identification of the various components in a variety of different settings, must await the systematic study of the social or spatial scientist.

Obviously the force of the pull between Yeats's polar types, those searching for general laws, the systematic scientific approach, and those seeking individual traits, varies from person to person. Most people have to make a choice between the two extremes since it seems impossible to span this dichotomy in one study. In the first place the language, the means of expression, has to be used quite differently. Even if this were not enough, the logic of justification, which is the key to scientific method, necessitates that the artistic appeal to the emotions, to feeling, plays no part in the scientific acceptance of a piece of work — except, perhaps, in preferences for alternative mathematical proofs.

The study of urban places, like most fields of endeavour, certainly spans Yeats's dichotomy. But within any individual, disciplinary subfield, such as urban geography, Yeats's dualism is too simplistic a contrast to account for the range of philosophical approaches that have been used — even on the systematic study side. For example, description ranges from the scientific, positivist emphasis of Berry (1970, 1972) to the

3

historical and humanistic perspectives of Vance (1977) and Wheatley (1974). To these essentially descriptive options must be added the prescriptive approaches of recent years. These range from the basically planning orientated, yet positivist approaches of Hall (1968) or Jackson (1972) to the radicalism and social justice orientations of Harvey (1973). One result of the adoption of such very different methods is that it is almost impossible to integrate the findings of even a single subfield in urban geography into a single body of systematic literature. Nevertheless, these alternative approaches must be welcomed. It would be unfortunate for any comprehensive understanding of cities if one approach was excluded to the detriment of others. Certainly the study of urban areas would be less rich than it is without these alternative perspectives. Yet at the same time the pluralism represented by these diverse philosophical and disciplinary perspectives creates a permanent and usually unresolved tension between exponents of the different methods, making it difficult to provide an integrated approach to urban studies or urban analysis.

(b) *Limited Conceptualization.* The second problem to be faced is that most of the definitions and characterizations of the nature of urban settlements are extremely limited; hence we do not possess very clear ideas of the limits of the phenomena we are dealing with. Several kinds of difficulties can be recognized among the urban concepts that have been identified. One set of ideas tends to be one dimensional, or are even data specific, in the sense that they only stress one aspect, or one set of information relevant to city character; for example, those definitions based on population size, political and economic character or even the 'interaction' emphasis of Mel Webber (1964). Another set are society specific, applying to only one type of society, the problem of criteria proposed by archaeologists, such as Gordon Childe (1950), historians such as Max Weber (1921), sociologists such as Louis Wirth (1938). Yet another set of ideas are really simple categorizations of urban variations, such as Sjorberg's (1962) pre-industrial and industrial city differentiation, which conceals as much of the variety of urban phenomena as it summarizes. Nevertheless, despite limitations, these conceptualizations are still useful in at least one academic sense; they allow students to sharpen their intellectual faculties by criticizing the ideas. At base, however, the limitations of these conceptualizations demonstrate the difficulty of putting bounds around, and hence adequately understanding, the urban places that are the objects of our attention. Perhaps the lesson to be drawn from this review is that if a viable set of concepts about the nature of cities ever emerges it will need to be free of specific societal, technological, value and environmental associations. Is this possible? Only time will tell. If such concepts *are* produced, they will be abstractions at the highest level — a level which still eludes us.

(c) *Homomorphus.* The third problem is that even where we can identify parallels in urban patterns and urban societies, it is often discovered that they are the consequence of quite different causes. For example, segregated ethnic groups may have the same urban spatial patterns but such patterns may be the product of voluntary or involuntary processes. Another good illustration is provided by a comparison of the contemporary urbanization of the third world with the experience of industrial countries at their phase of maximum urbanization in the late nineteenth century. In the crudest sense, as statistical aggregations of people, the agglomeration of population into cities looks the same, albeit at a different scale. In practice, Kingsley Davis (1972) and others have shown that the process of growth is quite different. In particular, it is the general population increase, as much as rural-urban migration, that accounts for the explosive growth of cities in the Third World — unlike the dominance of city growth by rural migration in the nineteenth century. So we look at third world urbanization through the experience of our own history at our peril; certainly we cannot erect models or produce projections of third world urban growth on the basis of the history of the advanced countries (McGee 1967). Even in the study of such a deceptively simple pattern as urban agglomeration a variety of different causes can be seen to have contributed to a similar end. This means we must be constantly aware of the need to identify the different ways of producing the same phenomenon or object. In a social science context this makes it that much more difficult to build a cumulative body of factual literature on the basis of past work (Davies, 1965). Indeed, previous work in identifying phenomena may even impede understanding of these new patterns — at least initially — since we might begin by assuming that the same processes have been at work. This means that past efforts are not the inevitable, or necessary stepping stones to future understanding of causes or processes that they often are in the physical sciences. This provides an important restriction on this study, namely that any investigation statistically measuring community character at any point in time must be wary of generalizing the results to assume a particular process is at work; very different processes can produce the same type of associations or patterns.

(d) *City and Society.* Fourthly, what of the relationship of the city to society? Again there is a division of opinion between those who conceptualize the city as a dependent variable (Sjorberg, 1962; Childe, 1950) where the city is dependent upon the society and technology of which it is a part, and those who view it as an independent variable, where the city produces a particular society (Weber, 1968; Hoselitz, 1955). Much of the character of cities depends upon which role the city played in any society. However, the debate between these two alternative perceptions (Castells, 1977) will never be resolved to the complete satisfaction of any one side. Rather it must be recognized that the city has been variously the 'creature of' and 'creator of' society through history. In both roles cities contain the basic stock of ideas, organizations and buildings that we consider to be the mark of civilization, and these qualities usually make cities the apex of any society. But the role in society cannot be a single relationship. To illustrate this point one need only compare the role of the city in the medieval society of West Europe with that of medieval China (Murphey, 1954). In the medieval Western Europe type of city, burghers sought, and frequently gained, economic and political independence from the rurally based feudal society in which they were embedded. This independence from the feudal maze of conflicting obligations was one of the forces that led to the transformation of feudal society. The contrast with the societal role of the Chinese city is quite

5

striking. Wheatley (1974) has provided a brilliant survey of urban origins in China in which he demonstrates that the traditional Chinese city supported the moral order of society. These Chinese cities may have been as functionally specialized as those in Western Europe but normally they did not have an independent role in society. Elsewhere, Lapidus (1969) has described how many of the organized community groups found in medieval Muslim cities were not exclusively based on the urban entities; membership transcended the built-up city to village communities. This led to societal schisms between the various groups *within* the city; there was a distinct lack of cohesion within the settlement. So location within the city does not automatically produce an integration of social function or purpose for the group or individual involved. Hence, if the whole historical sequence of urban development is taken into account, it is unduly restrictive to assume there is one relationship between cities and societies. There must be many relationships. Indeed, much of the character of an individual city will depend upon the particular societal role it plays and its relationships to people located outside its boundaries.

(e) *Symbolism and Value Orientations.* The reference to the historic Chinese urban form as described above can be extended to illustrate a fifth point about the complexity of urban phenomena. Cities, or parts thereof, have a symbolic and experiential role as well as a simple material and rational existence. Wheatley (1974) has eloquently described the way in which the Chinese urban form was underlain by a complex of ideas he calls astrobiology. These represented an attempt to achieve a parallelism between the order of the cosmos, as exemplified by the astrological sequence of heavenly bodies, and the disorder of the real world. Cities played an important role in achieving this parallelism, for they were laid out as replicas of what the cosmos was believed to be. Differences in belief inevitably produced detailed variations in the specific morphology for individual societies, but the comparable element was the transformation of part of the realm of the profane, the earth, into the realm of the sacred. Hence, even the morphology of the city possessed an existential as well as a geometrical order. In the lay-out of the specific urban forms certain common elements can be distinguished — grid, central axes, towers reaching to 'heaven', gates symbolizing entry to the sacred enclosure — whilst the segregation of the priestly class within the latter was a typical feature. These elements provided the material framework for carrying out the rituals that sustained the harmony between the cosmos and earth — a harmony that was supposed to ensure prosperity. Wheatley (1974, p. 418) succinctly summarizes this point by a quotation from the *Book of Li Chi:* 'rites obviate disaster as dykes prevent inundation'.

Clearly, therefore, the form of the city was a supportive element for society in a symbolic sense, and the particular morphology reflected the beliefs and values considered to be important by that society.

The symbolic values are, of course, difficult to study in other than an individualistic way. But it must not be thought that such symbolisms are only limited to past societies, or to cities with religious associations such as Mecca, Jerusalem, or even Salt Lake City. All cities, and many city areas, have positive and negative emotional values, as Lynch

(1960) has reminded us in his classic study, *The Image of the City*. Incidentally, the influence of this work testifies to the way in which the artistic, individualistic perceptions of cities were ignored by students of urban character for many years. Yet Lynch was not content to look at the image in literary terms; he attempted to identify analytically the various components of urban images for further study. Similarly, Hunter (1974) and Suttles (1968) have showed how symbolic and emotional attitudes can be conceptualized, and how these ideas apply to areas within cities.

These symbolic values are, of course, often deliberately emphasized and promoted by annual festivals. In an internal city context the palio of Sienna represents a tradition of intra-urban rivalry going back to the medieval period. For cities and towns the promotion of city fairs or festivals has made a comeback in recent years, as the extra business they generate becomes more clearly appreciated. In this respect, the small town of Llangollen with its International Eisteddfod, or the metropolis of New Orleans with its Mardi Gras, provide obvious examples. So does Calgary with its annual July Stampede. In this latter case a general characteristic of city festivals can be identified. Annual celebrations are often based on cultures or economies of eras, in this case ranching, which have long passed away. Certainly the city of Calgary is still an important retail and wholesaling centre for its agricultural hinterland, but this economic contribution has been outweighed by its importance as the administrative centre of the Canadian oil and gas industry, and increasingly with the financial strength accruing from this service-based economy. Yet the annual re-creation of youthful, frontier exuberance contributes most to the image of Calgary in Canada, if not the world, and is an essential, if increasingly factually fraudulent part of its character. At this point it is difficult not to point to a little known result of the festival, namely the rise in the monthly birth rates in April. This is a cyclical phenomenon that has nothing to do with spring or astro-biology; it is simply the latent or unintended consequence of the Stampede festivities nine months after the celebrations! In this contribution to the population growth of the city it can be argued that the symbol attains material form and reinforces itself.

(f) *Particularism.* Finally, the place-particular features of cities must be remembered. In the last resort all cities have some elements of environmental character, or some peculiar combination of historical circumstance, that impart an element of uniqueness to cities. Examples of the way unique characterizations have been made by poets and novelists have already been provided. But some urban scholars also find their greatest reward in describing, or should one say emphasizing, this uniqueness as part of the richness of human experience. In this context the tradition established by the University of Oklahoma Press in its 'City in Civilization' series (e.g. D. Young's *Edinburgh in the Age of Walter Scott,* 1965) is an outstanding illustration of this approach. So are the arguments for individualism recently presented by the historian Richard Cobb (1975) in *A Sense of Place,* the perceptual-individualist type of approach described as 'topofilia' by the geographer Y. F. Tuan (1974), or the detailed analysis of building fabric and materials presented by A. Clifton-Taylor (1980). These studies come very close to the particularistic descriptions of the poet or novelist since emotion and attitude are vital elements of the characterization. Obviously a comprehensive understanding of urban character — it can never be considered as complete if we accept conditions of epistemological dualism (Davies, 1972) — whether for the city as a whole, or sub-areas, requires an investigator to take all these issues into account.

This re-emphasis upon the individual approach can be seen in quite a different way. The old geographical tradition of monographs on individual city areas (Blanchard, 1935) seems to have been revived. One example is provided by the recent Canadian series of studies of urban areas (e.g. R. P. Blaine, Calgary, 1972); another by the case studies of metropolitan areas in the U.S.A. (Adams, 1976) that were produced as part of the survey of cities based on the 1970 census. However, we must not forget that exponents of the historical approach have kept alive the tradition of individual urban vignettes, as can be seen illustrated by Vance's seminal study of San Francisco (1964), or Carter's study of Dubrovnik (1972). Although the geographical expertise behind these studies inevitably produces a very different emphasis, this type of study comes very close to the individualistic urban descriptions produced by planners such as Rayner Banham in Los Angeles (1973), or writers such as James Morris, in either his superb study of Venice (1960), or his essays on *Cities* (1963). Such approaches provide the necessary complement to the systematic study of urban character in which intra-urban generalization, not uniqueness, is the focus of attention. However, it is difficult to see how both approaches can be integrated within the confines of a single book, from the mind of a single author at one point in time.

These six problems provide an overview of the problems of content and philosophy that are faced by all students of the city. They certainly illuminate, and hopefully confirm one of the earliest statements made in this essay about the nature of urban settlements, namely, that we are dealing with a complex, multi-faceted phenomenon, and it is extraordinarily difficult, if not impossible, to interweave all these aspects into a single body of systematic literature. The result is that most urban scholars would agree with David Harvey (1974, p. 195) that

> urbanism is far too complicated a phenomenon to be subsumed easily under some comprehensive theory.

Obviously there are theories and systematic bodies of literature on selected aspects of urban phenomena, but there is a glaring gap in the integration of these parts. Even in the area of interest of this study Timms (1971, p. 251) observed that:

> given present knowledge no attempt to produce an integrated theory of residential differentiation is likely to be successful . . .

The pessimism revealed in Timms's statement is based on the recognition that any complete study would have to interlink individual behavioural and macro-sociological conditions. In addition we can see that any general theory would have to be general enough to encompass both socio-economic, spiritual, and environmental character. The generalizations produced would have to be carefully linked to the idiosyncrasies of cities before all aspects of urban places are understood. Not surprisingly, the urban literature tends to be polarized or specialized into distinct areas of interest, each set looking at one part of the complexity of cities from a particular point of view.

For exponents of the holistic approach to urban studies, this discussion offers little comfort; it demonstrates that it is virtually impossible simultaneously to incorporate all aspects of urban character within the confines of one study. Yet this should not be thought of as a negative or indeed unique conclusion. For example, the psychologist Hitt (1968) has shown how the study of man is polarized into at least two schools of thought that are often mutually antagonistic; approaches he describes as the 'existential' and 'behavioural' models. His review concludes that neither approach is complete in itself; man is complex enough to need elements of both approaches. Similarly, sociologists such as Daniel Bell (1974) have emphasized the separation of what he calls 'structural' as opposed to 'value-attitudinal' approaches in modern society, the former refer to the patterns of tangible phenomena, the latter to the values and preferences of individuals and groups. Hence it is not surprising that man's works, in particular cities, must be looked at from a variety of different perspectives. Recognition of the need for a pluralist approach in attitude, if not in practice, therefore, resolves the impact of many of the difficulties previously described. The range of variation in urban conceptualization is only important if an investigator is searching for the Grail of complete understanding, an impossible dream. This means that *the specific problem of measuring the social character of urban communities can be viewed as being one area to be investigated in a whole range of alternative issues, problems, and approaches to the study of urban areas.* Recognition of this point means that individual analyses must be judged on their own terms. It is as pointless to criticize quantitatively minded urban ecologists for not dealing with experiential or policy issues as it is fruitless to condemn socially relevant reviews of spatial variations in housing policies for not producing urban typologies. Individuals certainly differ in the priority they give to each type of study — but it should be recognized that these priorities relate to the values of the investigators at the time of the study — not to the rigour or utility of the individual studies.

## 2. The Systematic Measurement of Urban Social Structure

The preceding discussion has made it clear that a choice has to be made between competing philosophies and methods in urban geographical studies. In the interests of clarity it is better to make such choices explicit. *In this monograph the emphasis will be upon the objective analysis of the systematic patterns or relationships expressed in the social character of Western urban areas.* As such it excludes non-Western forms although the methods can be applied to such cities. To some extent this interest in 'systematic' study and 'social character' may be considered to be contradictory since one approach implies the adoption of the nomothetic method, whilst the other has an idiographic emphasis. In addition, the range of possible sources of differentiation within cities is so immense, and relates to such different phenomena, that it is difficult to see how they can be integrated into one

9

set of generalizations. The difficulty can be illustrated by two quotations from quite different approaches to the study of inter-urban variation.

Charles Booth (1902), describing his individual studies of districts in the East End of London, pointed out that:

> each district has its character — its particular flavour. One seems to be conscious of it in the streets. It may be in the faces of the people, or in what they carry — perhaps a reflection is thrown in this way from the prevailing trades — or it may lie in the sounds one hears, or in the character of the buildings (1902, Poverty Series, I, p. 66).

Zorbaugh (1926, p. 188), writing in the heyday of the Chicago urban ecological approach, maintained:

> the individual city . . . is built about. (a) . . . framework of transportation, business organization and industry, park and boulevard systems and topographical features. All these break up the city into numerous small areas . . . Railroad and industrial belts, parks and boulevard systems, rivers and rises of land acting as barriers to movements of population tend to fix the boundaries of these natural areas . . . each natural area of the city tends to collect the particular individuals pre-destined to it. These individuals in turn give to the area its peculiar character . . .

This is not the place to comment on Zorbaugh's apparently deterministic assumptions of pre-destiny. Nor is it necessary to do more than to point to the methodological discrepancy between the individualistic description of London's districts implied by Booth's statement, and the quantitative assessment of the 'social condition' of these districts found in his Presidential Address to the Royal Statistical Society in 1895 (Davies, 1978). What is more important is that both statements describe a 'particular' flavour or 'particular' character, thereby implying that each area is unique. In the last resort it *is* possible to accept that all areas have something different about them, but this does not necessarily mean that all things about the areas are different. On *a priori* grounds, it is just as easy to accept the alternative position that there is a great deal of similarity between many urban areas, allowing investigators to search for the comparable patterns. This is the viewpoint taken in this study. It is not denied that there are symbolic, spiritual or experiential qualities of areas; however, these are considered to represent unique, often individualistic features that are difficult to study in a systematic fashion. Attempts have, of course, been made to identify the structure of urban images (Lynch, 1960), but since they represent a patterning of the image, rather than a patterning of area, they are not dealt with here. Instead the *focus of this study is upon the measurement of the systematic social regularities in city areas and urban regions* in which as much as possible of the social complexity of the areas is dealt with — rather than dealing with individual patterns such as ethnicity (Peach, 1975) or single areas such as the ghetto (Rose, 1972).

This concern with the regular patterning of urban areas and the development of this interest into a systematic framework of enquiry has a long history. The work of social commentators such as Engels (1845) or Mayhew (1862) can be considered as representing the beginnings of interest in the subject in the modern period. But such studies were primarily designed to draw attention to the problems of urban poverty; they were hardly systematic enquiries in the sense of developing concepts or generalizations appropriate to the field, or integrated bodies of either the substantive literature or methodological reviews. This means that we must associate the development of systematic interest in the field of urban social differentiation with the work of Charles Booth (1902) in late nineteenth century London, and Burgess, Park and their fellow urban ecologists at the University of Chicago after World War I (Park, 1925).

Most texts still claim that the so-called 'Chicago' school of urban ecology represented the first major breakthrough in the study of urban social variation as a separate field of enquiry. Certainly the development of the classical ecological concepts such as invasion and succession, or centralization, went beyond the specifics of individual city examples and illuminated the process of urban change; schemes such as the concentric zone generalization of Burgess (1925) provided a spatial model of the social patterning of cities (Figure 1). Yet equally important was the fact that critics of these initial ideas, particularly Hoyt (1939) with his emphasis upon the principles of sectoral growth, and Harris and Ullman (1945) with their multiple nuclei model, created alternative spatial models which have subsequently been shown to be important complementary ideas for urban structure. Nevertheless, any dispassionate review of the urban ecology literature will reveal that much of the traditional ecological approach had become rather sterile by the World War II period. Not only were the ecological concepts of change regarded as too general in scope, but the failure of most ecologists to provide precise quantitative evidence of their spatial models led to serious questioning of the relevance of the patterns that were identified (Alihan, 1938). In this respect, perhaps, Hoyt's study should have been seen as a way out of the ecologists' dilemma, since Hoyt was a land economist who based his generalizations upon an empirical study of 142 U.S. cities. However, the limitation of the study to changes in the location of residential areas meant that the analysis was only of limited scope for the study of social differentiation in general. In addition, the rather confusing description of certain concepts, such as the natural area idea (Timms, 1971, p. 7), did not help retain confidence in the traditional ecological approach. A further blow came from the attack of sociologists such as Firey (1945) who emphasized the need to incorporate the social valuation of space into any model of change. This demonstrated the way in which the ecologists had over-emphasized the tangible social environment in their concepts and spatial models, although it does seem they had successfully dealt with many behavioural issues in their related studies of urban groups or areas: for example, Shaw's study of delinquency areas (1929) or Thrasher's study of gangs (1927). From World War II onwards, therefore, it seems that there is a dichotomy between the utility of the various parts of the urban ecological approach. The behavioural studies have continued to represent a major contribution to understanding — in which the recent work of Suttles (1963, 1972) on territorial groupings in ghetto areas represents an outstanding example — whereas the tradition concerned primarily with the classification of social areas has been revealed as having major limitations.

Since the objective of this study lies in the classificatory approach these criticisms of

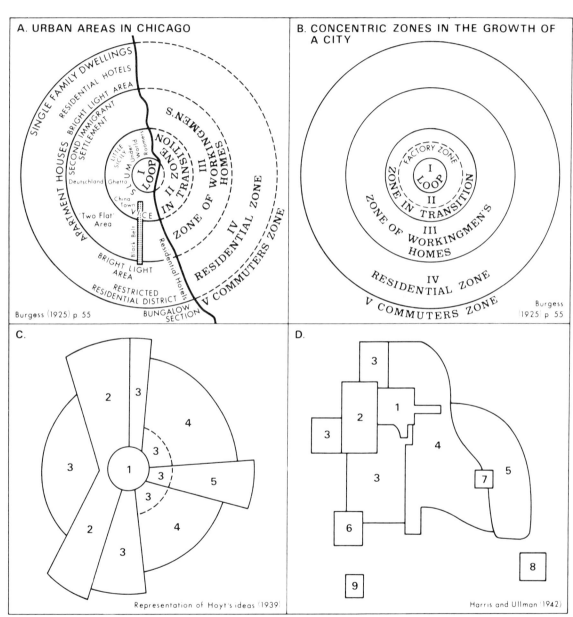

FIGURE 1 SPATIAL MODELS OF URBAN LAND USE AND SOCIAL STRUCTURE. THE NUMBERS IN MODELS C
AND D CORRESPOND TO THE FOLLOWING ZONES : 1. CENTRAL BUSINESS DISTRICT; 2. LIGHT
INDUSTRY, WHOLESALE; 3. LOW STATUS RESIDENTIAL; 4. MIDDLE STATUS RESIDENTIAL; 5. HIGH
STATUS RESIDENTIAL; 6. HEAVY INDUSTRY; 7. OUTLYING COMMERCIAL DISTRICT; 8. RESIDENTIAL
SUBURB; 9. INDUSTRIAL SUBURB.

the classical urban ecological approach are important. In retrospect, perhaps, it can be seen that many of these problems could have been resolved if the 'Chicago school' had paid more attention to the work of Charles Booth (1902). A quarter of a century before Park's work Booth produced a classic series of portraits of working class life and labour in late nineteenth century London. But of more interest than his individual descriptions of groups or areas, or his pioneering of social survey method (Simmey, 1969), were his detailed maps of poverty in London; these were compiled on a street-by-street basis. From this basis Booth went on to use several census variables which he combined to produce an aggregate score of what he called 'social condition' for each area in London (Booth, 1893). Given his interest in the classification of areas on as precise a basis as possible, Davies (1978) has claimed it was Booth, not Park or Burgess, who should be regarded as the originator of modern social area analysis. Unfortunately, Booth's ideas were not adopted by the Chicago ecologists or subsequent workers. Part of the reason must be linked to the very size of Booth's study in a different country to the one that developed the field of urban ecology. But Booth's philosophical preference for the ruling scientific methodology of his day — the compilation of facts and the refusal to generalize or to speculate — must also have had a major effect. Indeed, Booth went so far as to state in his final volume:

> the dry bones that are scattered over the long valley we have traversed together lie before my reader. May some great soul, master of a subtler and nobler alchemy . . . put them together.
>
> (Booth, 1902, vol. 18, p. 216.)

The modern phase of the systematic analysis of urban social structure can be said to have begun in 1955. In that year two influential studies were published, namely, Shevky and Bell's *Social Area Analysis* (an extension of previous work carried out by the senior author in Los Angeles in 1949 (Shevky and Williams, 1949)) and Tryon's *The Identification of Social Areas by Cluster Analysis*. Although they both dealt with the problems of defining social areas in cities in different ways they were alike in seeking a quantitative measurement of the social character of urban areas using census based variables. This had the effect of focusing attention upon one part of the overall field of urban ecology; that of understanding the recurring patterns of urban social differentiation rather than the behavioural or land use concerns of urban ecology in general.

The most important part of Shevky and Bell's work was that it linked the study of social variations in urban areas with a theory of social change (Figure 2) — one of the major deficiencies of the whole urban ecological tradition. From this they identified three axes of variation, originally called Social Rank, Urbanization (or Family Status) and Ethnicity. Since each area was measured on these axes of variation the method provided a clear demonstration of the need to separate the study of social dimensionality — the sources of axes of differentiation in cities — from the spatial patterns of these dimensions as expressed in the relative scores of each area on the axes. Today the limitations of the Social Area approach are well known (Timms, 1971). For example, the

## (a) Shevky and Bell

| Postulates Concerning Industrial Society 'Aspects of Increasing Scale' (1) | Consequences (of Statistics) of Trends (2) | Resultant Changes in the Structure of a Given Social System (3) | Summarized as Constructs (4) | Indicators (Related to the Constructs) (5) | Derived Measures (from col. 5) (6) | Combined as Index (7) |
|---|---|---|---|---|---|---|
| A. Change in the range and intensity of relations | Changing distribution of skills: lessening importance of manual productive operations — growing importance of clerical, supervisory management operations | Changes in the arrangement of occupations based on function | SOCIAL RANK (Socio-economic status)* | Years of schooling Employment status Class of worker Major occupation group Value of home Rent by dwelling unit Persons per room Plumbing and repair Heating & refrigeration | Occupation Schooling Rent | Index I |
| B. Differentiation of function and specialization | Changing structure of productive activity: lessening importance of primary production — growing importance of relations centred in cities — lessening importance of the household as economic unit | Changes in the ways of living — movement of women into urban occupations — spread of alternative family patterns | URBANIZATION (Family status) | Age and sex Owner or tenant House structure Persons in household | Fertility Women at work Single-family dwelling units | Index II |
| C. Complexity of organization | Changing composition of population: increasing movement — alterations in age, sex distribution, increasing diversity | Redistribution in space — changes in the proportion of supporting and dependent population, isolation and segregation of groups | SEGREGATION (Ethnic status) | Race and nativity Country of birth Citizenship | Racial and national group in relative isolation | Index III |

*Source:* Revision of Shevky and Bell (1955)    *Shevky and Bell's terms given first

## (b) McElrath

| Master Trends | Consequences of Trends | Indicators of Trends (Possible Variables) | Dimensions or Constructs of Social Differentiation | Indicators of Social Variables of Dimensions |
|---|---|---|---|---|
| A) Industrialization | (i) Changing distribution and reward of skills | Literacy; Further education; Commerce workers; Non-manual workers | SOCIAL RANK | Occupation Education |
|  | (ii) Changing structure of productive activity | Non-agricultural workers; Industrial diversity; Wage and salaried workers | FAMILY STATUS | Fertility; Women in workforce |
| B) Urbanization | (i) Aggregation of population | Urban and metropolitan concentration | MIGRANT STATUS | Migrants; Age/Sex Selection |
|  | (ii) Increasing external ties and dispersion of resources | External contact Immigration rates | ETHNIC STATUS | Culturally visible minorities |

*Source:* Revision of McElrath's ideas (1968, p.35); 'Societal scale and social differentiation', p.35.

FIGURE 2  THE THEORETICAL DERIVATION OF SOCIAL DIMENSIONS

utility of the particular theory of social change used by Shevky-Bell can be questioned, as can the logic by which the individual constructs and hence indicators were derived. Also, alternative deductions of the constructs and the indicators can be made, and it is difficult to see why 'ethnicity' is favoured over 'migration' in the third axis. In addition, the ratio measures used to define the axes represented relatively little advance on the ideas of Booth since there was no guarantee that the individual indicators that were added together to form the index of social variation co-varied. If these indicators had low correlations with one another the index is obviously spurious. Nevertheless, although the particular procedures can be criticized, the Social Area approach deserves an important place in the history of the analysis of urban social differentiation. Yet the development of the Social Area method cannot be exclusively linked with the work of Shevky and Bell (1955).

McElrath (1968) revised the original model to produce a four axis structure in which migration was added to the list of the original constructs from rather different master trends in society (Figure 2). Timms (1971) used these four constructs to construct a family of social area types based on the degree of separation of these axes. Figure 3 shows that most of these types relate to historical or non-Western societies rather than to modern Western structures which could be represented by a split of Timms's four axes into a series of post-industrial indicators. Few empirical studies have addressed themselves to this typology; its utility has not been tested. The result is that despite its initial breakthrough the Social Area approach has floundered because of the inability of the technical procedures suggested by Shevky and Bell to confirm the various ideas.

Tryon (1955), by contrast, took the opposite tack. His concern was primarily with the classification of areas and as such his study can be considered to represent an Area Taxonomic method. In his study of San Francisco he used a set of thirty-three variables to define the social variation in two hundred and forty-three census tracts. A similarity index was calculated between each pair of areas on the basis of their similarities over the set of variables, and cluster analysis was used to group these areas into a limited number of categories. Tryon's particular similarity and cluster procedures are now rather dated, given the recent technical advances in the field (Sokal and Sneath, 1973). But the importance of the work is that unlike Shevky and Bell, Tryon placed the study of urban social differentiation firmly within the developing literature on multivariate analysis. However, comparatively few workers followed this lead in the 1960s and early 1970s, outside the field of inter-urban classifications (Smith, 1965), and a weakness has been that most studies have tended to provide individual classifications of the study area, with little reference to the more rapidly developing literature on the dimensions of urban social variation. A recent study of wards and parishes in England and Wales (Webber, 1977), based on a forty variable set from the 1971 census, demonstrates this problem. Although the study must be praised for its scope in classifying each ward and parish of Britain into thirty-six clusters, which are themselves grouped into nine families of areas — a result only made possible because of the size of contemporary computers — there are many weaknesses in the technical arguments, and these limit its effectiveness. For

**Type A: Modern city**

| *Construct* | Social rank | Family status | Ethnicity | Migration status |
|---|---|---|---|---|
| *Indicants* | Occupation<br>Education<br>Income | Fertility<br>Working women<br>Marriage | Culturally-<br>visible<br>minorities | Native migrants<br>Age-sex imbalance<br>Mobility |

**Type B: Feudal city**

*Construct* — Single axis of differentiation

| *Indicants* | Occupation<br>Education<br>Income | Fertility<br>Working women<br>Marriage | Culturally-<br>visible<br>minorities | Native migrants<br>Age-sex imbalance<br>Mobility |
|---|---|---|---|---|

**Type C: Colonial city**

*Construct*    Social rank — Ethnicity     —    Migration status    Family status

| *Indicants* | Occupation<br>Education<br>Income | Culturally-<br>visible<br>minorities | Native migrants<br>Age-sex-im-<br>balance<br>Mobility | Fertility<br>Working women<br>Marriage |
|---|---|---|---|---|

**Type D: Immigrant city**

*Construct*    Social rank    Family status  — Ethnicity  —  Migration status

| *Indicants* | Occupation<br>Education<br>Income | Fertility<br>Working women<br>Marriage | Culturally-<br>visible<br>minorities | Native migrants<br>Age-sex imbalance<br>Mobility |
|---|---|---|---|---|

**Type E: Pre-industrial city**

*Construct*    Social rank — Family status    (Ethnicity  —  Migration status)
  ?

| *Indicants* | Occupation<br>Education<br>Income | Fertility<br>Working women<br>Marriage | (Culturally-<br>visible<br>minorities) | (Native migrants<br>Age-sex imbalance<br>Mobility) |
|---|---|---|---|---|

**Type F: Industrializing city**

*Construct*    Social rank    Family status    (Ethnicity)  ?  (Migration status)
  ?      ?

| *Indicants* | Occupation<br>Education<br>Income | Fertility<br>Working women<br>Marriage | (Culturally-<br>visible<br>minorities) | (Native migrants<br>Age-sex imbalance<br>Mobility) |
|---|---|---|---|---|

**Type G: Post-industrial city**

Social rank, Family status, Ethnicity and Migration status split into more detailed types. New indicants are required.

*Source:* Extension of Timms (1971 p.146)

<small>FIGURE 3 A 'FAMILY' OF SOCIAL AREA TYPES</small>

16

example, the precise cluster techniques are not described in detail, although one can infer from various diagrams that the standard Euclidean distance measure of similarity followed by Ward's hierarchical cluster method was adopted. In terms of the vital decision of any cluster method, namely the number of groups or clusters chosen for analysis, the author provides even less satisfactory evidence:

> it is difficult to explain just how the number thirty-six was chosen to constitute the number of clusters to which wards and parishes were assigned . . . a rough rule . . . is that the fusion of the most similar pairs of clusters should not contribute more than 0.30% of the total loss of variance.
>
> (Webber, 1977, p. 6.)

Such a statement hardly inspires confidence in the stability of the results although one cannot fail to have some sympathy with the author, given the enormous scope of his study. Nevertheless this failure to provide justification for the cut-off procedures and for the choice of hierarchical methods when non-hierarchical approaches (Barker, 1976) seem more flexible is disappointing.

In many ways the recent use of other grouping methods, such as Multi-Dimensional Scaling (M.D.S.) (Rushton and Golledge, 1972; Johnston, 1979) or Q Analysis (Atkin, 1975), represent a continuation of this areal taxonomic tradition. They have been developed to resolve some of the problems associated with cluster methods. But in addition they focus attention on some difficulties of factorial methods — such as the assumption of linearity in the data, or the independence of samples, which is crucial for the inferential approach to factor analysis. The development of non-metric factor analysis (McDonald, 1967) may help resolve the former restriction, although Cattell's (1978) comprehensive statement on the scientific rather than the statistical use of factor methods has pointed to the overall robustness of the factor model. Indeed, issues such as sampling conditions are really only relevant when factor methods are used inferentially; if factor analysis is used in the exploratory context they have less impact. Since these features help mitigate some of the difficulties experienced by factor analysts, the case for a revival in the Area Taxonomy approach is weakened. Moreover, Gould (1980) has shown how Q Analysis reveals the complexity of intra-urban structures rather than the simplistic results produced by other methods. As yet the new methods do not resolve the basic problem of the Area Taxonomic methods — irrespective of whether the new scaling approaches replace cluster analysis. This is that the taxonomic method — by itself — does not identify the separate dimensions, or sources of social variation, in the way pioneered by the Social Area approach: sources which are derived from, rather than imposed upon, the data by factor analysis methods. Certainly the summary characteristics of the groups of towns can be identified, but it is difficult to relate these to any theory of urban social differentiation, or any survey of the dimensionality of places. This means that the Area Taxonomy approaches — using whatever techniques — only really focus upon one part of the urban differentiation problem, namely, the classification of areas. A comprehensive approach needs to combine the definition of social dimensions or constructs with the spatial patterning of areas. This was the initial advantage of the factorial ecology approach over other methods. This approach is generalized into the Multivariate-Structural method in Chapter 2, and used in Chapters 4 and 5 to interpret the social differentiation of towns in Wales within the context of the specific problems described in Chapter 3.

At a time of technical fervent in the whole field of multivariate synthesizing procedures it is possible in the future that new methods will replace those used here. The problem is that *all* techniques have disadvantages as well as advantages, and until each procedure is comprehensively tested it does not seem appropriate to abandon procedures that have stood the test of time, and whose limitations are understood and allowed for. This is particularly relevant when the objective of a study is to contribute to the construction of a systematic body of literature, for the use of new and untried techniques makes it difficult to derive generalizations that can be systematically linked to the previous literature. This attitude should *not* be construed as providing a plea for the retention of old out-moded procedures, rather that their replacement must be accompanied by a careful and accepted demonstration of the relative advantages of any new procedures. At the time this research was carried out the authoritative survey of factor methods provided by Cattell (1978) suggested the continued utility of these procedures, particularly in the context of defining the sources of differentiation and separating the general from the specific sources of variation. Multi-dimensional scaling has the disadvantage of using nominal or ordinal rather than interval scale metrics, so much of the detail of a data set could be lost, whilst, like Q Analysis, it deals with all the variation in the data, not just the general sources filtered out by the preceding factor analysis. More to the point both techniques are essentially areal taxonomic devices, not procedures designed to identify the common sources of variation in a data set. It is possible to reverse these procedures to provide groupings of the variable sets, but as yet these M.D.S. methods do not provide a simultaneous derivation of variable similarity found in the factors, and the scaling of the importance of the areas on these factors. On balance, therefore, the need to deal with the social dimensionality, as well as the areal grouping of the areas, tilted the balance in favour of the factor-cluster procedures dealt with here. If an areal taxonomy alone was required it seems that other methods such as Q Analysis may be more appropriate, although the necessary comparative work in technical evaluation, providing unequivocal evidence of their superiority has still to be carried out.

## CHAPTER 2

# THE MULTIVARIATE-STRUCTURAL APPROACH TO URBAN DIFFERENTIATION

In the late 1960s a new methodological approach to the study of urban social differentiation was defined. Called 'Factorial Ecology' (Sweetser, 1965) because it applied *factor* analysis to urban *ecology* the method became a standard approach in the quantitative analysis of urban social character and has been extended to include all applications of factor analysis to ecological problems (Rees, 1971). The origins of the application of factor analysis methods to urban and regional studies can be traced back to the late 1930s and 1940s (Kendall, 1939; Price, 1942; Hagood, 1943). But the factorial method was rarely used since it was not particularly well known outside the field of psychology, where it has been extensively developed to define the dimensions of intelligence and personality, etc. (Cattell, 1978). From the 1960s onwards much of the subsequent popularity of the use of factorial approach in urban analysis can be attributed to Sweetser's pioneering studies of Boston and Helsinki (1965a, 1965b), the work of Gittus (1962) and Moser and Scott (1962) in the United Kingdom, and particularly to the efforts of B. J. L. Berry and his students at the University of Chicago which culminated in four sets of essays or books (Berry and Horton, 1970; Berry, 1971; Berry, 1972; Berry and Kasada, 1976).

This re-emergence of interest in the factorial approach can be linked to two features. Firstly, to the diffusion of quantitative methods to the social sciences, and secondly to the addition of larger and faster computers in research centres, with the associated growth of 'package' factor analysis programmes. These developments broke the previous barriers to the use of such sophisticated multivariate procedures, namely, the problem of recreating all the necessary statistical routines, and the need to spend simply enormous amounts of time calculating the results by hand, or with simple calculators. Lengthy reviews of the factorial ecology approach have been provided in several articles and books (Rees, 1970; Berry, 1971, 1972, 1976; Timms, 1971; Hunter, 1972; Robson, 1973; Clark, Davies and Johnston, 1974; Johnston, 1977). At its simplest level the factorial approach can be considered to be empirically based since the variable set used in the analysis is not necessarily dependent upon a particular theory of social change. This flexibility extends the scope of any factorial study as the method can incorporate a large number of variables and is really a synthesizing, rather than an analytical procedure. Since these techniques are used in this study a summary review of the approach and the extension of these purely factor analysis procedures to grouping procedures is required. The result is that eight stages (Figure 4) can be identified in a methodology designed not only to derive the social dimensions — or constructs — from the data, but also to synthesize the spatial variations into a limited number of areal categories.

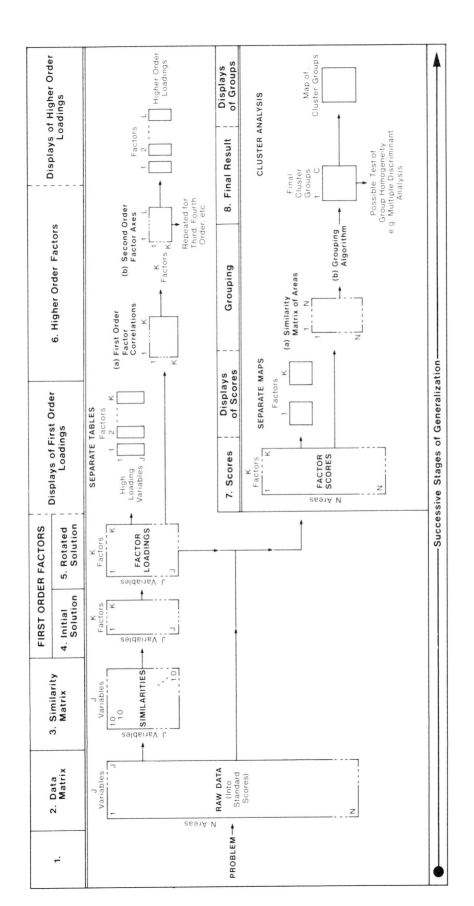

FIGURE 4 STAGES IN THE MULTIVARIATE METHODOLOGY

## 1. A Multivariate Methodology

Once the *problem* of the study has been carefully formulated the *first stage* of the method consists of the measurement of j variables — in this case of social character — over k observations, in the geographical case, areas. Normally these variables either index some theoretical construct which cannot be directly observed, for example, occupation or education variables which index social status, or provide a comprehensive coverage of assumed sources of differentiation without reference to any theory. This information is reduced to a j × j similarity matrix, the *second stage* of the analysis. Two options are present here: one relating to the choice of similarity measure, the other to the mode of the analysis. In the former case correlation coefficients appropriate to the data set are usually used, although many other types of similarity measure have been adopted in specific circumstances, such as the cos theta measure of proportional similarity (Clark, 1973). In terms of the mode of analysis it is traditional to use the R mode procedure, in which the similarities are calculated between the columns or variables of the data matrix. The opposite approach, the Q mode, calculates similarities between each pair of areas so that the similarity matrix is a row by row measure. These are the most popular modes of analysis, although Cattell (1952) suggested the P, R, S, T modes in which time is introduced as an additional source of variation to go with either cases or variables.

In the *third stage* the j × j similarity matrix is 'collapsed' via one of the possible factor methods to a smaller space consisting of j variables and p factors (where p is less than j). These factors, which can be regarded as surrogate variables, are basically mathematical constructs that identify and measure the separate sources of variation within the similarity matrix. The factors, sometimes called axes or vectors, can be best understood in terms of the following equation since they show how the correlations between one variable and all other variables are linearly reproduced.

$$Z_j = a_{j1} F_1 + a_{j2} F_2 + a_{j3} F_3 + \ldots \ldots a_{jq} F_q$$

Where: $Z_j$ is any variable j;

$a_{j1} F_1$ is the factor coefficient (weight or loading) of variable j on Factor 1

The equation shows that the variation in variable j is partitioned into separate, and additive, sources of variation associated with each factor $F_1, F_2. \ldots \ldots F_q$. Each factor loading $a_{j1}$ represents the *weight* attached to each factor, in other words the amount of the variability in variable j that is associated with this axis. There is an equation for every variable j in the data set so there are as many rows or factor equations as there are variables.

The equations are similar in form to the multiple regression expressions (King, 1968) where each variable is also described as a linear combination of other variables, plus a residual which accounts for the variance unexplained by the equation. However, in the regression model each variable is described in terms of the *original* variables. By contrast each variable in the factor equations is described by a *new* set of vectors, the mathematical constructs, called factors. In essence they describe the axes of differentiation that are latent within the data set, a set of axes that are derived from, rather than imposed upon, the data.

In theory there are as many factors as there are variables, but in practice the analyst usually finds that only some of the factors contain high loadings or variables with large weights. The factors which do not have large weights are usually discarded. Since loadings run on a scale from $-1.0$ through $0.0$ to a $+1.0$ a figure of $\pm0.3$ is often used by investigators to identify the lower bounds of acceptability, but no single procedure for determining the minimum acceptable size of loading exists. The $\pm0.3$ value is the nearest to a 10% cut-off limit since the square of the loading measures the amount of variance of the variable explained by, or associated with, the factor. In a $j$ variable R mode situation, therefore, the $j \times j$ similarity matrix is reduced to a $j$ variable $\times p$ factor matrix where $p < j$. From this $j \times p$ factor matrix the sum of the squares of the loadings can be used to measure the variance explanation of the solution. If these calculations are made by rows, across the factors for any variable, the *communality* is found, namely, the amount of variation of each variable explained by the $j \times p$ factor solution. If the calculations are made by columns, along the variables for any factor, eigenvalues are obtained. Each eigenvalue measures how much of the total variation of the $j$ variables is accounted for by each individual factor, or vector.

A basic distinction must be drawn between the component and common factor *models,* and in each of these a series of *different factoring methods* can be recognized. The former approach really represents a re-writing of the original similarity matrix into a more concise or parsimonious form. As such it is used extensively by factorial ecologists as an exploratory measure to identify the latent structure of data matrices without any prior assumptions about the final results. The Principal Axes factor method, strictly speaking the component method, is the most popular factoring procedure of this approach. A series of 'rules of thumb', such as the 1.0 rule and scree test (Rummel, 1971; Davies and Barrow, 1973; Cattell, 1978) have been proposed to help investigators choose an appropriate place to stop factoring, but these are only guidelines, not rigid tests. By contrast, the common factor approach, or factor analysis proper for the pure statistician, is designed to test some hypothesis: either that there are a certain number of common factors, or that certain levels of common variance or sizes of communalities occur in the data set. In these common factor models the decision to stop factoring is made on the basis of some statistical test of significance. The important feature of the common factor approach is that the variance of any variable $Z_j$ is partitioned into three parts.

$$Z_j = a_{j1} F_1 + a_{j2} F_2 + a_{j3} F_3 \ldots . + b_j S_j \ldots \ldots \ . \ + e_j E_j \ldots . .$$
$$Z_j = \text{Common Factors} \ldots \ldots . + \text{Specificity} \ldots . + \text{Error}$$

The common factor model is concerned primarily with the *common variance,* not with *specific* variance associated with the particular variables or areas, or with the *error* associated with the solution. In the component approach this distinction between the variance of the common factors and specific factors is not explicitly made; a series of components are identified and these are a hybrid mixture of common and specific variance. A variety of common factor methods can be recognized, each using different ways to abstract factors. One set of methods directly calculates the common factors from the similarity matrix. They either need the communalities to be defined, as for example in the Principal Axes method, or a number of axes have to be specified, such as in the Maximum Likelihood or Minres methods (Harman, 1976). Another set of methods adjusts the matrix before calculating common factors by a series of different procedures, such as Image, Alpha or Rao's Analysis (Nie et al, 1975). Giggs and Mather (1975) as well as Davies (1978) have reviewed the utility of these various factoring methods for geographical analysis.

The *fourth phase* of an investigation usually involves the rotation of the initial component, or common factor solution to new positions in the multi-dimensional space of the factors to make them easier to interpret. No variance is lost in this procedure; it is simply redistributed from one axis to another. The factors are then named, usually by generalizing from the type of variables having high loadings with the factor. There are two basic types of rotation: orthogonal rotations, in which the axes are rotated as a set at right angles to one another; or oblique rotations, in which the individual axes are allowed to vary independently so that they can be oblique to each other. In both types a variety of alternative methods have been proposed (Rummel, 1971), although the standard techniques now seem to be Varimax for the orthogonal approach and Direct Oblimin (with gamma set at 0.0) for the oblique. One advantage of the use of oblique rotation is that orthogonal factor structures are not imposed upon the data set. This means that the axes can be oblique to one another — probably a more appropriate relationship in most real situations. In addition, the oblique approach leads to the production of a factor correlation matrix, measuring the correlations between the factors, or axes. This, in itself, can be factor analyzed to produce the *fifth phase,* the derivation of successively higher order solutions. These generalize the results even further (Cattell, 1968; Davies and Lewis, 1973).

So far the discussion has only been phrased in terms of the variables, in the R mode case leading to the derivation of factor loadings which identify the interrelationships between the variables. The *sixth phase* involves the calculation of factor scores. These measure the importance of the factors on the areas or the original urban units. Again a variety of alternative methods have been proposed to calculate scores (Harman, 1976), a basic difference between them being that common factor scores have to be estimated whereas component scores can be obtained directly. The basic derivation is given by the following formula:

Where:

$$S_{p1} = \sum_{j=1}^{n} \frac{a_{jp}}{\lambda_p} . Z_j$$

$S_{p1}$ is the factor score for factor p on area 1;
$a_{jp}$ is the loading for variable j on factor p;
$\lambda_p$ is the eigenvalue for factor p;
$Z_j$ is the standardized score for variable j;
n is the number of variables.

The factor scores are usually standardized to zero mean and unit variance to make them comparable to one another, although it is obvious that each scale is of more or less importance according to the eigenvalue of the factor. If a set of scores proportional to the importance of each factor is needed the scores can be weighted by the various eigenvalues. In the R mode example, the scores complement the loadings, since they explicitly deal with the relative importance of each area on the individual factors. The relative nature of these measurements can be appreciated by the fact that in the Q mode approach the scores identify the variables scoring highly on factors which are clusters of similar areas. Whether the R or Q mode route is chosen it should be apparent that some of the basic problems faced by generations of students of urban social structure are very clearly identified by the factorial method. The R mode loadings and factors identify and measure the *collectivities of the data set,* the separate sources of variation. The R mode scores identify and measure the distribution of factors, specifically *the spatial patterns* of all these collectivities or sources of social variation. In addition, two factor models, the component and common factor approaches, give investigators the flexibility of using the exploratory or confirmatory (or hypothesis testing) routes.

It has already been noted at the end of Chapter 1 that other multivariate techniques have been applied to the problem of measuring urban social structure. Cluster Analysis, another family of related procedures, has been used by Tryon (1955) as an alternative to Social Area Analysis and, more recently, Atkin (1975) has proposed the use of Q Analysis. The problem with these approaches is that they produce a series of clusters of similar areas, but fail to provide the investigator with either a quantified statement on the relationships between the variables or a precise measurement of the importance of each source of variation to each area or cluster. However, cluster analysis does have an important part to play in the Multivariate-Structural approach. It can be applied to the factor score matrix as a *seventh stage* to produce a final grouping of urban sub-areas. Normally the factor scores are used directly, since each set measures a separate source of variation, but some researchers have weighted the scores according to the eigenvalues (Smith, 1972). Presumably this decision is made to take into account the importance of each source of variation. Since the 'importance' of an axis depends upon the variable set, which may be biased in favour of certain characteristics, there is no necessity to weight scores in this way if the investigator is trying to provide equal balance to all sources of variation. Again, there are many alternative similarity measures which can be applied to the factor score matrix, as well as a variety of different clustering methods that can be used on the similarity matrix. These alternatives have been reviewed elsewhere (Sokal and Sneath, 1972; Wishart, 1975). Here it is enough to note that the wide choice may cause problems if the advantages and disadvantages of approach are not recognized. In general, however, the alternatives do provide a great deal of flexibility for any investigator. Finally, it is often useful to apply discriminant analysis to 'test' the utility of the final groupings if the various factors are not too highly correlated. This may be an *eighth stage* in the study.

This brief summary of the factorial and cluster analysis methods as applied to the study of urban social structure demonstrates that there cannot be a single 'best' technique or solution covering all eventualities — there are many options. The choice of options has to be carefully justified with respect to the particular problem being investigated if the results of any study are to be used in the development of a systematic body of literature. Comparatively few of the existing studies broadly labelled as 'factorial' have been convincing in this respect, and much of the early factorial work was really based on the Social Area method, since they attempted to establish the validity of the Shevky-Bell model of urban social differentiation, with its three constructs of Urbanization or Family Status, Social Rank, and Ethnicity. Later work (Anderson and Bean, 1961; Murdie, 1968) showed how the spatial patterns of the scores on these axes corresponded to the distribution originally proposed in one of the classical urban ecological models. In other words, Family (or Urbanization) Status was linked to concentric zonation (Burgess, 1925); Social Rank (or Socio-Economic Status) was associated with sectors (Hoyt, 1939); and Ethnicity was distributed in the cluster pattern favoured by the multiple nuclei theory (Harris and Ullman, 1943). Although these original patterns were often linked to land use as well as social variations the patterns cannot be considered to represent confirmation of the original ecological theories. The results indicate that these patterns are useful ideas in indexing the spatial structures of separate parts of urban social structure. By contrast very few multivariate analyses have been produced in which the total community or areal structures (as opposed to individual dimensional patterns) are related to these or other spatial generalizations. Most urban typologies are content to describe the final patterning of areas at a place-particular level.

Any review of the factorial evidence for the three axis model of the urban social differentiation reveals that the extent of support for this idea is not very convincing. Bell (1963), using the same data set for San Francisco analysed in his earlier Social Area Analysis study with Shevky (1955), maintained that the factorial results showed that the three axis model of Economic Status, Family Status and Ethnicity was appropriate, in the sense that the three axes were discrete factors of variation. The same conclusion was reached by Hunter and Latif (1972) in Winnipeg, this time using fifteen variables to index the three postulates.

Despite these positive findings about the utility of the Social Area constructs, empirical example after example showed that the three axis model (or for that matter McElrath's (1968) four axis model which added Migration Status to the constructs) is only a partial description of the social differentiation of cities. Many additional axes have been found, as for example in Davies and Lewis's studies of Leicester (1973, 1974). Figure 5 shows that eight first order axes were identified from a factor analysis of sixty variables. How, therefore, can these additional axes of differentiation be reconciled with the three or four axis proposition? Part of the explanation lies in the fact that most tests of the Shevky-Bell model used very small variable sets. This ensured that only part of the potential differentiation in cities was dealt with. Nevertheless the use of higher order factor methods on large variable sets — as in the Leicester study (Figure 5) — demonstrated that some of these more specialized axes collapse into the traditional

## Successive levels of generalization

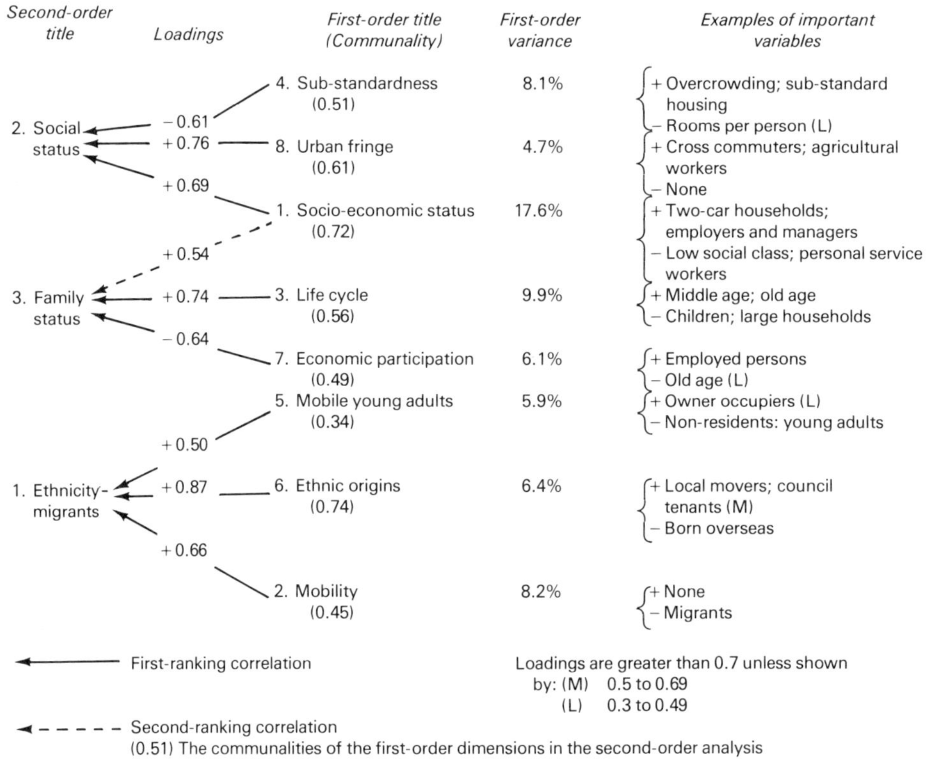
Second-order title
Loadings
First-order title (Communality)
First-order variance
Examples of important variables
2. Social status
−0.61
+0.76
+0.69
+0.54
4. Sub-standardness (0.51)
8.1%
+ Overcrowding; sub-standard housing
− Rooms per person (L)
8. Urban fringe (0.61)
4.7%
+ Cross commuters; agricultural workers
− None
1. Socio-economic status (0.72)
17.6%
+ Two-car households; employers and managers
− Low social class; personal service workers
3. Family status
+0.74
−0.64
+0.50
3. Life cycle (0.56)
9.9%
+ Middle age; old age
− Children; large households
7. Economic participation (0.49)
6.1%
+ Employed persons
− Old age (L)
5. Mobile young adults (0.34)
5.9%
+ Owner occupiers (L)
− Non-residents: young adults
1. Ethnicity-migrants
+0.87
+0.66
6. Ethnic origins (0.74)
6.4%
+ Local movers; council tenants (M)
− Born overseas
2. Mobility (0.45)
8.2%
+ None
− Migrants
First-ranking correlation
Second-ranking correlation
(0.51) The communalities of the first-order dimensions in the second-order analysis
Loadings are greater than 0.7 unless shown by: (M) 0.5 to 0.69
(L) 0.3 to 0.49

## (b) Higher-order Principal Components solution

| *Components* | *1* | *2* | *3* | *4* | *5* |
|---|---|---|---|---|---|
| % variance | 21.86 | 15.93 | 13.03 | 10.95 | 9.74 |
| Cumulative variance | 21.86 | 37.82 | 50.84 | 61.79 | 71.53 |

## Second-order correlations matrix: biquartimin solution

| | *1* | *2* | *3* |
|---|---|---|---|
| 1. Ethnic migrant | 1.00 | | |
| 2. Social status | 0.10 | 1.00 | |
| 3. Family status | −0.15 | −0.07 | 1.00 |

*Source:* Davies and Lewis (1973)

FIGURE 5 AXES OF DIFFERENTIATION IN LEICESTER, ENGLAND (1966)

Shevky-Bell axes at higher levels of generalization, whilst Davies (1978) has claimed that the more modern structures found in Canadian Prairie cities are reflected in four higher order axes which parallel McElrath's (1968) ideas. This would seem to indicate that a static or simplistic view of Western urban social structure, reflected in a single dimensional model, is inappropriate. Also it is worth remembering that twenty-five years have passed since Shevky's work, and Daniel Bell (1974) has maintained that the greater specialization of Western society means that it is more appropriately described as *post-industrial* in nature. This can be linked with the suggestion that Western cities are becoming more complex and finely differentiated in their spatial structures (Johnston, 1972) — implying that simplistic spatial models no longer apply. This makes it more and more important to measure the social differentiation of cities and regions in as detailed and comprehensive a fashion as possible.

Despite the initial breakthroughs provided by the factorial approach any dispassionate review will reveal that the term 'factorial ecology' is neither precise enough, nor comprehensive enough, adequately to summarize the developments produced by the application of multivariate statistical methods. For example, other multivariate methods, such as cluster analysis, have frequently been used in conjunction with the factor procedures, so 'factor analysis' alone is no longer an adequate descriptive definition. The term 'multivariate' appears to be much more suitable since it focuses upon the use of many variables and the general application of multivariate statistical procedures. In addition it is clear that the 'factorial ecology' approach does not cover all avenues of inquiry defined by the term 'urban ecology'. The review of the 'Chicago School' of urban ecology in the previous chapter demonstrated that the field contains behavioural studies of various social groups in cities, and profiles of urban associations or organizations. These seem to be as important to the urban ecology approach as studies of the spatial distributions of social groups. In such a situation it is hard to see how the 'factorial ecology' approach can ever claim to be a major contribution to such analyses of urban behaviour or associations. Instead, it illustrates the need to restrict the focus of enquiry to those areas which can be adequately handled by the multivariate methods.

After reviewing the alternative possibilities, the decision was made to restrict the application of these multivariate methods to urban structural analysis. When this is welded to the multivariate methodology already described it is apparent that a revised approach to the study of urban social differentiation is being proposed. This can be described as the *Multivariate-Structural Approach*. It cannot, of course, be claimed that the approach is completely original, after all it uses some of the same techniques that were used by the 'Factorial Ecology' and 'Area Taxonomy' methods. However, since it integrates and extends these two approaches within the much more specific framework of the 'structural' social tradition (Blau, 1976) it represents a sufficiently distinctive method to deserve the dignity of a new title. Since the 'multivariate' part of the title has been described it remains to look in more detail at the meaning of the 'structural' approach in terms of the content area and scales of investigation, its assumptions and the dangers of restricting geographical interest to this one perspective.

## 2. What is the Structural Approach?

One of the recurring problems in the development of interest in urban social differentiation was the ambiguity caused by the lack of comprehensive definitions of the content area and perspectives of the studies. In addition, key concepts, such as the 'natural area' idea, were confusing because the criteria used to define them lacked clarity. Such sources of confusion provide much greater problems for the development of a systematic study than the individual technical difficulties found in each phase of endeavour. Techniques, after all, can always be improved. But without explicit definitions and objectives of study it is difficult to define the frame of reference of any analysis or to relate it to the wider corpus of knowledge. Hence the first task of any attempt at systematizing the literature on the social differentiation of urban communities is to identify the various components — or parts — and approaches that contribute to the similarity or differentiation of places. Davies (1970) provided a conceptual model of the alternative approaches to urban geography which can be used for this task. Figure 6 shows the three components or parts that were defined.

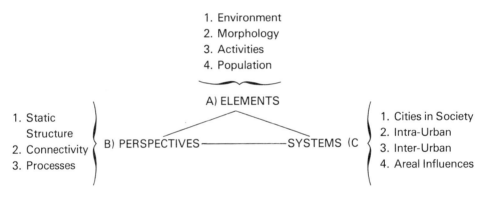

FIGURE 6   A CONCEPTUAL MODEL OF URBAN DIFFERENTIATION

This diagram shows that the static structure approach is defined as one of three alternative *perspectives* of study although structures can also be isolated from connectivity patterns. The intra-urban approach is shown to be one of four *systems* of study. It is in the *elements*, however, that one finds the content of any investigation. These four elements, or sets of differentiating features, attempt to account for all the variations found in urban areas. These are called: Environment; Morphology; Activities; Population. By summarizing and extending Davies's original ideas (1970) the range of phenomena to which the social structural approach can be applied is clarified.

(i)  The term *Environment* relates to the physical environment, and deals with all the environmental features, hills, rivers, soil condition, climate, forests, etc., that provide the physical geography of the area.

(ii) *Morphology* describes the man made 'skeleton' of the city, the pattern of roads, the layout, and architectural style of buildings.

(iii) *Activities* include both the *behaviour* of people, which can basically be expressed in terms of flows of people or information, the *organizations* of these activities, as well as the consequences of these actions, the *land uses* of cities with their specialized areas and activities.

(iv) *Population* relates to the social differences of the people in the areas. As such it encompasses what can be called the *social attributes* of the population (the age, sex, economic or ethnic differentiation) their *attitudinal* or preferential characteristics, as well as the *organizational* differentiation, such as the roles or status of individuals.

For students of the ideographic approach, the whole range of these elements forms the bedrock from which the nuggets of individual characterization are mined. This philosophical position means that there is little interest in either being comprehensive, that is summarizing the range of variation, or even of organizing and systematizing the knowledge that is identified by searching for the repetitive patterns or relationships. This latter approach is the focus of this particular study; it is part of the tradition described as 'structural' by social scientists.

Unfortunately the terms 'structural' or 'social structure' do not summarize a single intellectual tradition, as can be seen from the rather diverse ideas contained in a recent set of essays on the topic written by some of the leading figures in North American sociology (Blau, 1976) or in recent reviews by geographers and sociologists (Blau, 1974, Johnston, 1977, and Rumley, 1979). A variety of different meanings for the structural approach can be identified, a problem compounded by the fact that the term is only defined implicitly in the various analysis. Nevertheless it can be suggested that three different connotations can be distinguished.

**(a)** The first is one of identifying the basic components in social life:

> social structure refers to the patterns discernible in social life, the regularities observed, the configurations detected.
>
> (Blau, 1976, p. 3.)

In other words the emphasis is upon the 'standardized or normative patterns' in which the vital orientation is to the definition of the component parts or relationships which describe the observable empirical features of groups or classes of people. As such:

> a social structure is delineated by its parameters. A structural parameter is any criterion implicit in the social distinctions that people make.
>
> (Blau, 1974, p. 615.)

The term 'social distinction' is still, of course, rather vague, but it is proposed that it relates most closely to the things that people, or in our case, aggregates of people in area, are, or do, rather than how they think or feel. The concept of 'structure' can be clarified by noting that any person occupies positions on several different parameters, age, ethnicity, occupation, family condition. Blau (1974, p. 616) explained that these social distinctions are not structures *per se* but analytical elements of it. This means that the 'structures' that we are searching for can be conceptualized as the 'collectivities' of these parameters, namely, the fundamental dimensions or patterns to which they belong. Thus if age completely determined family condition, or ethnicity a type of occupation, there would be at least two, not four, structures involved. Blau (1974, p. 616) also maintains it is the differentiation rather than the configuration of these parameters that is all important. For example, it is ethnic heterogeneity not ethnic background, occupational position not character, that are the key features in the structural approach. In view of the areal focus of this study the concentration upon the degree of differentiation, rather than configuration, may be more obvious. Each part of the city, or the whole city for that matter, will have a position on each paramater defined by the characteristics of the aggregate of people in the area, such as a certain percentage in an ethnic group. The search, therefore, is for the repetitive social patterns or structures based on areal differences that underlie these individual social variables.

The use of this social structural method, with information compiled on an areal basis, does mean that certain restrictions are placed upon the content of the study — at least when compared to the social character approach, or even to the structural approach for non-areal social data. Environmental elements are excluded since the systematic study of their variations relate to non-social processes. Moreover the effect of the environment upon social variation is difficult to study on an areal basis. Morphological variations are also usually excluded, with the exception of different sizes of houses or housing amenities. In the last resort it could be argued that the morphological variations are the product of social preferences for particular urban designs, but morphology describes a set of phenomena of quite different characteristics and they need to be treated separately. This leaves the elements summarized as Population and Activities in Figure 6. Again it does not seem appropriate to treat all of them as structural features in the context of this areal study. For example, the behaviour or organizations that occur in cities frequently have territorial aspects but they are movements *in areas,* not the products *of areas.* These restrictions mean that the primary orientation of the social structure approach is to the 'attributes' of the population in areas, to the tangible features of these units. This normally excludes the attitudinal aspects of social life. Preferences are certainly expressed by groups or individuals for areas; they are not really the preferences *of areas,* although such preferences could, perhaps, be measured in this form. In other words, there seems little doubt that the structure of behaviour in cities, or preferences, are more profitably organized upon some other basis than the strictly areal one adopted here, in the same way that the spatial analysis of human phenomena in general has been liberated from the bounds of a purely regional study. Social structure, therefore, is treated in this study in quite a restricted way. So although it is possible to refer to behavioural structures or to land use structures and patterns they are not the focus of concern in this study. Also it can be acknowledged that these behavioural or land use patterns may be related to the social structures found in cities but they are considered to be issues of a different order that will not be explored.

The type of 'structural' approach that is dealt with here has been described by Blau (1974, p. 615) as being:

> merely the basis for a theory yet to be constructed to explain these conditions.

As such, the approach can only be considered to represent a partial view of the characteristics that are being described and is an interpretation of 'structure' that is usually traced back to the work of Radcliffe-Brown (1940).

(b) The second interpretation of structure is drastically different and is associated with the work of investigators such as Levi-Strauss (1952). In Blau's words this alternative interpretation means that:

> social structure is a system of logical relationships among general principles which is not designed as a conceptual framework to reflect empirical conditions but as a theoretical interpretation of social life.
> (Blau, 1974, p. 615.)

In this interpretation 'structure' is used to describe *the underlying principles or substrata of society,* the set of norms and values which govern social life and development and which obviously condition such specific societal issues as the one considered here, the patterns of communities in cities. In essence these are the types of underlying conditions which govern the societal interpretations made by Karl Marx in the nineteenth century or Talcot Parsons (1964). It is the type of structure that has achieved some recent popularity in geography because of the work of Harvey (1973) and Castells (1977).

To avoid confusion it is worth clarifying the differences between these two interpretations of structure by means of a familiar example, that of land use differentiation in cities. For the follower of Radcliffe-Brown it would be enough to identify the structure, or pattern of land issues in the city, the area dominated by particular land use combinations. For exponents of the 'underlying sub-stratum' view, the attempt would be made to identify the causes of these regularities. In a capitalist society one can point to the controlling influence of the bid-rent mechanism as a fundamental force in the concentric patterning of cities (Muth, 1969) with the central area attracting the greatest economic value. However, it makes much more sense to go beyond the specifics of economics and suggest that, in our society, it is the social valuation placed on these economic variations that really leads to the differential use and control of areas which underlies the land use patterns. In other societies, for example those with a theocratic basis, a similar zonation with a central city focus has also been found, but this time the pattern is reversed. The higher prestige associated with a central city location seems to have led to the concentration of a particular group of people, and hence land uses, in the inner city — this time the religious elite and their buildings. This prestige was often linked to the valuation of a central point in the city since it was the place closest to the heavenly cosmos from which power emanated (Wheatley, 1972). Hence in both the capitalist and theocratic city there is a high valuation placed on the city centre, one expressed in cultural mores, the other in economic terms. Social valuation is the structure that can be used to subsume these explanations since the term is broad enough to cover both manifestations. Such issues are not, however, of primary concern to this discussion; it is enough to have clarified the two meanings of structure.

(c) A third interpretation of structure has recently been made by Rumley (1979), this time in the geographical literature. It is primarily concerned with 'structural effects' in the sense that it investigates the way in which the attributes of space or spatial patterns affect individual behaviour. As such the idea describes the approach more generally known as 'contextual' or 'compositional' (Przeworski and Soares, 1971; Cox, 1968). Robson's (1969) study of Sunderland provides an example of the approach in which the influence of parental attitudes to education were studied in an urban ecological context. Attitudes towards the eleven plus examination were shown to be affected by the character of areas (as measured by factor techniques) in the sense that some areas inhibited the development of favourable attitudes, whereas these were encouraged in others. Similarly, Herbert (1976) demonstrated a contextual relationship between delinquency and social areas in Cardiff. The obvious primary concern of these studies is with behaviour or attitudes rather than area *per se* — hence Rumley's description of 'structural effects'. But as always, the difficulty is of measuring the precise amount of this effect. For example, Giggs (1973 and 1975) showed how schizophrenics were concentrated in low status inner areas of the city of Nottingham. He suggested that it is easy to fall into the trap of arguing for the re-inforcement or even the creation of the mental illness because of the areal characteristics. Giggs was careful to show that the association may be a product of individuals with these tendencies moving into the area and that only a behavioural study following case histories would be able to tease out the relationships. It would seem that investigators need control populations of people with similar tendencies who are located outside these areas before any unequivocal conclusions about areal effects can be provided. The argument, of course, takes one close to the nature: nurture discussion of the relative effects of genetic inheritance versus environment, one that still causes dispute among psychologists. Despite Rumley's enthusiasm for specifically geographical contributions, research by geographers in this area does seem rather limited and must involve other social scientists.

The presence of these three approaches, all using 'structural' or 'structuralism' to some degree in their descriptions, obviously causes confusion to any investigator. Hence the particular approach favoured in any research needs to be justified. The study of *structural effects* would best seem to be accommodated by the more traditional title of *contextual* study, whilst *structuralism* is best reserved for the Levi-Strauss ideas of deep seated *theoretical causes*. The terms *structure* or *structural*, therefore, can be reserved for the type of *pattern,* or *construct seeking* approach described in the first section of this review. Obviously there are associations between all three approaches in the sense that the structures or patterns dealt with here are the product of the underlying bases of society and these structures seem to influence behaviour quite markedly. In fact, Rumley (1979, p. 356) called for:

> a more systematic definition of spatial structures whose influence or behaviour is being tested . . . A tentative typology might derive from categories based on physical structures such as the home and workplace, *social structures such as occupation and ethnicity,* behavioural structures such as crime and voting behaviour, attributes of space such as crowdedness and relative location, and external inputs such as a change in the law or party activity. Analytical frameworks would then be developed for each structural sub-category.

Although it would seem the phrase in italics describes variables, not structures in our sense, the case for the analysis of structures seems made. But now that the differences between these three different approaches have been identified it is important to decide on which type of structure is being investigated. The one dealt with here is the *structural* or *pattern seeking* approach in which the attempt is made to define the types of social structures involved — not by predetermined key variables as in Rumley's example — but by the multivariate methods previously described. In many ways, perhaps, the 'underlying principle' or 'Levi-Strauss' approach to 'structuralism' may appear to be the more fundamental for explaining the differentiation of society. Yet it appears to be of more limited geographical value in the search for methods which tell us how one area or settlement differs from another. This explains the preference for Blau's approach to the study of structures (Blau, 1976). In essence, the structural approach adopted here searches for the social structures and patterns found in urban areas — defined empirically by Factor Analysis as the collectivities of the variables and by Cluster Analysis as the similarity of the areas over a set of measures. To put this approach within the context of empirical study it means that *the objective is to isolate the general features which best describe social variations.* For example, one might assume — on intuitive grounds — that family or economic variations are the best ways of describing these patterns. The approach adopted here rejects these vague subjective or descriptive categories. Instead, it uses a comprehensive variable set that is sorted in such a way that the basic categories of variables are identified as factors, and the variables are put in order of importance in terms of their contribution to these sources of differentiation. In structural terms, therefore, the differentiating variables are first indentified, then synthesized to contribute to some overall construct, rather than being assumed on *a priori* grounds. Returning to the example of land use distribution in cities, it is obvious that the concentric form is not the only pattern or structure involved in the social differentiation of cities. Hence it is argued here that we need to understand the variety in the patterns of social differentiation in society and their areal manifestations *before* we search for the mechanisms of these patterns. If a theory only described part of the urban social variety it is obviously not as comprehensive as it could be. It is far from trite to remind ourselves of Sherlock Holmes's advice to Dr Watson:

> It is a capital mistake to theorize in advance of the facts (in *The Adventure of the Second Stain,* A. Conan Doyle, Vol 2, 1977 Reprinting).

Two points should be made about this statement. Firstly, philosophers of science delight in debate about the nature of a fact. This is not the place to enter into the discussion. To allow the quotation some meaning in the context of this discussion, a fact can be treated simply as one of the components or patterns in the social structures of cities. So one of the tasks of this study is to identify the very diverse and complex forms these structures take.

As such this monograph follows Blau's dictum (1974, p. 616) that the:

> complex configuration of elements that comprise social structures cannot be understood unless analytical dissection precedes synthesis.

Secondly, theorists of a deductive persuasion will vigorously disagree with Holmes's advice. But the difference between the deductive and inductive approaches is rarely as clear cut in terms of the *history* of research — as opposed to the way the results are finally presented — as it would initially seem. Since there is no single path to knowledge, alternatives should be explored. Once the structures have been identified one can move on to describe and ultimately to explain these patterns.

## 3. Assumptions of the Structural Approach

This interpretation of the structural approach to the social differentiation of urban areas, summarized as urban social differentiation, is not complete without making explicit the assumptions upon which it is based.

**(a)** The first assumption is that patterns of regularities *can be,* and, perhaps more importantly, *are* identified to the satisfaction of other workers. This represents an appeal to the logic of justification. It is proposed that there *are* persisting (but not permanent) social structure regularities in cities, instead of only chaotic, idiosyncratic variations. In part the assumption can be related to the continuing debate among historians about the way patterns or regularities can be found. It has, of course, been argued that:

> philosophers of history and social evolutionists to the contrary, long-term directionality tend to be in the beholder's eye, not in the materials themselves.
>
> (Nisbet, 1969, p. 284.)

Undoubtedly, Nisbet was criticizing the concept of the wider processes of history, which go beyond our definition of structure, since it is more relevant to the Levi-Strauss conception. Nevertheless, it is as well to emphasize that the idea of regularity in the social structure of areas and the resultant spatial patterns is not necessarily an obvious, or fundamental, element in urban patterning. The review of the history of ideas in urban ecology will reveal that not all researchers have accepted the assumption of regularities; Davie's critique of Burgess's concentric zones (1938) is, at base, a plea for particularism. Given the possibility of rejecting the idea of a patterned regularity it is vital to use a method which will either unequivocally produce a pattern from the data, or demonstrate that none exists. It is in this sense that the factorial method already reviewed in the first section has proved useful, since it inductively derives the patterns and measures the amount of explanation involved in the model. Instead of simply asserting that this particular method is the most appropriate for the objectives of this monograph, a lengthy justification is provided. It is argued that without such methodological justification there would be little to recommend the results of the study. Naturally, it should go without saying that not all the patterns found in any city can be part of the regularity; unique, place-particular distortions complement the general features. It is trite, but nevertheless worthwhile, to emphasize again that cities are composed of both general and particular patterns; the concern here is with the former.

**(b)** The second assumption is an implicit one in most scientific studies; it is the acceptance of 'epistemological dualism'. A succinct summary has been provided by Lovejoy (1930, p. 379):

> whatever knowledge we have of real objects is indirect or representative, the datum whereby . . . we . . . know any such object is not identical with the object known.

Even in an empirical study the adoption of such a position helps one to appreciate that the individual variables used in any study are not the final, definitive answer to the characterization of an area. According to exponents of the dualist position the 'reality' can never be completely observed; instead it is only operationally defined by the variables chosen by the analyst. Yet a moment's reflection will confirm that a multitude of different variables and operational definitions could be used since there is an infinite number of properties of areas. Even restricting the choice to part of the characteristics of areas with the adoption of the social structural approach only marginally cuts down the scale of the problem. Nevertheless, most scientists assume that there is some order behind this multitude of variation. Sets of scientific concepts called 'constructs' are proposed, each of which summarize, or account for, part of the individual variations. These constructs are not observable; they are only defined in theory since they are building blocks from which scientific theories are constructed, the theories being the most complete form of the scientific representation of the reality. In other words, a five-fold division can be recognized in this interpretation of the areal variation in socia character.

First, the sense perception of the differences between the areas, which has been restricted to the tangible social attributes of the urban areas, not to the land use, morphological or attitudinal variations.

Second, the operational definitions of the variables used to measure these perceived differences.

Third, the identification of the collectivities of these variables, the constructs.

Fourth, the logical interrelationship of these constructs. This forms a theoretical representation of the last stage.

The fifth and last stage is the reality, or rather the scientific perception of the reality.

It cannot be claimed that this division is the only perception, or even organization, of the reality being dealt with. Each of these stages involves an inferential jump from one level to another, jumps that become progressively more difficult to justify in any absolute sense since the relationships have, in the last resort, to be assumed. Nevertheless, the essence of the scientific method is to derive connections and conclusions which are clear and precise enough to convince the rest of the scientific community that such relationships are acceptable ones. This appeal to a collective judgement differs drastically from the intuitive approach, the 'beauty to the eye of the beholder' premise that justifies so much of the subjective or artistic approach. Yet in the last resort the fact that these links or relationships are assumed must be emphasized. Complete objectivity is an illusion and the majority of scientists accept this fact — even if their critics rarely acknowledge it.

(c) The third assumption is that a particular scale or range of vision is employed, namely, a medium scale approach. Given that continuities in society exist, it is easier to summarize this scale by looking at it within the context of the polar positions. By searching for the empirical interrelations and patterns lying beyond the social parameters, this medium scale approach obviously conflicts with the microscale view, which deals with the behaviour of individuals, or the macroscale perspective, which identifies the external characteristics of the global society and environment — the 'structural' approach of Levi-Strauss. This means that three very different scales of analysis could be used, each of which contain phenomena that determine social structure. For example, it is possible to take the individual, behavioural view and investigate the residential choices of individuals as a decision-making activity conditioned by their psychological make-up, and the alternatives available in the city. To some extent the day-to-day maintenance of the social structure depends on these choices. At the other extreme lie the external conditions of society, in which an obvious example is provided by the technological status of society. It will be shown that Shevky and Bell (1955) used the idea of industrialization and the attendant divisions of labour and mobility as the basis for their derivation of structural axes of social character. However, this is not necessarily the only societal condition. For example, sociologists such as Talcot Parsons (1961, p. 34) point to the primacy of the cultural system, to the patterns of meaning, of values, of norms, organized knowledge and beliefs that lie behind the different structures of individual societies. To these we can add the natural environment which, in its variations, can produce different economies. These may condition the character of the urban places or regions lying within it. Between these macro and micro extremes lies what Blau (1976, p. 5) called the 'intermediate' range of social structure or conditions, which is the search for the structures upon which micro-social behaviour can be based and to which macro-social processes can be addressed. Yet it is worth noting that even the adoption of this type of scale still leaves many technical questions unanswered, such as the level of aggregation, the size of the city area to be used as collecting cells, or even whether the ideas can be extended to the analysis of whole cities.

Recognition of the differences in scale between these various approaches to the study of urban social differentiation must leave one very wary about the comprehensiveness of the type of medium scale structural explanation attempted here. This leads to a related assumption, one that has been succinctly summarized in one of Merton's stipulations about structural analysis.

> [It] . . . can lay no claim to being capable of accounting exhaustively for social and cultural phenomena.
>
> (Merton, 1976, p. 36.)

A complete explanation of the social differentiation of urban areas would presumably have to take into account the behaviour of individuals in cities, and long-term or macro-societal trends — apart from all the elements already excluded — and also the idiosyncratic urban characteristics usually ignored by students of systematic patterns. To integrate such diverse features seems to be an impossible task at this time. But Merton's view demonstrates that there is no need to seek such a comprehensive solution. An analogy with the type of knowledge we have on the structure of the human body will illustrate the point. Micro-physical processes at the cell level constantly create and regulate the structure of the organs and parts of the body. Yet a macro-evolutionary view is needed to explain how these structures have been produced. Which has primacy, cell chemistry or long-term evolution? This is the classic chicken/egg argument found in many disciplines. These micro-physical or evolutionary considerations are important, but should not lead investigators to ignore human anatomy, or structure. This can be an important emphasis in its own right. Hence an important research question is the identification of the structure or recurring patterns of urban areas. There is no necessity to ask questions about how this structure functions, or how it evolves; they are issues of a different order which are difficult to intregrate into a single study. Since it is quite likely that quite different processes operate at the various scales, the separation of these approaches may be a sensible analytical move at this point in our understanding. Feyman (1965, p. 32-3) succinctly illustrated the same type of point in relation to the discipline of physics:

> the behaviour of matter on a small scale obeys laws quite different from things on a large scale. People have not succeeded in completely making a theory which is consistent with the uncertainty principles and the quantum mechanical principles.

If physicists are prepared to accept such scale differences in their explanations of gross matter and fundamental particles it is difficult to deny the need for different approaches to studies of deep seated societal theories, social structural patterns and the behavioural dynamics of small groups. In other words, Merton's opinion that an all-embracing theory is likely to elude researchers is accepted. Intellectual 'monism' is out of fashion; it is more practical to work towards a series of limited scale paradigms.

Despite this methodological conclusion, which will be an assumption of the case studies, many urban researchers have found it tempting to assume that scale-dependence does not exist; that the behaviour of individuals or groups is directly related to the character of the area in which the behaviour is found. This danger is one to which urban ecologies have been particularly prone since the study of the social structure and patterns of cities has often been subservient to behavioural analyses. For example, Burgess's (1925) classic concentric zone generalizations were primarily designed as an introduction to the study of the behaviour of groups in cities. Even recent investigators who are careful to distinguish between the scales of analysis admit that the interest in urban structure is secondary rather than primary (Timms, 1971, p. vii). Hence it must be emphatically stated that *the focus of interest of this study is upon the social structures of areas, not the behaviour of groups,* and that a direct relationship between the behaviour of individuals and the character of areas (Palm, 1973) cannot be assumed. The whole history of the neighbourhood concept provides a warning in this respect, for there was often an implicit link made between the behaviour of people and the influence of a particular urban design. This is not to deny that urban behaviour and urban communities or social areas share mutual relationships. For example, the classic study by Festinger, Schachter and Back (1950) showed that the association between friendship patterns and spatial proximity was influenced by the design of housing units for groups of similar socio-economic levels. Also, Greer (1956, p. 22) demonstrated that differences in the family status of areas affected the degree of participation of the population in a set of different types of social associations. Bell and Force (1956, p. 34) came to the conclusion that:

> the economic characteristics of a neighbourhood population as a unit may be important indicators of the economic reference group of those living in the neighbourhood and may provide a set of expectations with respect to the residents' associational behaviour.

The use of the word 'may' represents an important qualifier. Similarly, studies of delinquency and crime from the time of Shaw and McKay (1929) onwards have revealed the concentration of these deviant behaviours in particular areas. They noted that,

> delinquency persists in these areas not only because of the absence of constructive neighbourhood influences and the inefficiency of present methods of prevention and treatment, but because various forms of lawlessness have become more or less traditional aspects of social life and are handed down year after year through the medium of social contacts. (Shaw and McKay, 1929, p. 596)

Such generalizations were not, however, really new. More than half a century earlier Mayhew (1862) had drawn attention to the localization of crime in the so-called 'rookeries' of London, places such as St. Giles, where people were supposedly born and bred to the criminal habit.

Yet the localization of a particular behaviour, such as crime or delinquency, or the preference of a particular economic or social group for a certain pattern of association, does not necessarily mean that *all* people in an area with such attributes have the same behaviour. To assume so is to accept an implicitly deterministic connection. Any characteristic of an urban sub-area or community is but one of several influences on the behaviour of individuals; the aspirations of the individual, the psychological 'make-up', the network of social influences such as family, job, friends, etc., must all be taken into account. It is true that the incidence of face-to-face contacts and the number of chances of meeting people of a certain character vary according to the composition of the community — using the word in its fullest spatial context. Hence there is little doubt that the characteristics of the community have some effect on behaviour. But the effect will vary considerably from individual to individual, area to area, or from urban character to urban character.

Many of these problems are summed up in the well-known ideas of ecological and individualistic fallacies (Robinson, 1950; Galtung, 1967). In the context of the areal aggregation used here, the ecological fallacy describes the situation when conclusions drawn from aggregative data, perhaps the character of areal groups, are applied to the individual scale. The individualistic fallacy would apply when conclusions about individual data are applied to aggregative data. Such problems are usually avoided when a precise scale is adopted — when limits are set around the phenomena to be investigated. Since it has been emphasized that this study is concerned with the systematic patterns found in the social differentiation of urban areas most of these fallacies are avoided. Yet it must not be thought that the areal approach adopted here is completely self-contained and does not have relevance to individual studies. The method known as contextual analysis — described earlier as structural effects — attempts to relate individual behavioural studies with the character of the areas in which this behaviour occurs and is a rapidly emerging area of interest which replaces the deterministic speculations of previous years. A vital part of the contextual approach would be the precise determination of areal character. Again, however, it must be observed that there is no necessity for a 'behaviour-area' connection to be found. Suttles (1968) has shown how relatively homogeneous areas of the black ghetto of Chicago are carved up into a very different set of territories associated with teenage gangs. In this example a complex behavioural space is founded upon a homogeneous social structural space.

(d) The fourth assumption is that areas can be treated in the same way as individual objects or people, in the sense that separate structures or properties can be identified from the aggregation of social characteristics found in these units. Areas can be described as having certain proportions of a set of social attributes, for example; percentage ethnic, percentage old age, and it is expected that these separate parameters can be generalized to the structures or dimensions of variation. Unfortunately, this assumption of equivalence between areas and individuals leads to three types of problems.

(i) The first, the extent of content scale dependence, has already been dealt with, namely, the problem of the ecological fallacy resulting from generalizing the results of the study to a different scale from the one studied.

(ii) The second problem is that the objects being described, the areas, can never be as definitive as the objects being studied in other sciences. The intra-urban communities, used here to describe the areas within cities upon which measurements are made, are usually abstracted from continuous distributions. Certainly some clear subdivisions within cities can be easily recognized; areas bounded by major barriers such as rivers, roads, rail lines, parks, etc. However, these units never form a complete set of *separate* territorial entities that can be used for ecological analysis. Many areas cannot be split into such easily defined units. Moreover, the very different sizes of these units cause problems, in the sense that different geographical scales are being combined. In addition, the behaviour of groups within these areas may vary by area and by group so that it cannot be assumed that the entities have any behavioural validity. Obviously a variety of criteria are needed to define the complex behavioural patterns that can be called 'community of interest' areas in cities. Also it must be emphasized that the areas in cities for which census data can be obtained are rarely defined on any community of interest or even morphological criteria. Most 'small area' data sets are based on enumeration districts, areas which were defined for the convenience of the census enumerator, not the analyst. Fortunately the growing practice of organizing data by block-face in North American censuses, and making this available at a series of different scales of aggregation, may help modify this general problem. The result is that it is imperative to treat the sub-areas within cities as operational taxonomic units (O.T.U.s), namely as modifiable units defined for a particular classification or operation. In other words, it is quite possible that a different size or shape of aggregation will produce different descriptions, and perhaps, different social structures. One of the essential tasks of any urban sub-area study, therefore, is to identify the extent of geographical scale dependence, the extent to which any set of results is unique to a particular scale of analysis. This type of problem can easily lead to depression about the utility of any intra-urban generalization. However, in the last resort the scale problem is not unique to students of the city; the plant ecologist faces it all the time. Even geologists may deal with entities recognized as rocks, but these are made up of combinations of chemical elements organized in particular ways. These are, in turn, combinations of atoms and, eventually, fundamental particles.

(iii) The third problem relating to an area is that most of the inferential statistical methods useful for the type of urban research dealt with here are based on the assumption of independence of samples or objects analyzed. Individuals can be easily thought of as separate, independent entities. Areas within cities are abstracted from essentially continuous social distributions, with the result that neighbouring units are likely to share characteristics. In addition, intra-urban studies usually deal with the complete set, or population, of areas, since one of the objectives is to produce a complete pattern of urban variation or a complete typology of areas. The result is that the areas being used in any analysis are hardly independent in any statistical sense. Hence the appropriateness of the significance tests linked to many quantitative methods must be placed in doubt. One way around the problem is to base the analysis upon sample areas — units derived by the adoption of some non-contiguous sampling method. This is one resolution of the difficulty, but it conflicts with the need to derive a complete typology of areas. Given this latter requirement the exploratory rather than the confirmatory methods of factor analysis were used in this study, although it will be shown that a comparison of the results of the two approaches led to the position that there was little difference in the substance of the conclusions.

(e) The final major assumption is the adoption of pluralist approaches. Two separate issues can be distinguished. The first relates to the results of any enquiry. On *a priori* grounds it would seem unlikely that a single set of structures will apply to all cities — even at one point in time — when particularistic phenomena are ignored. Yet a great deal of the literature in the study of social areas assumes this type of 'structural monism', whether in Burgess's (1925) ecological zonation or Shevky and Bell's (1955) axes of differentiation. Both models were accepted with alacrity by sociologists and geographers alike, and their persistence suggests a longing for a single all-embracing model or theory of relationships. A plurality of structures is, however, a more likely finding, given the variety of urban societies and forms.

The second area in which a pluralist attitude is worth cultivating relates to the methods of enquiry. No particular methodological or indeed theoretical approach can be assumed. Homans (1976, p. 59) was being critical of the multiplicity of definitions of structure when he pointed out that the structural approach does not imply:

> the use of any general method of research or analysis that can be distinguished from other methods of social science as specifically structural.

In the history of academic endeavour in the field of urban social structure the variety of alternative methods that have been used bears witness to this point. Yet this must not be thought of as condoning a methodological eclecticism; this study makes a case for the utility of a multivariate approach using factorial and cluster analysis methods.

## 4. Problems of the Structural Approach

As with all decisions to adopt a particular approach, the use of this type of structural approach is not without its dangers.

(a) The most obvious is the charge of reductionism, although this is, of course, the problem of all science. René Dubos the biologist has succinctly described the issue in his book, *So Human an Animal.*

> The reductionist scientist tends to become so involved intellectually and emotionally in the elementary fragments of the system, and in the analytical process itself, that he commonly loses interest in the phenomena, or the organism which had been his first concern. For example, the biologist who starts with a question formulated because of its relevance to human life is tempted, and is indeed expected, to progress seriatim to the organ or function involved, then to the single cell, then to sub-cellular fragments, then to molecular groupings or reaction, then to the individual molecules and atoms.
> (Dubos, 1968, p. 242.)

Dubos (p. 242) criticized this progression, believing that

> the most pressing problems of humanity . . . involve . . . situations in which systems must be studied as a whole in all the complexity of their interactions . . . when life is considered only in its specialized functions the outcome is a world emptied of meaning.

In view of the dominating position that science occupies in modern life and the problems of this method in the social sciences, it is difficult not to feel some sympathy with this plea for the holistic approach. The reductionist approach does produce a society of specialized individuals or workers. However, sympathy should not be allowed to cloud the fact that it is difficult to conceive of a situation in which primary attention is paid to these 'complete' systems. This would surely provide the death knell for rapid extensions of our understanding. Our current knowledge of the world, with all its flaws, has been built-up by this reductionist approach. Such an expression of personal values should not be construed as implying that Dubos's plea for the holistic and humane approach should be ignored. It *is* an important research task that has been neglected; but it is not one that is dealt with here. Indeed, it is difficult to see how the charge of reductionism can be avoided if the particular problems of this study are to be adequately solved.

(b) A related problem of the structural approach is the over-emphasis upon patterns of uniformity, especially in relation to spatial or temporal changes. Coser (1976, p. 215) has observed that the prevailing orthodoxy among sociologists has been to accept Talcot Parsons's ideas about the inevitable and uniform effects of modernization and industrialization. This results in traditional societies being replaced by a relatively uniform societal type similar to the North American model. This appears to be an underlying assumption in the Shevky-Bell schema. However, it is increasingly recognized that such a uniform response has not occurred. In Coser's words:

> it has turned out that societies do not develop in a stately progression of orderly structural stages towards modernity; they exhibit startling incongruities and discontinuities in the course of their development.
>
> (Coser, 1974, p. 216.)

The result is that:

> in such situations of change there develop not just one possibility of the restructuring of forces and activity but rather a great deal of possibilities.
>
> (Einstadt, 1973, p. 306.)

These opinions reinforce the assumption already made that it is unlikely that a single set of relationships can ever represent the complete range of societal structures in the Western world. An important research task, therefore, is to identify these alternative patterns in the various societies.

(c) A third danger is the possibility of over-emphasizing the static, cross-sectional, approach, thereby neglecting the social processes involved, whether these processes are looked at at the structural scale used here, or at the micro- or behavioural-scale and the macro- or society-scale. Similarly the linkages between these scales are not systematically developed, such as the way in which the social patterns influence choice and behaviour, or give potentials for change. Undoubtedly the approach used here does lay itself open to such a charge of neglect, whilst the failure to pursue the linkages between these scales or to investigate the way in which social patterns influence choice and behaviour and give potentials for change represent other limitations. Yet it is difficult to cover all possible types of enquiry. Here it is argued that without a clear indentification of the various social structures in urban areas, and the scale issues involved, there is little profit in *initially* speculating about the causes or relationships of these structures. At a time when the hypothetico-deductive method is given such kudos among adherents of modern scientific methods, this reversal to what is almost an inductive method for identifying the social patterns of cities from data sets, may seem like heresy. But the methodological contrast is more one of illusion than substance. In practice, many scientists do not always work from first principles, deduce patterns and test these patterns in the real world. Instead there is a great deal of interrelation between these alternatives. Nevertheless as scientists usually write their reports in this deductive mould the approach is usually assumed to be the most appropriate one for investigators to follow.

The conclusion must be that the structural approach to the study of urban social differentiation is not without its limitations and pitfalls; but no approach is ever free of such problems. Compared to previous urban social investigations it has the advantage of setting some very precise bounds around the area of interest. Although these restrict the scope of the approach within the general framework of urban ecology, they make it easier to develop a systematic body of literature. Now that these bounds are identified and the multivariate technical procedures have been defined it is necessary to turn to the stages of investigation involved in any analytical study, principally to the way in which the various social, spatial, and typological aspects of the problem can be integrated in the confines of a single study.

## 5. A Paradigm for the Study of Urban Social Differentiation

Many of the problems associated with the study of the structure of urban social areas can be attributed to the fact that the various alternatives in the field have not been clearly identified. In addition further confusion is associated with the way particular words, such as 'space' and 'area', are used, for Shevky and Bell's (1955) use of the terms left much to be desired. Even in the factorial ecology literature similar types of confusion about the meanings of 'space' and the various components of urban analysis can be identified. For example, Berry and Rees (1969) identified four separate 'spaces': Social Space (Units for Individuals or Families); Housing Space (Units or Dwellings); Community Space (Tracts or Larger Sub-Areas); Locational or Physical Space (Tracts or Larger Sub-Areas). Although this classification of the residential location decision process has been widely adopted in the standard text books (Johnston, 1971, pp. 344-5; Yeates and Garner, 1977, p. 306) it is neither a comprehensive, nor clear summary of the alternative types of 'spaces' when applied in a social area classification context.

Figure 7 shows that Berry and Rees's first and third "spaces" confuse the various components or elements that compose the structure of spaces with the alternative scales of investigation. For example, the so-called Social Space refers to the relative location of *individuals or families* whereas Community Space deals with the position of *areas*. This is really a difference in the type of aggregation employed. Both represent alternative "social spaces" in the sense that the social attributes of individuals or areas are used to locate one unit in relation to one another; the spacing simply refers to a relative positioning using different levels of aggregations. Nothing necessarily geographical is implied by the term 'space'. Certainly the use of factor analysis to classify the communities, as shown on the Community Space diagram, does not automatically confer such geographical or locational status.

A second major problem relates to the first and second 'spaces', the Social and Housing Spaces. It is clear from the subdivisions in Figure 7 that individual variables or parameters are used to position the individuals with respect to one another in these spaces. Hence they are not really 'structures' in the meaning employed here. The objective of the factorial approach is to search for the collectivities of the variables, to identify the underlying patterns or structures beyond the individual indicators or variables. In this sense the descriptions of Social Housing Space are not structures since each is composed of two major sets of indicators. Moreover, they are hardly comprehensive since many other variables could be used. For example. ethnicity would produce Ethnic Spaces. Hence, rather than using individual variables, it is more appropriate to identify the *structures* that lie behind these variables. An individual, or community, or any other type of aggregation for that matter, would have a position on the social structures identified — such as Socio-Economic Status, Life Cycle, Ethnicity and Migration, etc. (In practice, of course, they would be located in the multivariate space of these axes of differentiation. But sets of simple two-dimensional pairings of the structural axes can be used to portray part of the relationships involved.) It is also worth noting that the evidence of the factorial literature throws doubt on the use of 'Housing' as a dimension, or construct, equivalent to the other sources of variation identified in the Social Space diagram. Few factorial ecologies outside the U.K. have identified separate housing axes, whilst the presence of two such axes seems most improbable. At an individual variable level the idea of a differentiation in housing conditions may be accepted — subject to the addition of other 'spaces' with different adjectival descriptions. At the social structural level the construct can be questioned. It could, however, be argued that Housing represents a different content area to the Social attributes. If this view is accepted there is no reason why the other elements identified in Chapter 4, such as Morphology, Environmental Conditions, etc., could not also be used.

A third problem associated with Figure 7 is that the Housing and Social Space diagrams contain several different types of criteria and assume a particular set of relationships. For example, in the Social Space diagram, the vertical axis uses occupational, educational, and income criteria, and, more importantly, relates them to a single scale. Three separate indicators seem to be involved here, and there is no guarantee that the variables are directly related to one another. This type of implicit assumption of a strong and linear correlation between the indicators was, of course, one of the problems associated with Shevky and Bell's (1955) decision to add variables together to

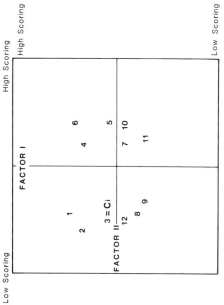

## SOCIAL SPACE
### (UNITS:INDIVIDUAL OR FAMILIES)

Si- individual i's position in social space.

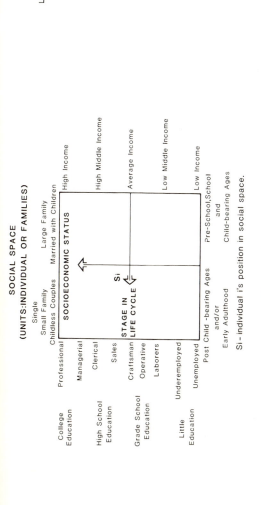

## HOUSING SPACE
### (UNITS:DWELLINGS)

Hi- individual i's position in housing space.

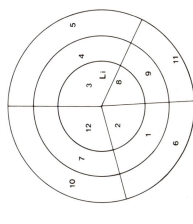

## COMMUNITY SPACE
### (UNITS:TRACTS OR LARGER SUB-AREAS)

Ci-the community in which i's home is located

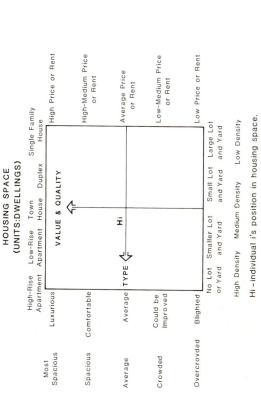

## LOCATIONAL OR PHYSICAL SPACE
### (UNITS:TRACTS OR LARGER SUB-AREAS)

Li-the zone in the community in which i's home is located

FIGURE 7  THE SOCIAL, HOUSING, COMMUNITY AND LOCATIONAL SPACES OF BERRY AND REES (1969)

45

form a composite index. Similar examples of the same problem can be found on the other diagrams. There is no evidence for these implicit associations. One advantage of the factorial approach is that the degree of linear interrelationships between variables can be measured directly, thereby removing the problem. In addition, Figure 7 shows that each diagram is organized in terms of orthogonal (or right-angled) relationships. This ignores the fact that the differentiating variables, or the factor axes, may be correlated with one another. In other words, a particular configuration is imposed on the data set in order to portray the relationship.

The fourth problem, or rather sets of problems, can be seen in the Locational or Physical Space diagram (Figure 7). At first sight it appears to be a representation of the position of each community area in some generalized geographical space. But there is no need to assume immediately such a diagrammatic representation. It is possible to plot the areas in their real world location and, perhaps, subsequently to generalize the pattern into a simpler representation — in terms of the zones and sectors as shown on the diagram. However, the empirical evidence on the spatial pattern of each factor axis implies that much more complex structures than simple zones and sectors are likely to be present. Moreover, it can be argued that the locational diagrams could equally well be applied to individuals, or families, or other scales of aggregation. In any case a single Locational Space diagram, or even a real world and diagrammatic representation, cannot deal with the very real differences between the maps of *individual* social structure patterns, the spatial patterns of socio-economic status, family status, etc., and the map of *aggregated* social structures. At the community scale this would involve a classification of the communities into a set of specific types. These could then be portrayed either on a single diagram, or on a set of diagrams if it was easier to treat each community type separately. Similar types of criticism can be made about other recent attempts to identify the structure of intra-urban variations. For example, Robson's (1975) idealized structure of the British city is based on the dimensions of Status, Age, and Housing although there is hardly any empirical evidence to justify the presence of Housing as being a separate and more important dimension of variation than, for example, ethnicity, whilst the sub-division of each construct into only two or three types restricts the flexibility of the approach. These problems mean that there is a need for an alternative interpretation of the intra-urban structural relationships that can be studied under the topic of urban social differentiation. This is summarized in Figure 8.

The first distinction that has to be made is between the *Content Area* of the investigation and the *Scale of Aggregation* being used. The content refers to the variables or indicators which measure the phenomena being investigated; the aggregation relates to the units used in the investigation. The individuals, families, or areas can be positioned in Social Indicator Spaces by plotting the social indicators one pair at a time. The examples in Figure 8 show bi-variate scatters produced by plotting the number of rooms in the house against the number of years spent in high school: firstly, by showing how individuals can be located in this social space by their characteristics; secondly, how communities can be located by their average values on those indicators.

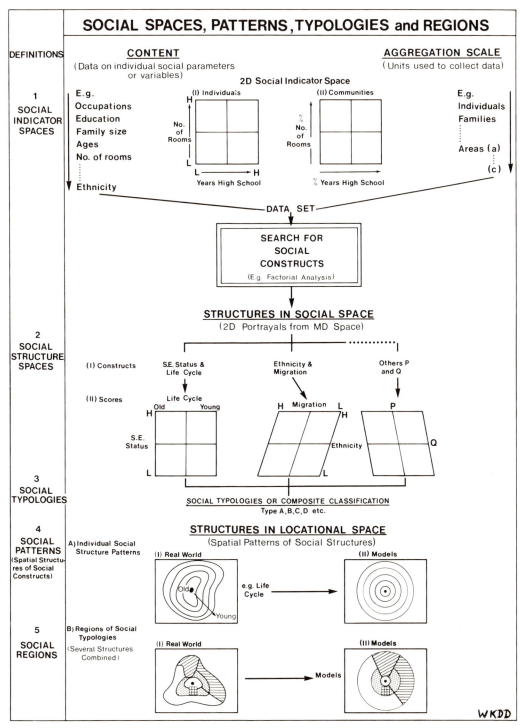

FIGURE 8   A PARADIGM FOR THE STUDY OF URBAN SOCIAL STRUCTURE

These two dimensional portrayals are obviously limited because they only deal with two indicators at a time. Methods, such as factor analysis, are available for defining the latent structure of a data set of social indicators. The social structures — or social constructs — that lie behind the individual indicators are identified and measured in this way. In Figure 8 a series of alternative social structures are identified, such as Socio-Economic Status and Life Cycle, etc. Depending upon the scale of the aggregation — individuals or communities can be used — the units can be located by their factor scores on these individual structures. Several examples show how two dimensional portrayals make it easier to conceptualize the relationships found in the multi-dimensional space. It is worth noting that some of these diagrams have angled axes to draw attention to the possibility of oblique relationships. These scores position the aggregation units with respect to one another on these social structures, so they are called *Social Structure Spaces,* although nothing geographical is implied by use of 'space' in this context.

The third stage identified in Figure 8 involves the construction of *Social Typologies.* These describe the composite classification of the units on the basis of all the scores, usually by cluster analysis methods. Separate Social Area Types can be identified. For example, at the community area scale, a Skid Row type of area is often found, one that is characterized by low or impoverished social status, mobility, family disorganization and substandard housing conditions. In the same way that areas are given summary characteristics so composite types can be derived from scale studies.

The fourth stage deals with 'space' in a geographical sense, namely, the structures that are found in locational space, the spatial patterns of the social structures. Each individual social structure or construct may have a separate type of spatial pattern; for convenience these variations are called Social Patterns. Figure 8 shows an example of a real world annular pattern of the distribution of life cycle in the city. This can be generalized into a simpler relationship in the concentric *Social Pattern Model* by assuming away the directional biases of the real world pattern. If all the Social Patterns are integrated, perhaps by cluster analysis methods, a series of typologies of areas can be produced. If these different types of area are located on a map then similar contiguous units can be joined together. Usually these types cluster in particular areas so that a set of composite social patterns, or *Social Regions,* are identified. These can be generalized into *Social Region Models.*

It is worth noting — by way of conclusion — that these analytical stages do *not* necessarily depend upon the particular multivariate techniques used in this study. The paradigm, therefore, should have an application beyond the use of factor or cluster analysis techniques. Now that the stages in the application of this Multivariate-Structural approach have been defined it is necessary to turn in the next chapter to the particular problems studied in Wales within the field of urban social differentiation.

## CHAPTER 3

BACKGROUND TO THE CASE STUDIES: AREAS AND PROBLEMS


The previous chapter has shown that there is a crisis of understanding in the urban social structure literature. Despite variations in the number of axes proposed, all the general models, whether Shevky and Bell (1955), McElrath (1968), or Timms (1971), assume that a single set of relationships is adequate for describing the social structures of Western cities. Yet such an assumption is contradicted by the accumulating factorial evidence that many additional axes of differentiation can be recognized. Moreover 'common sense' interpretations produce structures such as a separate Young Adult age group component that are not accommodated by the models. In part, Berry's (1972) work provides one way out of this impasse. He argued against a single set of relationships by proposing variations in the dimensionality of cities according to the 'degree of welfare' in societies. At the urban system level this idea certainly breaches the assumption of a single model — but it is limited to one additional source of differentiation. Any review of the available literature on cities will reveal that there are many other sources of variation which are likely to modify the social structures of Western cities, for example: the degree of modernization of society; the level of welfare or government intervention in social conditions; the size of the cities; the degree of cultural heterogeneity. Given the technical problems associated with many studies much of the evidence for these variations cannot be counted as being entirely conclusive. In other words, there is a definite need to demonstrate, as conclusively as possible, that societal variations in Western intra-urban structure can be found. This led to the major proposition of this study, namely, that Western cities do not have a single, uniform, urban social structure modified only by place-particular variations. Instead, there are systematic variations in Western urban structure.

One way of exploring this general proposition would be to compare the social structures of cities by taking examples from different societies. This approach was rejected in favour of a study of the dimensionality of centres in one area, Wales. This single area example appeared to be more useful in contributing to the knowledge of urban social structures in general, since it was more effective in dealing with a number of related problems to the main proposition of the study. These problems were: the inter-relationship between the axes of differentiation found at both the intra-urban and regional scales of analysis; the degree of technical dependence in results; the links between spatial and societal differentiation; the derivation of community typologies from inter-urban sources of differentiation. Each of these issues is dealt with in more detail in the various sections of this chapter. Before dealing with these problems, however, it is important to explain why Wales was chosen as the study area and to describe the differentiation of towns at the inter-urban level. This discussion of the dimensionality of the urban system not only provides the context from which the case

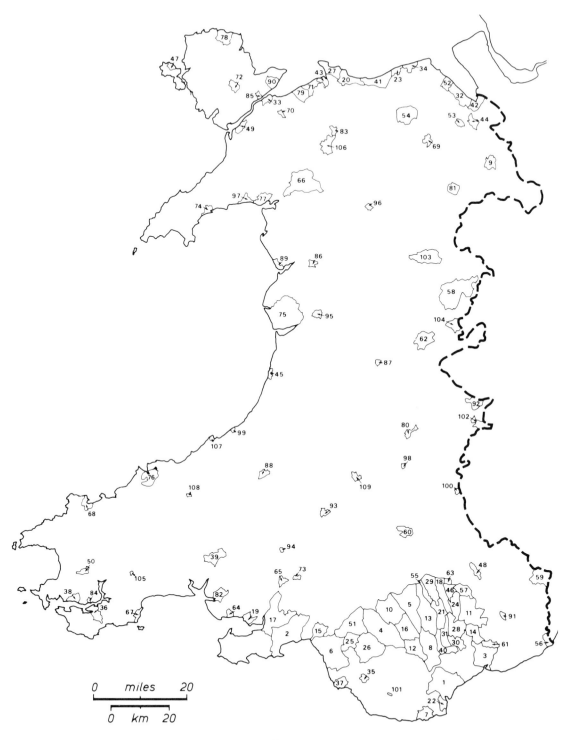

Figure 9   Urban Administrative Areas in Wales in 1971

## Key to Figure 9

| | | | |
|---|---|---|---|
| 1. Cardiff | 29. Tredegar | 56. Chepstow | 83. Llanrwst |
| 2. Swansea | 30. Risca | 57. Blaenavon | 84. Neyland |
| 3. Newport | 31. Mynyddislwyn | 58. Welshpool | 85. Menai Bridge |
| 4. Rhondda | 32. Flint | 59. Monmouth | 86. Dolgellau |
| 5. Merthyr Tydfil | 33. Bangor | 60. Brecon | 87. Llanidloes |
| 6. Port Talbot | 34. Prestatyn | 61. Caerleon | 88. Lampeter |
| 7. Barry | 35. Bridgend | 62. Newtown | 89. Barmouth |
| 8. Caerphilly | 36. Pembroke | 63. Brynmawr | 90. Beaumaris |
| 9. Wrexham | 37. Porthcawl | 64. Burry Port | 91. Usk |
| 10. Aberdare | 38. Milford | 65. Ammanford | 92. Knighton |
| 11. Pontypool | 39. Carmarthen | 66. Blaenau Ffestiniog | 93. Llandovery |
| 12. Pontypridd | 40. Bedwas and Machen | 67. Tenby | 94. Llandeilo |
| 13. Gelligaer | 41. Abergele | 68. Fishguard | 95. Machynlleth |
| 14. Cwmbran | 42. Connah's Quay | 69. Ruthin | 96. Bala |
| 15. Neath | 43. Conway | 70. Bethesda | 97. Criccieth |
| 16. Mountain Ash | 44. Buckley | 71. Penmaenmawr | 98. Builth Wells |
| 17. Llwchwr | 45. Aberystwyth | 72. Llangefni | 99. Aberaeron |
| 18. Ebbw Vale | 46. Nantyglo | 73. Cwmamman | 100. Hay |
| 19. Llanelli | 47. Holyhead | 74. Pwllheli | 101. Cowbridge |
| 20. Colwyn Bay | 48. Abergavenny | 75. Towyn | 102. Presteigne |
| 21. Bedwellty | 49. Caernarvon | 76. Cardigan | 103. Llanfyllin |
| 22. Penarth | 50. Haverfordwest | 77. Portmadoc | 104. Montgomery |
| 23. Rhyl | 51. Glyncorrwg | 78. Amlwch | 105. Narberth |
| 24. Abertillery | 52. Holywell | 79. Llanfairfechan | 106. Betws y Coed |
| 25. Maesteg | 53. Mold | 80. Llandrindod Wells | 107. New Quay |
| 26. Ogmore and Garw | 54. Denbigh | 81. Llangollen | 108. Newcastle Emlyn |
| 27. Llandudno | 55. Rhymney | 82. Kidwelly | 109. Llanwrtyd Wells |
| 28. Abercarn | | | |

study examples were chosen but — in part at least — provides an additional type of scale comparison which complements the intra-urban and regional analyses.

## 1. The Study Area

At first sight the decision to carry out a set of multivariate-structural studies in Wales may seem rather unusual to some people. Welsh towns are hardly spectacular models of urban form, or trend-setting examples of Western urban life (Carter, 1965). Nevertheless, they have important advantages for the primary proposition of this study since they have a peripheral location in the economic and social life of the Western world. For three generations most Welsh towns have experienced lower levels of prosperity than their counterparts in southern England. One consequence has been that lower levels of modernization are particularly evident in the urban fabric, in addition to high levels of government intervention in the housing market. A decade ago the Welsh Housing Condition Survey (Welsh Office, 1969) showed that 32.0% of the houses in Wales were substandard, whilst the census of 1971 showed that 29.6% of the houses in Wales were built and owned by Public Authorities (the so-called 'Council Houses'). Moreover, a cultural difference is shown by the fact that 29% of the population over 5 years of age in 1971 were Welsh-speaking. Yet the cultural difference implied by the figure must not be exaggerated. Not only are those able to speak Welsh concentrated in the west of the country (Bowen and Carter, 1974) but the lifestyle and economy of the

51

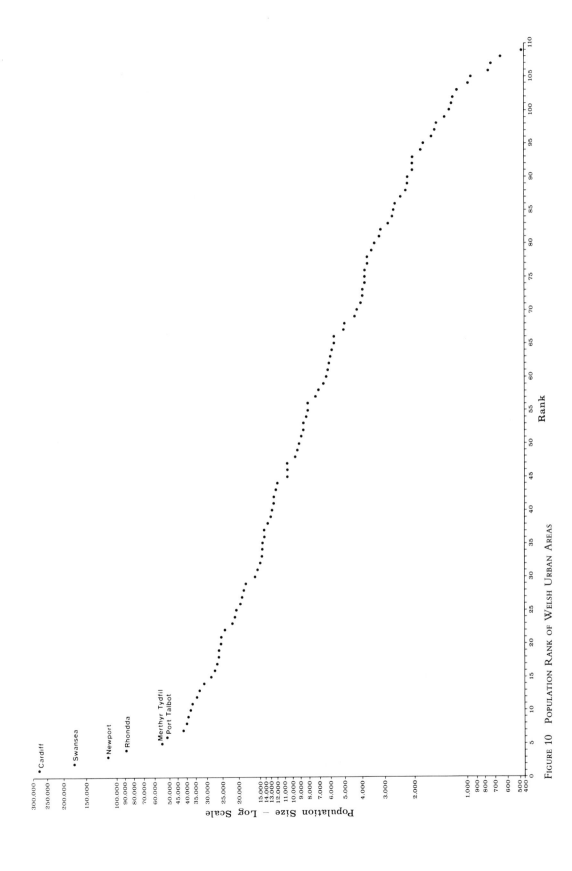

FIGURE 10 POPULATION RANK OF WELSH URBAN AREAS

Welsh-speaking groups are indistinguishable from the rest of the population; for centuries the cultural differences in Wales have manifested themselves in the non-material context, namely, in language and literary issues. Indeed, it could be argued that in 1971 Wales had lower levels of societal separation due to cultural heterogeneity than other parts of Britain with equivalent economies. This is a consequence of the low levels of New Commonwealth immigration into Wales (Jones, 1978). For example, even Cardiff, the largest city, only had 1.9% of its population in this immigrant category. Nevertheless, the Welsh dimension means the area is characterized by economic and cultural variations which set it somewhat apart from the mainstream of British or even western society. Berry (1972) has argued that British towns are different from North American cities because of higher welfare conditions and lower modernization levels. If this is the case it can be hypothesized that the towns of Wales have even greater variations from any 'standard' North American type, so Wales represents an appropriate area in which to investigate the primary proposition of this study.

Rather than simply accepting this descriptive background and assuming that the towns of Wales provide a suitable area in which to test the general proposition of this study it can be shown that there is some evidence for the idea that Welsh towns differ from the standard Western model — at least at the inter-urban level — making Wales a particularly useful case study area. The evidence for this view came from an inter-urban study using a 107 area × 26 variable data matrix, in which the 107 areas consisted of the urban administrative units for the Principality in 1971 (Figure 9). The 26 variables (Table 1) were chosen as indicators of 8 of the hypothesized dimensions of inter-urban character proposed by the two major works on inter-urban structure, namely, Hodge (1968) and Berry (1972). Three of the postulated dimensions shown in Table 1 were not used. Despite Hodge's support of the 'Geographical Situation' dimension it seems more sensible to regard this as a source of regional, not societal, variation produced at the factor score level, whilst suitable variables could not be obtained from the small area U.K. census data source for the other two axes; namely, 'Male Participation' and 'Education'. This was not considered to be a major disadvantage since few other studies of the urban system have identified these axes (Davies and Welling, 1977).

Table 2 shows the axes obtained from the oblique rotation (Direct Oblimin) results of a Principal Axes component analysis of the 107 area × 26 variable matrix for Welsh towns and provides a more complete statement of previously reported results (Davies, 1977). The two largest factors combine four of the expected axes. The largest dimension abstracted integrates the characteristics of 'age' and the 'major economy', whether manufacturing or distribution and service. The second most important axis separates growth and mobility features as opposed to stagnation and substandardness. Hence the title *Degree of Renewal* is used for the latter axis, Component II, whilst *Age and Major Economy* is used to describe the largest dimension. Of the other axes, the separate *Tenure* construct reflects the dominant presence of the various levels of government in the housing market in Welsh towns. More closely related to other studies of inter-urban character is the *Size* dimension, whilst the presence of two axes primarily linked to

Table 1

## Categories and Variables Used in the Urban System Analysis

| *Categories* | *Variables* |
|---|---|
| 1. *Size* | 1. Population size in 1971<br>24. Retail Trade turnover in 1971** |
| 2. *Age and Family* | 8. Children (% population 0 – 14 years)<br>9. Old Age (% population over 65 years)<br>10. Young Adult (% population 15 – 24 years)<br>4. Female Ratio (number per 1000 males) |
| 3. *Physical Structures or Development* | 27. Large Dwellings (dwellings > 7 + rooms)<br>26. No Bath (% households without baths)<br>19. Unemployed (% unemployed among economically active)*<br>3. Persons per room (density average for area) |
| 4. *Economy* | 11. Mining and Quarrying (% of employed population)*<br>12. Manufacturing (% of employed population)*<br>15. Service and Distribution (% of employed population)*<br>16. Government and Defence (% of employed population)*<br>13. Construction, Transport, Utilities (as above)* |
| 5. *Ethnicity* | 5. Welsh speakers (% in population >3 years)<br>21. Born in Wales (% of population)*<br>22. Born in Ireland (Numbers per 1000 residents)* |
| 6. *Welfare (Housing Tenure)* | 7. Council housing (% households)<br>6. Owner Occupied (% households) |
| 7. *Growth and Mobility* | 17. Local Movers (% households moving within local authorities in the previous 5 years)<br>18. Distant Movers (as above, but between local authorities)<br>25. Visitors (non resident visitors per 1000 persons)*<br>2. Population Change (absolute change 1951-71) |
| 8. *Females* | 20. Economically Active Females (% adult females)*<br>25. Young, Single Females (% females, 20-30 years who are single) |
| 9. *Education* | Not included |
| 10. *Male Participation* | Not included |
| 11. *Geographical Situation* | Not included |

Sources:   County reports of 1971 Population Census unless marked
   **1971 Retail Trade Census.
   * Aggregated from the 1971 Census Enumeration Area Tables. The economic figures are based on a 10% sample.

Table 2

**Table 2**

**Welsh Towns in 1971: Axes and Loadings**

| Title and Variables | Loadings for Different Factoring Methods (Oblique Rotation: Direct Oblimin 0.0) | | | | |
|---|---|---|---|---|---|
| | Principal Axes | | Image | Rao | Alpha |
| **1. AGE & MAJOR ECONOMY** | Component* | Factor | | | |
| Order of Axis | 1(1) | 1 | 2 | 1 | 1 |
| 4. Female Ratio | 84(73) | 74 | 73 | 78 | – 77 |
| 9. Old Age | 82(81) | 80 | 79 | 81 | + 79 |
| 15. Service-Distribution | 73(80) | 72 | 70 | 66 | + 75 |
| 27. Large Dwellings | 67(79) | 66 | 62 | 63 | 62 |
| 5. Welsh Speakers | 49(56) | 49 | 50 | 44 | 48 |
| 25. Young, Single Females | 46(67) | 51 | 54 | 40 | 50 |
| 23. Visitors | —(54) | — | 34 | — | — |
| 7. Council Housing | – 33( – 49) | — | – 31 | 30 | — |
| 11. Mining | – 37(– 38) | – 32 | — | – 33 | – 31 |
| 10. Young Adults | – 48(—) | – 46 | – 33 | – 50 | – 46 |
| 12. Manufacturing | – 60( – 72) | – 58 | – 55 | – 53 | – 59 |
| 8. Children | – 71(– 82) | – 73 | – 75 | – 70 | – 66 |
| 3. Persons/room | – 78( – 88) | – 81 | – 77 | – 78 | – 75 |
| **2. DEGREE OF RENEWAL** (Substandardness, Growth) | | | | | |
| Order of Axis | 2(2) | 2 | 5 | 2 | 2 |
| 26. No Bath | – 84(83) | – 78 | 66 | – 77 | – 82 |
| 21. Born in Wales | – 61(65) | – 57 | 63 | – 58 | – 54 |
| 11. Mining | – 60(64) | – 54 | 65 | – 55 | – 55 |
| 19. Unemployed | – 46(45) | – 35 | 37 | – 33 | – 37 |
| 17. Local Movers | – 38(38) | – 34 | 30 | – 35 | — |
| 2. Population Change | 60( – 68) | 62 | – 49 | 65 | 62 |
| 18. Distant Migrants | 79( – 80) | 76 | – 67 | 75 | 73 |
| 15. Service Distribution | —( – 33) | | | | |
| **3. SIZE (and GROWTH)** | | | | | |
| Order of Axis | 4 | 4 | 1 | 3 | 5 |
| 24. Retail Turnover | 99(97) | 100 | 100 | 95 | 100 |
| 1. Population Size | 98(96) | 98 | 99 | 94 | 96 |
| 2. Population Change | 43(44) | 35 | 36 | 38 | 34 |

**Table 2** *(continued)*

| Title and Variables | Loadings for Different Factoring Methods (Oblique Rotation: Direct Oblimin 0.0) | | | | |
|---|---|---|---|---|---|
| **4. COLLEGE-RESORT TOWNS** (Young Adult-Visitors) | *Principal Axes* | | | | |
| | *Component* * | *Factor* | *Image* | *Rao* | *Alpha* |
| *Order of Axis* | 3 | 3 | 4 | 4 | 3 |
| 10. Young Adults | 89(90) | 93 | 83 | − 82 | 91 |
| 23. Visitors | 79(70) | 72 | 69 | − 76 | 73 |
| 25. Young, Single Females | 70(58) | 65 | 59 | − 71 | 64 |
| 4. Female Ratio | —( − 36) | — | — | — | — |
| **5. SPECIALIZED ECONOMIES** | | | | | |
| *Order of Axis* | 5(4) | 5 | 7 | 6 | 4 |
| 13. Construction, Transport & Utilities | 84(77) | 77 | 80 | 71 | 71 |
| 22. Irish | 71(66) | 53 | 52 | 49 | 58 |
| 16. Government, Defence | 56(72) | 57 | 37 | 65 | 57 |
| 12. Manufacturing | − 39( − 50) | − 54 | − 30 | − 54 | − 51 |
| 20. Economically Active Females | − 39( − ) | — | − 30 | — | — |
| **6. TENURE** | | | | | |
| *Order of Axis* | 7 | 7 | 6 | 7 | 7 |
| 7. Council Housing | − 80(78) | − 87 | 79 | − 77 | − 85 |
| 17. Local Migrants | − 47(48) | − 34 | 33 | − 40 | − 34 |
| 8. Children | —(33) | — | — | — | − 34 |
| 6. Owner Occupation | 89( − 87) | 85 | − 80 | 84 | 87 |
| **7. WELSH CENTRES** | | | | | |
| *Order of Axis* | 6(7) | 6 | 3** | 5 | 6 |
| 5. Welsh Speaking | − 46(51) | − 37 | | 43 | 40 |
| 21. Welsh Born | − 31(31) | − 29 | | 30 | 28 |
| 12. Manufacturing | − 31(—) | — | − 57 | — | — |
| 13. Construction, Utilities | —(31) | — | | 34 | — |
| 17. Local Movers | —( − 34) | — | — | — | — |
| 15. Service, Distribution | —( − 35) | — | 43 | — | — |
| 16. Government, Defence | 59( − 35) | 30 | 49 | — | − 30 |
| 20. Economically Active Females | 60( − 75) | 59 | — | − 63 | − 58 |

*Figures in brackets represent loadings for Varimax solution.
**Image Analysis title should be 'Major Economy'.

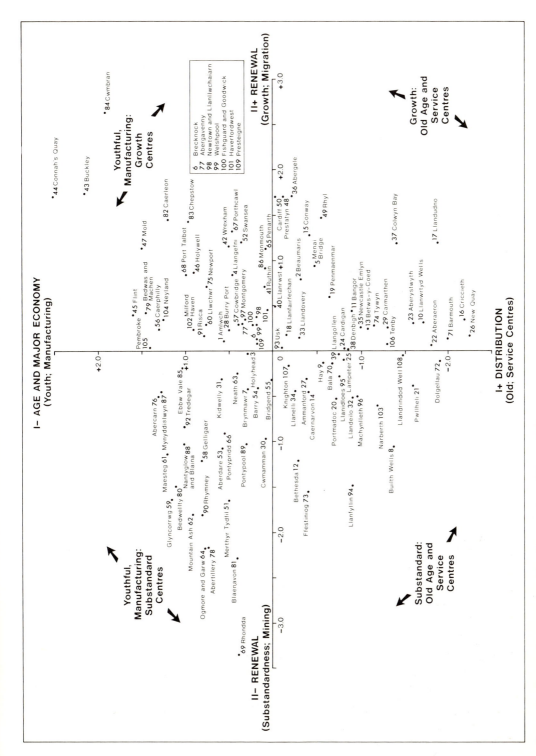

FIGURE 11  FACTOR SCORES FOR THE TWO LARGEST AXES: WALES, 1971

57

## Table 3

### Factor Scores and Percentages on the Minor Axes

#### (a) Component 5: Specialized Economy Towns

| Towns | Component Scores >1.5 | Construction | Utilities and Transport | Public Administration and Defence |
|---|---|---|---|---|
| 100. Fishguard | 4.17 | 14.5 | 24.3 | 19.7 |
| 105. Pembroke | 3.12 | 21.3 | 13.2 | 13.4 |
| 3. Holyhead | 2.16 | 7.7 | 27.4 | 7.2 |
| 6. Brecon | 2.36 | 11.6 | 5.9 | 25.4 |
| 102. Milford Haven | 1.95 | 16.7 | 15.0 | 10.9 |
| 41. Ruthin | 1.81 | 11.5 | 7.9 | 22.6 |
| 104. Neyland | 1.87 | 18.8 | 5.8 | 11.6 |
| 57. Cowbridge | 1.61 | 14.0 | 10.5 | 15.8 |
| 1. Amlwch | 1.53 | 23.4 | 10.6 | 3.5 |
| 101. Haverfordwest | 1.44 | 11.7 | 11.1 | 11.4 |
| 94. Llanfyllin | 1.40 | | | |
| 108. Llandrindod | 1.38 | | | |
| 96. Machynlleth | 1.02 | | | |
| 34. Llanelli | − 1.43 | 4.9 | 6.1 | 3.9 |
| 85. Ebbw Vale | − 1.56 | 4.5 | 2.7 | 2.8 |
| 91. Risca | − 1.56 | 5.1 | 6.1 | 2.5 |
| 10. Llanwrtyd Wells | − 1.74 | 10.0 | 0.0 | 0.0 |
| 35. Newcastle Emlyn | − 2.06 | 5.5 | 5.5 | 0.0 |
| Averages for Welsh Towns | | 8.9% | 8.6% | 7.0% |

#### (b) Component 4: College-Resort Centres

| Towns | Component Scores >1.5 | % Young Adults* |
|---|---|---|
| 23. Aberystwyth | 5.2 | 28.1 |
| 11. Bangor | 3.59 | 24.7 |
| 25. Lampeter | 3.94 | 22.8 |
| 33. Llandovery | 2.71 | 16.0 |
| 13. Betws-y-Coed | 2.34 | 17.1 |
| 10. Llanwrtyd Wells | 1.39 | 13.3 |
| 35. New Quay | − 1.39 | 9.2 |
| 36. Llanidloes | − 1.52 | 9.9 |
| 48. Prestatyn | − 2.05 | 9.5 |
| Average for Welsh Towns | | 13.6% |

*Young Adults: Population between 15 and 24 years.

**Table 3** (*continued*)

## (c) Component 6: Housing Tenure

| Towns | Component Scores | Percentage Houses in: | |
|---|---|---|---|
| | | Council Ownership* | Owner Occupation |
| 84. Cwmbran | 3.03 | 77.3 | 18.6 |
| 4. Llangefni | 2.96 | 64.4 | 26.4 |
| 72. Dolgellau | 1.98 | 47.2 | 31.3 |
| 21. Pwllheli | 1.85 | 31.7 | 36.9 |
| 14. Caernarvon | 1.80 | 39.8 | 42.5 |
| 59. Glyncorrwg | 1.76 | 47.2 | 37.6 |
| 70. Bala | 1.55 | 39.1 | 41.8 |
| 11. Bangor | 1.51 | 45.6 | 36.4 |
| 36. Abergele | − 1.63 | 14.4 | 74.3 |
| 69. Rhondda | − 1.65 | 15.8 | 67.8 |
| 67. Porthcawl | − 1.84 | 10.0 | 71.0 |
| 100. Fishguard | − 1.87 | 18.6 | 65.2 |
| 43. Buckley | − 1.87 | 21.3 | 69.3 |
| 48. Prestatyn | − 2.02 | 9.7 | 78.1 |
| 10. Llanwrtyd Wells | − 2.30 | 3.1 | 68.7 |

*Council (or public) housing includes houses owned by New Town Corporations.

## (d) The 'Welsh Speaking Towns'

| Percentage Population (>3 years) that is Welsh speaking | | | |
|---|---|---|---|
| Llangefni | 93.1% | Holyhead | 57.7% |
| Cwmamman | 85.8 | Betws-y-Coed | 56.2 |
| Blaenau Ffestiniog | 87.4 | Menai | 55.3 |
| Bethesda | 82.5 | Llanfairfechan | 53.7 |
| Caernarvon | 82.6 | Denbigh | 53.2 |
| Bala | 86.3 | Bangor | 51.1 |
| Newcastle Emlyn | 82.9 | Llandovery | 51.9 |
| Pwllheli | 80.0 | Barmouth | 51.7 |
| Portmadoc | 77.9 | Burry Port | 50.1 |
| Aberaeron | 77.6 | Carmarthen | 50.0 |
| Dolgellau | 73.7 | Towyn | 50.7 |
| Ammanford | 71.6 | Ruthin | 47.4 |
| New Quay | 71.3 | Llanwrtyd | 47.1 |
| Criccieth | 69.8 | Llanfyllin | 47.2 |
| Kidwelly | 69.2 | Penmaenmawr | 44.7 |
| Cardigan | 65.6 | Llanelli | 44.4 |
| Lampeter | 67.6 | Aberystwyth | 43.8 |
| Llanrwst | 65.3 | Llwchwr | 42.9 |
| Amlwch | 64.9 | Welshpool | 41.9 |
| Machynlleth | 63.5 | Beaumaris | 39.3 |
| Llandeilo | 65.0 | Conway | 33.3 |
| | | *Mean* | *29.6%* |

particular economic characteristics and their consequences, namely, the *College-Resort* and *Specialized Economies* axes, demonstrate the importance of treating economic variations as a series of separate vectors, not a single source of dimensional variation. None of these axes can be regarded as being technique dependent since substantially the same characteristics were found when four very different common factor methods were applied to the same data set or when varimax rather than oblique rotation was used. This parallelism in the results did not, however, characterize the seventh axis shown in Table 2. Since it has such low loadings and also varies by technique the axis cannot be considered to represent a primary source of variation.

These results demonstrate that the dimensionality of Welsh towns differs from the set of relationships proposed by previous students of Western inter-urban character. It is tempting to place the study within the context of Berry's (1968) 'transitional' type which was applied to countries such as Chile and Yugoslavia, areas half way between the under-developed and developed world. But since the pattern of the axes is more likely to be a consequence of Wales's heritage of economic depression and stagnation, it is more likely that the combination or overlap of the largest axes is a type of lapsed state, a reversal to a more traditional type of inter-urban pattern. Only a temporal analysis could confirm this point. What is more relevant for this study is the fact that the analysis has provided unequivocal evidence for the view that Welsh towns differ from the normally accepted 'standard' Western model — at the urban system level.

Although the general study area has been chosen, the particular set of towns within Wales to be used in subsequent analyses has not been identified. The results of the inter-urban analysis were used to help with this selection. Figure 11 shows the classification of the centres on the basis of the component scores of the two larger axes, whilst Table 3 pinpoints the scores and associated key variables for the highest scoring towns on the minor axes. Given the very specialized nature of many towns in Wales, as shown by the high component scores on the minor axes (such as economy or tenure), there is little point in using these centres in the analysis since the resultant patterns may be distorted by reason of these local peculiarities. More importantly, most of the towns in Wales are quite small; only three centres, Cardiff, Newport and Swansea, have over 100,000 population (Figure 10). Since the full range of inter-urban characteristics identified for Western centres are unlikely to be found in the smaller centres, attention was focused on these larger places. Cardiff was eventually chosen as the primary case study area since it was the largest centre and was presumably the one with the greatest range of urban characteristics. Moreover, it scored quite highly on the Growth-Migration side of the Renewal axis, yet was only located halfway on the Age and Major Economy axis. This meant that it was one of the more modern centres in Wales with relatively low sub-standardness, but possessed rather average values in terms of its general population structure and economy. Any variations found in the inter-urban structure, therefore, could not be attributed to place-particular or unique features.

In terms of the regional analysis scale it would have been ideal to have identified an area in which a complete cross section of the major types of Welsh towns was found. No such area could be identified, given the spatial separation of the fourfold division of types shown in Figure 11. Hence the decision was made to analyze the area immediately adjacent to Cardiff, an area roughly defined as its city-region on the basis of journey-to-work flows (Davies and Musson, 1978). In an ecological or geographical context one advantage of using this area was that it enabled the study to incorporate the commuter settlements found outside the boundaries of most major cities. In addition, the area contained an extensive area of recent urban growth, the Vale of Glamorgan, as well as a major portion of the South Wales Coalfield with its heritage of declining industrial centres. An additional advantage, in terms of the objective of producing community typologies, was the fact that previous attempts had been made to define the regional characteristics of the area (Carter, 1974). Less satisfactory was the fact that the area did not contain examples of the Old Age — Substandard or Growing Service centres identified in Figure 11; such centres are found almost exclusively in the north and west of Wales.

## 2. The Postulated Axes of Differentiation

The fact that the inter-urban axes of differentiation in Wales deviate from the standard types laid down for more modern Western societies provides partial support for the major proposition of this study. It is not conclusive because the results in the previous section apply to the *inter*-urban, not to the *intra*-urban scale. Yet there is already some limited factorial evidence that bears out the general patterns that have been identified. For example, Davies (1975) has shown how the largest factor axes in a study of Swansea displayed greater factorial overlap (meaning lesser degrees of axial separation) than equivalent studies of prosperous English centres. But many other factorial studies in Wales have not shown such characteristics (Herbert, 1970; Evans, 1973; Carter, 1974). Since these previous studies only used unrotated (or orthogonal) rotations, overlapping axes would be missed. The resultant imposition of orthogonality upon data sets could have meant that the data was forced to conform to a particular model, thereby failing to identify the variations of interest here. In other words, the orthogonality of the axes in the studies by Herbert, Evans and Carter may have been a consequence of the technical solutions chosen. Additional studies are, therefore, needed to resolve this problem. This conflicting evidence provided another justification for the choice of study area.

Reference back to the major proposition of this study, that societal or regional differences led to variations in the structure of intra-urban axes, does not, of course, answer the question of which particular axes are expected. This question of the *expected axes* is another major problem of the study. From the previous discussion it might be assumed that the regional or societal variations in Wales will produce axes rather different from those in the most modern, culturally heterogeneous, private enterprise society, as in parts of North America. For example, it could be hypothesized that the dimensions in the Welsh towns are likely to be fewer in number, will show more general character, and will display less specialization. They are also likely to overlap with one another. However, it is much more difficult to answer questions about the appropriate number of axes, or which axes are likely to appear in a particular society. At this stage in our understanding of urban social differentiation we do not have enough knowledge of the particular range and type of axial variations expected in Wales. So it seemed more logical to organize the study on the reverse premise, namely, that if a single type of urban structure was an appropriate description for all Western societies, then the complete set of Western city axes should be present in Wales. The specific axes proposed as representing the standard Western typology are a set of factors either identified in previous factorial ecologies, or deduced from concepts of post-industrial society. In other words, a Western urban structure standard is proposed and deviations can be measured from this standard. Given the proposition of the study, it is to be expected that the case studies of Welsh towns will *not* conform to the proposed structure, thereby providing evidence for variations in Western urban structure.

Table 4 shows the set of axes that were proposed. Each potential dimension is indexed by between two and four variables. Ideally, more variables should be used to identify the axes, but the limitations of the data source made it impossible to find additional indicators. To ensure comparability of measurement all the twenty-seven variables used in the study of intra-urban variation were obtained from the unpublished enumeration district tables of the 1971 census. By explicitly postulating a series of axes in this way, the analysis avoids one of the basic problems of many factorial ecologies, namely, over-emphasizing one type of characteristic, a fact that is inevitably reflected in the factor axes. For example, two-fifths of Evans's forty variable study of Cardiff (1973) relate to household or dwelling condition so the axes obtained reflect this bias. In addition it must be noted that the set of variables shown in Table 4 are the final set of indicators; a pre-screening process eliminated some highly skewed variables which were replaced by conceptually equivalent indicators (Clark, 1973; Bennett, 1977). Each of the final variables was carefully measured to avoid those problems of redundancy and closed number systems which produce the spurious correlations described by Dent and Sakoda (1973).

Table 4 shows that seven other axes were identified apart from the four dimensions noted by McElrath (1968), namely: *Socio-Economic Status* (I), *Urbanization* or *Family Status* (IV), *Ethnic* (VIII), and *Migrant* (VII). Two of the additional axes measure the extent of family related specialization in modern society: first, a *Young Adult* (or pre-family) construct, which should identify the extent to which young adults have left home and have found their own accommodation (V); and, second, a *Late Family* axis (VI), which picks out areas where the aging family unit remains with higher levels of economic participation because the children are working, or where two person households remain after the children have left home. Two more axes are linked to economic status differentials. The *Substandardness* (or Non Affluence) dimension (II) represents the seemingly irradicable 'trailing edge' of society left behind whilst the majority have improved their living standards, and is an axis measured primarily by poor housing conditions, low income levels and even family breakdown. The *Urban Fringe* axis (III) recognizes the fact that urban economy and life have spilled beyond the city

**Table 4**

**List of Variables and Postulated Axes: Intra-Urban and Regional Scales, 1971**

| Possible Axis | Variables (Short Title) | Description of Variables |
|---|---|---|
| I Socio-Economic Status | + T28 Two Car Households | Percentage of households with two or more cars. |
| | + T29 High Employment Status* | Percentage of households with head in Socio-Economic Groups 1 to 4. (Employers, Managers, Professionals, etc.). |
| | − T33 Unskilled* | Percentage of households with head in Socio-Economic Group II. (Unskilled, Manual Workers). |
| II Substandardness (Non-Affluence) | + T16 No Bath | Percentage of the total number of dwellings without a bath. |
| | + T18 Small Dwellings | Percentage of the total number of households having less than 4 rooms. |
| III Urban Fringe | + T37 Commuters* | Percentage of employed people working outside the local authority area of residence. |
| | + T38 Agriculture* | Percentage of the employed persons working in agriculture. |
| IV Life Cycle and Family Status | + T25 Large Households | Percentage of the total number of households having more than 6 persons. |
| | + T10 Children | Percentage of the total population under 15 years of age. |
| | − T13 Old Aged | Percentage of the total population over 65 years of age. |

**Table 4** *(continued)*

| *Possible Axis* | *Variables (Short Title)* | *Description of Variables* |
|---|---|---|
| V   Young Adult (Residentialism) | + T14 Single Adults | Percentage of the adult population who are single, widowed, or divorced. |
| | + T11 Young Adults | Percentage of the total population between 15 and 24 years of age. |
| VI  Late Family | + T17 One Person Households | Percentage of the total number of households with only one person. |
| | + T12 Middle Aged | Percentage of the total population from 40 to 50 years old. |
| | + T27 Economically Active Females | Percentage of adult females over 60 years of age who are economically active. |
| VII  Mobility (Migrant) | + T35 Local migrants* | Percentage of households in which the head moved *within* local authority during the previous five years. |
| | + T36 Distant migrants* | Percentage of households in which the head moved *into* the local authority during the previous five years. |
| VIII Ethnicity | + T03 English | Percentage of the total population born in England. |
| | + T04 Welsh | Percentage of the total population born in Wales. |
| | − T05 Born Overseas | Percentage of the total population born outside the United Kingdom. |

**Table 4** *(continued)*

| *Possible Axis* | *Variables (Short Title)* | *Description of Variables* |
|---|---|---|
| IX  Females | + T08 Female | Females as a ratio of males. |
|  | + T46 Single Females | Percentage of oadult females under 65 years of age who are single, widowed, or divorced. |
| X  Tenure | + T20 Owner Occupied | Percentage of the total households that are owner occupied. |
|  | – T21 Council Housing | Percentage of the total households that are council owned. |
| XI  Economies | T39 Mining* | Percentage of the employed persons working in Mining and Quarrying occupations. |
|  | T40 Manufacturing* | Percentage of the employed persons working in Manufacturing. |
|  | T43 Distribution/Service* | Percentage of the employed persons working in Distribution and Service. |
|  | T45 Local Government* | Percentage of the employed persons working in Government and Defence. |

*Calculated from 10% sample tables.

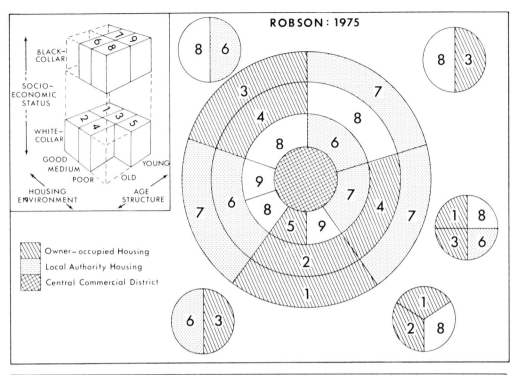

ROBSON: 1975

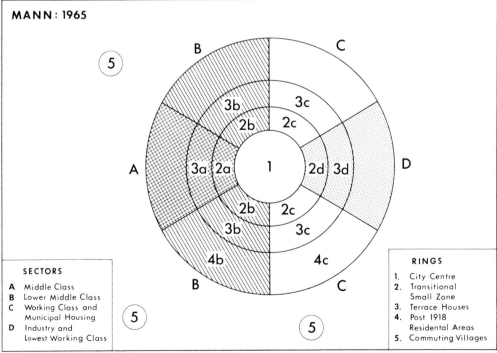

MANN: 1965

SECTORS

A Middle Class
B Lower Middle Class
C Working Class and
  Municipal Housing
D Industry and
  Lowest Working Class

RINGS

1. City Centre
2. Transitional
   Small Zone
3. Terrace Houses
4. Post 1918
   Residental Areas
5. Commuting Villages

FIGURE 12 SOCIAL AREA SPACES IN AN IDEALIZED BRITISH CITY. (SOURCES: ROBSON, 1975; REVISED FROM
MANN, 1965).

boundaries. High status people, in particular, have moved to surrounding villages and commute to the larger commercial centres, and this means that rural areas outside the town have a mixture of rural and urban economies. The next axis is one that seems to be worth proposing for British towns alone; it is a *Tenure* dimension (X) which recognizes the dominance of the public housing sector in British society. In addition a separate *Female* axis (IX) is postulated, since a specialized axis of this type has been identified in several factorial ecologies (Berry, 1972; Davies and Lewis, 1975). Finally, a set of variables measuring *Economy* (XI) or economic base differences in the workforce is added. Previous chapters have already shown that the economic indicators are important in differentiating between settlements at the urban system level of analysis (Hodge, 1968). The addition of these variables to an intra-urban analysis ensures that the link between the results at the regional, intra- and inter-urban scales of analysis is kept open.

## 3. Spatial Patterns of Dimensions and Community Typologies

The third problem dealt with is more closely related to geographical or ecological considerations. Two related issues are involved: First, the spatial patterns of the axes; second, the classification or typology of communities.

(a) It is well known now that the individual axes of differentiation found in cities are associated with quite different spatial patterns. The intra-urban case study will, therefore, determine the extent to which these singular patterns can be recognized in Cardiff. Unfortunately, it is difficult to provide any set of comparable generalizations for the analysis at the regional level; the typology at the city regional level is bound to be related to the unique resource imbalance in the area and is unlikely to display many general spatial patterns that would be common to all city regions.

(b) The discussion of the Area Taxonomy method illustrated how community typologies can be produced in any area, but emphasized that the areal classifications are not really integrated with the dimensionality of places. It has been shown that the Multivariate-Structural Method can be used to resolve this problem. The individual factor scores can be interrelated to form a community area typology by applying cluster analysis methods to the matrix of scores. Most factorial studies imply that the taxonomies produced are specific for the local area being analyzed, whilst some of the most commonly used typologies — such as Mann's (1964) and Robson's (1975) ideas shown in Figure 12 — have only been identified by intuitive, descriptive means, as either no link is made between the social dimensions and typologies, or statistical evidence for these results is lacking. But if there is a general patterning in cities, and if there are systematic relationships between indicators, constructs, social patterns, typologies and regions, as shown in Figure 8, then the community typologies should be made up of particular combinations of the social constructs that have been proposed.

Table 5 summarizes the results of some of the major taxonomic studies of Western urban social structure. From this summary Table 6 identifies a set of fifteen types that represent the most important categories. These are made up of high or low values on

67

# Table 5

## Areal Taxonomies Proposed for Western Cities

| Burgess (1925) Concentric Zones 5 Zones | Harris-Ullman (1945) Multiple Nuclei 9 Areas | Shevky-Bell (1955) Social Area Analysis 64 Areas (Example of Polar Types from Social Rank, Urbanization, Ethnic) | Rees (1972) Chicago Factor-Subjective 9 Groups | Johnston (1966) Melbourne 4 Types | Jones (1969) Melbourne Factor 3 Groups 20 Sub Groups | Robson (1975) Subjective | Norman (1972) London Factor 6 Groups | Davies (1978) Edmonton Factor 9 Groups | Herbert (1973) Cardiff Factor 9 Groups | Webber (1977) UK Area Taxonomy (15 out of 36 types relevant to Cities) | Davies (1980) (Proposed Typology) |
|---|---|---|---|---|---|---|---|---|---|---|---|
| 1 C.B.D (Retail, Wholesaling, Factory Zones) | 1 C.B.D<br>2 Wholesaling-Manufacturing | | | | | | | | | | A Central City (i) Retail and Offices (ii) Wholesaling (iii) Industry |
| 2 Transition Zone (Ethnic Areas) | | | A Apartments/Townhouses<br>1 Skid Row<br>B Black Ghetto | | | 5 Student Bed-sits<br>9 Rooming House | | A Central City<br>1 Non Family and Migrant<br>2 Ethnic and Non Affluent | 6 Shared<br>5 Rental<br>1 Decayed Old Age/Foreign | 29 Rooming House, High Status<br>27 Immigrant, Multi-Occupied<br>11 Inner City Poor Quality<br>29 High Status, Rooming House | B Inner City<br>1 Transient -Rooming House<br>2 Immigrant<br>3 Decayed and Low Status<br>4 Ageing Status<br>5 Private Renewal<br>6 Old Council Housing<br>7 Local Authority Renewal |
| 3 Working Class (Ghetto, Ethnic Areas) | 3 Low Class | 1A Low Social Rank No Children (a) Non Ethnic (b) Ethnic | 4 Old Working Class<br>9 Ethnic Areas | 1 Low S.E.S. -Average Family -Immigrants | III Variables S.E.S. -Low Familism -High Immigrant | 8 Private Rented Low Status<br>6 Inter War Council/ Inner City C. Flats<br>1 Inter War Owner Occupier | 1 Bed Sitting Room<br>2 Poor | B Inner City<br>4 Stable and German<br>5 Stable and E & S European | 7 Established Council Estates-Low Ethnicity | 21 Inner City, Council<br>22 Council, Single People<br>8 Edwardian<br>31 Mock Tudor | |
| 4 Better Residences | 4 Medium Class | 4A High Social Rank No Children (a) Ethnic (b) Non Ethnic<br>1D Low Social Rank Children (a) Ethnic (b) Non Ethnic | 2 Old, Middle Class<br>3 Rich, Few Children<br>B Outer City-Suburbs<br>7 Working Class | 3 High S.E.S. -Low Family -Few Immigrants<br>4 Above Av. S.E.S. -Low Family -Few Immigrants | | 1 High Status Owner Occupier<br>7 Post War Council/ Inner City High Rise | 3 Stable Working Class<br>4 Upper Class | 5 University<br>6 High Status<br>C Outer City<br>B Suburban Old Fringe | 9 Highest Status-Old<br>3 Mixed Private/Council<br>2 Middle City/ Better Residences | 34 Very High Status<br>20 Inter War Local Authority | C Middle City<br>8 Established Family/Middle Status<br>9 Established Council Housing<br>10 Established High Status |
| 5 Commuters | 5 High Class<br>6 High Class Residential<br>7 Outlying Business<br>8 Residential Suburb<br>9 Industrial Suburb | 4D High Social Rank Children (a) Ethnic (b) Non Ethnic | 6 Middle Class<br>5 Upper Class | | 1 High S.E.S. -Av. Familism -Low Immigrants<br>II Low S.E.S. -High Familism -Variable Immigrants | 3 Post War Semi O' Occupier<br>4 Post War Owner Occupier | 5 Local Authority Housing<br>6 Almost Suburban | 7 Suburban- Middle Status<br>9 Suburban | 4 New, Status Suburbs | 30 Modern, High Status<br>16 Overspill Estates<br>4 Modern Low Cost Owner Occupied<br>13 Villages with Some Agric. Employ'nt<br>23 Rural, Established High Status | 11 New, Council Housing<br>12 New, Middle Status<br>13 New, High Status<br>E Fringe<br>14 Council Overspill<br>15 Rural/High Status (Rural/Urban Fringe) |

several dimensions. No attempt was made to restrict the choice of axes used in identifying the typical categories but in practice between three and six axes were used. Socio-Economic Status and Family Status are the major differentiating axes, following Gans's (1962) ideas, with Ethnicity and Migration the minor ones. Obviously a whole variety of alternative social area types could, in theory, be produced. The justification for the categories identified comes simply from the fact that all the structures have been previously recognized in some multivariate analysis. In addition, it would be possible to be much more systematic in ecological terms by demonstrating how the individual dimensions are localized in areas and how these axes overlap so as to produce a typical location for the postulated types. This was only partly carried out here; in this case by linking the postulated types to four different categories of urban space, inner, middle, outer city and fringe. The concentric zonation this implies does not mean that sectoral or cluster patterns are ignored. For example, if seven different types of area are to be located in the inner city they are fitted into the zonation by some kind of cluster or zone. In other words, this rather primitive locational reference system can be used when the directional element in the postulated scheme is absent.

(i) The inner city is postulated as the area of most complex character since seven different types of area are proposed for the zone. Table 6 shows how these areas were derived and the titles summarize their characteristics: Transient; Decayed and Low Status (or Substandard); Immigrant; Old Council Housing; Aging Status areas. Two renewal areas complete the set, the first is the so-called 'Local Authority or Council Renewal', the second is called 'Private Renewal', since it is the product of so-called 'gentrification' process, the 're-colonization' of the inner city by middle to high income groups (Berry, 1971).

(ii) In the middle city, three types are proposed: Established Council Housing Estates; Established (or Late) Family Communities of Middle Status; and Established Family High Status Areas.

(iii) In the outer suburban area three types are suggested. The first is the peripheral New Public Housing (or Council) Estates, the second and third are the New Status Areas, both Middle and High Status.

(iv) Finally, in the rural-urban fringe outside the area of continuous or built-up city, are two other areas: the Commuter Villages, composed of high status areas of young families mixed in with people engaged in rural occupations; and the Overspill Council (Public Housing) Estates located beyond the city boundaries.

These fifteen different types arranged in four geographical zones obviously only deal with residential areas and do not produce a complete breakdown of intra-urban space. The variations found in the Central Business District, or those caused by industrial and recreational land uses do not form part of the schema.

Only one intra-urban area is being analyzed here so this community typology needs to be modified for British cities above a quarter to half million population size range. Only thirteen of the fifteen types proposed are expected in this case study. 'Private Urban Renewal' in the inner city has not been large enough to be recognized at the scale

69

# Table 6

## Postulated Typology of Intra-Urban Residential Areas

| Location | Characteristic Social Dimensions | Short Title |
|---|---|---|
| 1. Inner City: | Low Status + Young Adult + Mobility + Service Sector + Substandardness + Female | 1. Transient, Rooming House |
| 2. Inner City: | Low Status + Substandardness + Old Age | 2. Decayed and Low Status |
| 3. Inner City: | Low Status + Substandardness + Immigrant | 3. Immigrant or Ethnic |
| 4. Inner City: | Low Status + Local Authority Housing + Manufacturing + Old | 4. Old Council Housing |
| 5. Inner City: | Low Status + Local Authority Housing + Younger Families | 5. Council or Local Authority Renewal |
| 6. Inner City: | High Status + Old Age + Female | 6. Aging Status |
| 7. Inner City: | Possible Middle-High Status + Younger Families | 7. Private Renewal (Gentrification) |
| 8. Middle City: | Low Status + Local Authority Housing + Late Family | 8. Established Council Housing |
| 9. Middle City: | Middle Status + Late Family + Non Mobile | 9. Established (Late Family) Middle Status |
| 10. Middle City: | High Status + Late Family + Owner-Occupation | 10. Established (Late Family), High Status |
| 11. Outer City: | Low Status + Local Authority Housing + Young Family | 11. New Peripheral Council Housing |
| 12. Outer City: | Middle Status + Young Family + Owner Occupation | 12. New Middle Status |
| 13. Outer City: | High Status + Young Family + Owner Occupation | 13. New High Status |
| 14. Fringe: | High Status + Young Family + Owner Occupation + Rural-Urban Fringe | 14. Rural-Urban Fringe (Commuter Villages) |
| 15. Fringe: | Low Status + Local Authority Housing + Young Family | 15. Overspill Council Estates |

employed, whilst 'Peripheral Council Housing' also subsumes the 'Overspill Council Estates' since public housing estates have been built on the edge of the city, not some distance from it. Finally, it must be observed that no attempt is made to mould the postulated structure to the local conditions of Cardiff by the identification of a separate 'old, inner city immigrant area', such as Tiger Bay in Cardiff's dockland. The reason is simply that the British census did not record the colour of person in 1971; only the data on 'country of origin' gives a clue to ethnic differentiation. Although the 'country of origin' is useful for picking out the new immigrant areas in British cities it means that older or established coloured communities, such as Tiger Bay, cannot be identified if census material alone is used. The ethnic information in the 1971 national census is, therefore, incomplete — a problem perpetuated in the 1981 Census since racial questions were omitted. This means that the results of this study must take the limitations of the data source into account in the final conclusions.

The typology of communities tested at the intra-urban level is not the only type of classification produced. Studies at the regional or city-regional scale are more closely linked to the unique resource imbalances between various parts of the area. Hence they are less likely to display general spatial patterns common to many types of areas. As a result there is little point in establishing any general regional standard in this section; instead, the expected community types are related to the sources of areal differentiation specific to the area.

## 4. Scale Dependence of the Axes

The fourth problem investigated is that of the *scale dependence* of the axes. The analysis carried out in Chapter 4 at the enumeration district scale in Cardiff is replicated at the ward scale, a difference between 541 and 20 areas. In addition, the intra-urban analysis — with basically the same variable set — is repeated for the 193 communities identified in Cardiff City-Region in Chapter 5. Presumably any region of Wales could be used to establish the intra-urban/regional congruence, but it seemed more sensible to use the region immediately around the intra-urban case study, since this would cut down on the place-particular distortions associated with different regions. Moreover, the choice of a city-region seemed appropriate to measure regional variations since this is a unit that has a high degree of urban functional cohesion.

At present there is a considerable degree of disagreement in the literature of Social Area and Factorial Ecology about the relationship between intra-urban axes and regional or urban system scales. It was originally implied that the axes were scale-free since Shevky and Bell dealt

> with the statistics of large cities not because of a belief that these cities were independent dominant factors, but because of a belief that the emerging characteristics of modern society were best observed in such areas of movement and expansion.
>
> (Shevky and Bell, 1955, p. 1.)

Both Udry (1964) and Timms (1971) investigated the applicability of the three

Shevky-Bell axes to inter-urban and regional studies and came to the opposite conclusion, namely, that not all these axes could be recognized at inter-urban and regional scales; they only applied to the intra-urban scale. However, the limited number of axes being investigated, the small number of variables used in both studies, and, in the case of Udry's study, the poor correspondence between the variables and the postulated axes, call for more comprehensive investigations into the problems. This is especially important since Hodge (1968) and Berry (1972) have shown that axes similar to the Shevky-Bell formulations represent some of the dimensions of intra-urban systems. By contrast, Rees (1970) and Hughes and Carey (1972) showed differences between the urban and metropolitan scales of analysis.

In a study more directly relevant to this analysis, Carter (1974) analyzed the dimensions of inter-urban variation in a study of Glamorgan (1974). He picked out four axes (Socio-Economic Status, Life Cycle, Economic Participation, Urban Fringe/City Centre) that were similar to some of the intra-city axes identified by Davies and Lewis (1973). The other two axes identified in Glamorgan, Growing Manufacturing Employment, and Employment, could be considered as indexing certain specific Growth and Economy dimensions noted by Hodge (1968) and Berry (1972) as being indicative of urban systems. This led Carter to call for:

> a series of carefully designed analyses with a great variety of scales so that it might be possible to argue for the organization of socio-economic space through the same components.
>
> (Carter, 1974, p. 72.)

The studies in the next two chapters represent an attempt to explore the problem of scale dependence.

## 5. Links between Social and Spatial Differentiation

The fifth problem is related to the *theory of social and spatial differentiation*. At present social analysts have not identified a satisfactory theoretical link between the theory of social change, whether the increasing 'scale' ideas of Shevky and Bell (1955), or the 'modernization' trends of McElrath (1968), and the consequent residential or sub-area differentiation. In other words, there is a hiatus between societal change and the spatial manifestation of these changes. Udry (1964) maintained that there were two co-ordinated theories involved, one of increasing scale applying to societal change, the other of sub-area differentiation relating to spatial differences. However, he was unable to provide a satisfactory solution to the theoretical connection between the two ideas. Moreover, the type of diffusion analogy proposed by Bell and Moskos (1964, p. 415) describes, but does not explain, the mechanisms involved.

One way of understanding the contrast between societal change and sub-area differentiation is to suggest the mediation of ecological processes. In other words, we can recognize that the specialization, or modernization of society, produces non-overlapping roles for both individuals and families, leading to the separation of identifiable axes as social rank, family, etc. (Timms, 1971, p. 143). But the crucial point we need to add here is that *these trends only produce sub-area or spatial differences if individuals with these specialized roles are unequally distributed in space.* If they are scattered equally throughout the sub-areas of the city one would find societal specialization, but no spatial manifestation of these changes. In other words, some ecological or geographical processes must work upon the various societal specializations to produce the residential or spatial concentrations; without such imbalances no sub-area differentiation will be recognizable.

Most of the ecological processes leading to spatial differentiation are known in general terms, for example, the 'trade-off' between accessibility (to central area jobs and entertainment) and the amount of space (in house, garden, and green space) which lies at the heart of the differentiation of family status throughout the city. In this case the central business district is assumed to be a major employment area and the city is growing by peripheral expansion of single family units. Yet to demonstrate the separation of these ideas of societal, as opposed to ecological, specialization in theoretical terms in more difficult. One approach, albeit a negative one, is to hypothesize that ecological effects are *not* present. If no ecological effects are found then the axes of societal differentiation found at one scale should be the same as those at another scale, since there can be no reason for differentiation to occur if societal differentiation is uniform throughout the area. This is the argument adopted for this study. The result is that all but one of the indicators used in the study of intra-urban variation in Cardiff are used to describe the socio-economic variations in the settlements of Mid and South Glamorgan, or Cardiff City-Region. The additional variable added was the percentage employed in Mining and Quarrying, an important addition to an area which has been so closely associated with mining. If the axes of differentiation that are produced in the two studies are not the same, and do not parallel other studies with similar data sets, then it can be argued that some ecological processes must be operating to modify the resultant dimensions. Obviously, care must be taken to avoid distortions produced by particular techniques. Hence several factoring methods should be used to establish that the variations are not statistical artefacts or the product of a single factorial procedure.

## 6. Degree of Technical Dependence

The last of the major problems dealt with in this study is the question of technical invariance. In order to avoid the charge that the results are technique dependent, several different factoring and rotation procedures are used. The Principal Axes component model was employed as the primary factoring technique since it has been shown to possess a number of advantages over more sophisticated methods (Davies, 1978) when used in an exploratory context. The most obvious advantages are that no assumptions have to be made about the amount of common variance whilst unique component scores are produced. Although this does mean that components contain both general and specific variance in the classical factor analysis sense, the extent of distortion in the resultant interpretations can be tested by using the common factor version of the factoring technique. In any case it has been shown (Giggs and Mather, 1975; Velicer,

1977; Davies, 1978) that the Principal Axes technique produces parallel results to those of other methods when the data set is well structured. Obviously it cannot be known in advance whether there is a strong degree of structure in the data so the Principal Axes results were compared to those produced from an Image Analysis, since Davies's (1978) comparison of eight methods showed that these two approaches provided the greatest differences in factor solutions. In many ways this resolves the vital criticism that can be made of the Principal Axes technique in the context of the problems of this study. In theory the attempt to establish the validity of a set of postulated axes for the study areas should lead to the use of the common factor method, since these methods have associated statistical tests which should confirm or deny the presence of the hypothesized dimensions. Obviously the precision of these statistical tests depends upon all the assumptions of the common factor model being upheld, not only the distributional requirements of the data but also the independence of the sample. It can be emphasized that any ecological study designed to classify all the urban areas as well as to identify the dimensions breaches the latter assumption. So it was considered more appropriate to reject what in this case would be the *apparent* rigour of the common factor method. Nevertheless, by comparing the components with common factor results, the degree of technical invariance of the solution can be derived. In addition, the use of oblique as well as orthogonal rotations ensures that orthogonality is not imposed on the results. In other words, it can be argued that if parallel results from the different methods are obtained then a stable, satisfactory, solution has been derived.

Higher order analysis was also carried out on the factor correlations of the oblique solutions to measure the degree of independence of the factor axes and to produce higher level factor generalizations. The adoption of the higher order approach also has the advantage of reducing the impact of the initial decisions made about the number of factor axes to extract, since higher order analysis often identifies the larger axes that would be picked out by underfactoring the data set (Davies, 1978). Although these technical issues interrupt the substantive discussion, satisfactory resolutions of the problems are necessary before any degree of confidence can be placed in the factorial results. Two final points of terminology need to be clarified. Strictly speaking, the results of the Principal Axes component solutions should be called 'components' rather than factors. The term 'factor' is often used as a general descriptive term, to avoid repetition of words, to cover both 'components' and 'common factors'. Where common factor methods are employed 'common factor' is used if the meaning is not obvious. In relation of the areas being used the term 'community' is often applied. This has no behavioural association; the word 'community' is simply used as an alternative for 'settlement'.

## Chapter 4

## SOCIAL DIFFERENTIATION AT THE INTRA-URBAN SCALE:
## A SOCIAL ECOLOGY OF CARDIFF IN 1971

This analysis of the social dimensions and spatial patterns of Cardiff is one case study of the proposition that cities in Wales show a rather different social dimensionality to those found in other parts of the Western world. If substantiated, this proposition provides empirical support for the more general concept described in previous chapters, namely, that the social differentiation of Western cities does not conform to a single, uniform type but displays systematic variations associated with individual societal characteristics. In the case of Welsh towns it is likely that the variations in urban social structure at various scales are due to lower levels of modernization and high levels of government involvement in the housing market, as well, perhaps, as some cultural heterogeneity. This study, therefore, concentrates on one of these scales, the intra-urban. Apart from the study of social dimensionality the case study also deals with the individual spatial patterns of the dimensions identified. Moreover, these individual patterns are integrated by means of a summary classification or typology of the social areas in the city. This typology is linked to the more general body of literature by explicitly relating it to the social dimensions and comparing it to previous social typologies established for Western cities.

The basic substantive aims are complemented by analyses of the degree of invariance in the factorial results. These studies are carried out at two levels. The first, the technical level, identifies the similarity of results produced by two different factor methods and two different rotations. The second, the geographical scale level, compares results at two very different scales, the 541 enumeration areas of the city and the 20 wards. If invariance rather than variation by factor method characterizes the results it helps to confirm the utility of the specific results of the case study and certainly eases the task of building a systematically related body of literature on the urban social structure of cities. To achieve these aims the chapter is divided into five parts. The first describes the study area and the postulated dimensions and typology; this is necessarily brief since much of the information has been dealt with in the previous chapter. The second section describes the analytical procedures used and the enumeration area results. The third summarizes the higher order analyses and the relationship of the results to the postulated axes. The fourth section repeats the previous analyses by replicating the study at the ward level. The final section describes the results of the classification of enumeration areas and wards on the basis of the factor scores and its relationship to the postulated ecological structure.

### 1. Study Area and Postulated Structures

The decision to deal with the above problems by an analysis of Cardiff was made primarily because Cardiff is the largest city in Wales, and in size terms should display the maximum degree of complexity. Moreover, its population of 278,221 in 1971 means that it is comparable in size with a set of parallel factorial studies in Britain (Davies and Lewis, 1973; Davies, 1975), and Canada (Davies and Barrow, 1974; Davies, 1975, 1977, 1978) using similar techniques, although it must be noted that these cities are well below the million or over population size of city most frequently analyzed in factorial studies of American cities. An added advantage for the choice of Cardiff was that there appear to be no cultural or specialized economy distinctions which could produce unique results. Cardiff is the primary commercial centre in Wales with a mixed economy that shows low levels of economic specialization. A final and important advantage was that Cardiff has already been the subject of several previous factorial studies using 1960 and 1966 data (Herbert, 1970; Evans, 1973; Herbert and Evans, 1973) providing, therefore, a much better basis for comparative research than is usually the case.

The study was organized around two postulated structures, one relating to the dimensionality of the urban social structure, the other to the way the dimensions combine spatially to produce a typology of community areas.

(a) A total of twenty-seven variables formed the data set (Table 1) and these indexed the eleven postulated areas of social differentiation shown in Table 7, namely, *Socio-Economic Status, Stage in Life Cycle, Ethnicity, Migration Status, Substandardness* (or *Non-Affluence*), *Pre-Family* (or *Young Adult*), *Post or Late Family, Tenure, Females, Economy, Urban Fringe*. These axes were considered to be as comprehensive as possible given the restrictions caused by the use of the single or census data source. To avoid misinterpretation it is worth re-emphasizing that the axes do not cover the 'quality' or 'perceptual' aspects of urban differentiation.

(b) Although a very large number of different combinations of the axes of differentiation could be postulated, in practice a limited number of distinctive areas can be identified in intra-city space, each area being associated with a restricted set of the social characteristics. In other words, only certain dimensions have very low or high values and these dominate the social character of areas. Using the postulated axes of differentiation, *twelve* different combinations of these axes described in Chapter 3 are proposed as forming the basic typology of the case study area. These twelve types were obtained by generalizing the results of the previous typologies shown in Table 5.

## 2. The Choice of Solution and Factorial Results

The first stage of the analysis consisted of measuring these twenty-seven variables over the 541 enumeration districts (E.D.s). Figure 13 shows the study area consisted of all the E.D.s in the city of Cardiff and those parishes immediately outside the city. In this way, the built-up, rather than the political, area of the city is used in the analysis. These units, with an average population of 520 people, represented the finest scale of mesh for which information was available from the 1971 census and is much more detailed than previous studies of Cardiff in which 119 (Evans, 1973) and 334 (Herbert, 1970) areas were used. However, to avoid bias in the calculation of percentage data from the use of very small

## Table 7
### Postulated Axes: Cardiff, 1971

| | |
|---|---|
| 1. Socio-Economic Status | 7. Mobility |
| 2. Substandardness (Non Affluence) | 8. Ethnicity |
| 3. Urban Fringe | 9. Females |
| 4. Life Cycle and Family | 10. Tenure |
| 5. Young Adult (Residentialism) | 11. Economies |
| 6. Late Family | |

(For detailed description of the variables composing those dimensions, see Chapter 3, Table 4).

## Table 8
### Choice of Component Solution for Cardiff, 1971

### (a) E.D.s Enumeration Districts

| Components Abstracted | Number of first ranking loadings >0.3 in solution | | | | Number of Communalities | | | Variance |
|---|---|---|---|---|---|---|---|---|
| | 0 | 1 | 2 | 3+ | >0.7 | 0.7 to 0.5 | >0.5 | |
| 8 | 1 | 2 | 1 | 4 | 17 | 10 | 0 | 74.8% |
| 7 | 0 | 2 | 1 | 4 | 15 | 11 | 2 | 71.3% |
| 6 | 0 | 1 | 1 | 4 | 13 | 10 | 4 | 67.0% |
| 5 | 0 | 0 | 1 | 4 | 12 | 8 | 7 | 62.4% |

### (b) Wards

| | | | | | | | | |
|---|---|---|---|---|---|---|---|---|
| 7 | 3 | 1 | 0 | 3 | 27 | 0 | 0 | 95.8% |
| 6 | 2 | 1 | 0 | 3 | 27 | 0 | 0 | 94.4% |
| 5 | 0 | 2 | 0 | 3 | 27 | 0 | 0 | 91.5% |
| 4 | 0 | 0 | 1 | 3 | 26 | 0 | 1 | 87.6% |

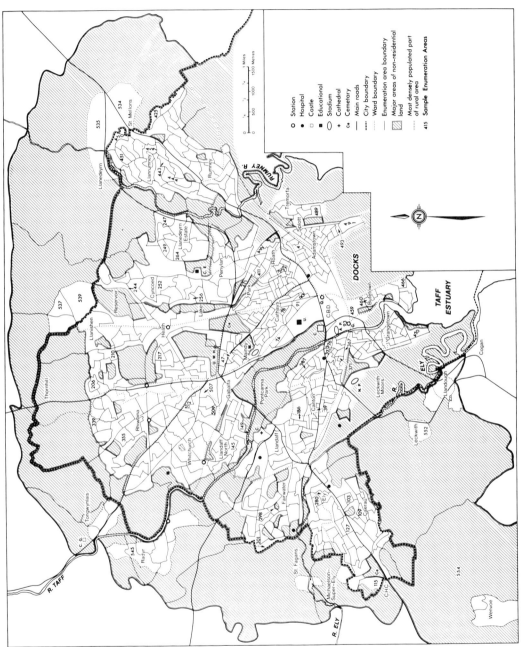

FIGURE 13   ENUMERATION DISTRICTS AND STUDY AREA: CARDIFF, 1971

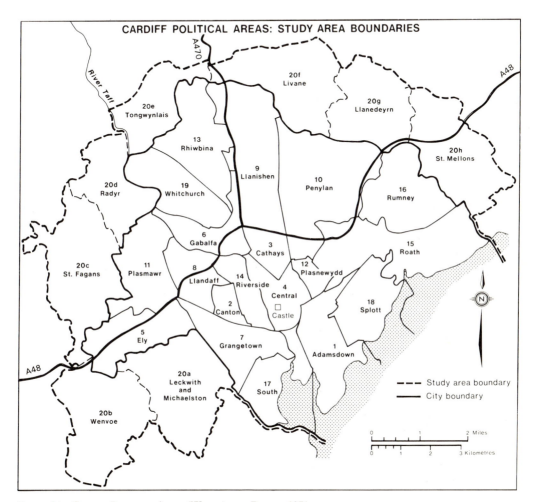

CARDIFF POLITICAL AREAS: STUDY AREA BOUNDARIES

FIGURE 14   CARDIFF POLITICAL AREAS (WARDS) AND FRINGE: 1971

enumeration areas, ten of the original enumeration units with less than 100 population were combined with adjacent units.

A two-fold procedure was used to produce the final set of factorial results that were interpreted, namely the use of R mode Principal Axes component and Image Analysis factoring methods followed by Direct Oblimin rotation. These two methods were chosen because the Principal Axes component approach based on the correlation matrix has been shown to produce results comparable to many other procedures (Giggs and Mather, 1975; Velicer, 1977; Davies, 1978) and does not necessitate making decisions about the size of communalities. The Image Solution, based on the co-variance matrix, is used as the comparison because it is a method that has shown the greatest deviation from the Principal Axes results (Davies, 1978). In this way, the results, if comparable, should not be subject to the criticism of being technique dependent. A mixture of distributional and interpretational criteria were used as the basis for the final choice of axes since no completely acceptable statistical test of the adequacy of a component solution has been invented; those that exist relate to common factor methods and are only really applicable if all the distributional requirements have been satisfied and the areas represent samples rather than a complete population. Even then there is always the problem discussed in Chapter 2 and by Harman (1976), namely, the distinction between statistical and substantive conclusions. Given these circumstances, therefore, this study cannot be considered to be a rigid statistical test of hypotheses. In the strictest sense it is only an exploratory study of the dimensionality and social topography of Cardiff, in which eleven possible axes are proposed as identifying the widest possible range of differentiation that can be measured from the available data set and twelve types of social area are proposed as representing the regional character of intra-urban space. Yet despite these reservations the use of a set of alternative factoring procedures does mean that if the results are shown to be invariant then a great deal of confidence can be placed in the conclusions — at least as far as this data set is concerned.

A six axis model was considered to produce the most acceptable results from the data set in the absence of a clear break of slope in the distribution of eigenvalues of the Principal Axes solution. Table 8 shows that a scree can be recognized between three and nine axes, so attention was focused on this range of factors. At five axes too many of the variables had communalities below 0.5. The seven and eight axis solutions produced very highly correlated vectors that could not be satisfactorily interpreted and had too many vectors containing fewer than 1 in 20 first ranking loadings (Burt, 1950). The six axis solution was, therefore, an acceptable compromise and was used as the final solution. One additional advantage was that each axis accounted for more than 5% of the variance. This seems to be a more standard guide than the 'eigenvalue 1.0' rule (Rummel, 1971) which produces such a fluctuating basis of comparison between studies using different numbers of variables.

The distribution of loadings for the Principal Axes and Image Analysis solutions, together with the varimax and oblique results for the former, are shown in Table 9 whilst the scores for each axis are shown in Figures 15 to 19.

## Table 9
### Loadings for the Solutions, Cardiff, 1971

| Component Titles | 541 Enumeration Districts | | | 20 Wards | |
| --- | --- | --- | --- | --- | --- |
| | Principal Axes | | | Principal Axes | |
| | Oblique | Varimax | Image | Oblique | Varimax |
| **1. SOCIO-ECONOMIC STATUS** | 1. | 1. | 3. | 1. | 1. |
| T03 English | 85 | 88 | 80 | 76 | 82 |
| T29 High Employment Status | 77 | 81 | 63 | 74 | 81 |
| T28 Two Car Households | 75 | 80 | 70 | 60 | 69 |
| T43 Distribution and Service | 68 | 63 | — | 92 | 88 |
| T36 Distant Movers | 64 | 65 | 60 | 48 | 53 |
| T37 Commuters | 44 | 50 | 48 | 31 | 38 |
| T20 Owner Occupation | 38 | 50 | — | 35 | 50 |
| T45 Local Government | — | — | — | 69 | 72 |
| T12 Middle Aged | — | — | — | 43 | 46 |
| T08 Female | — | — | — | 40 | 45 |
| T35 Local Movers | — | — | — | 35 | — |
| T21 Council Housing | — | − 36 | — | — | — |
| T25 Large Households | — | − 37 | — | − 38 | − 50 |
| T33 Unskilled | − 49 | − 54 | − 30 | − 88 | − 90 |
| T16 No Bath | − 50 | − 47 | − 35 | − 78 | − 70 |
| T40 Manufacturing | − 65 | − 63 | — | − 94 | − 92 |
| T04 Welsh | − 73 | − 69 | − 72 | − 56 | − 52 |
| **3. LIFE CYCLE and TENURE** | 3. | 2. | 4. | 2. | 3. |
| T10 Children | 71 | − 77 | − 68 | − 73 | − 81 |
| T25 Large Households | 63 | − 66 | − 58 | − 80 | − 82 |
| T21 Council Housing | 37 | − 44 | — | − 91 | − 90 |
| T04 Welsh | — | — | — | − 39 | − 45 |
| T05 Born Overseas | — | — | — | 38 | 41 |
| T16 No Bath | — | — | — | 46 | 41 |
| T20 Owner Occupation | − 32 | 39 | — | 76 | 74 |
| T45 Local Government | − 32 | 32 | — | 30 | 38 |
| T46 Single, Widowed, Divorced Females | − 42 | 46 | 38 | 30 | 35 |
| T17 One Person Households | − 68 | 67 | 64 | 52 | 54 |
| T08 Female Ratio | − 69 | 67 | 57 | — | — |
| T13 Old Aged | − 90 | 89 | 85 | 94 | 91 |

**Table 9** (*continued*)

| Component Titles | 541 Enumeration Districts | | | 20 Wards | |
|---|---|---|---|---|---|
| | Principal Axes | | | Principal Axes | |
| | *Oblique* 2. | *Varimax* 3. | *Image* 2. | *Oblique* 4. | *Varimax* 2. |
| **2.  YOUNG ADULT & NON FAMILY** | | | | | |
| T11  Young Adult | 85 | 82 | 77 | 98 | 91 |
| T14  Single Adult | 75 | 74 | 70 | 89 | 91 |
| T18  Dense Occupation | 73 | 76 | 60 | 91 | 91 |
| T46  Single, Widowed, Divorced Females | 72 | 72 | 69 | 79 | 81 |
| T17  One Person Households | 44 | 52 | 34 | 71 | 81 |
| T05  Born Overseas | 42 | 49 | 47 | 76 | 77 |
| T16  No Bath | | | | | 41 |
| T29  High Employment Status | | | | | − 38 |
| T08  Female Ratio | — | — | — | − 42 | − 44 |
| T28  Two Car Households | — | − 30 | — | − 35 | − 45 |
| T10  Children | − 31 | − 33 | − 32 | − 34 | − 39 |
| T04  Welsh | − 35 | − 38 | − 36 | − 45 | − 77 |
| T20  Owner Occupied | − 51 | − 48 | − 48 | − 43 | − 36 |
| T12  Middle Aged | — | — | — | − 51 | − 65 |
| **5.  LATE FAMILY/MOBILITY** | 5. | 5. | 5. | 3. | 5. |
| T12  Middle Aged | 65 | − 64 | 39 | — | — |
| T27  Economically Active Females | 54 | − 52 | 30 | − 88 | 82 |
| T08  Female Ratio | — | — | − 43 | − 51 | 55 |
| T46  Single Females | — | — | — | − 39 | 38 |
| T04  Welsh | — | — | — | − 35 | 40 |
| T36  Distant Movers | — | — | — | 37 | − 41 |
| T18  Dense Occupation | − 33 | 35 | — | — | — |
| T10  Children | − 36 | 35 | − 33 | 32 | − 31 |
| T35  Local Movers | − 68 | 66 | − 41 | 33 | — |
| **6.  URBAN FRINGE** | 6. | 6. | 5. | 6. | 4. |
| T38  Agricultural | 74 | 73 | — | 83 | 87 |
| T37  Commuters | 54 | 52 | — | 78 | 82 |
| T36  Distant Movers | 38 | 36 | — | 62 | 72 |
| T28  Two Car Households | — | — | — | 34 | 45 |

**Table 9** *(continued)*

| Component Titles | 541 Enumeration Districts | | | 20 Wards | |
|---|---|---|---|---|---|
| | Principal Axes | | | Principal Axes | |
| | Oblique 6. | Varimax 6. | Image 5. | Oblique 6. | Varimax 4. |
| **6. URBAN FRINGE** *(continued)* | | | | | |
| T40 Manufacturing | — | — | 61 | — | — |
| T03 English | — | — | — | — | 33 |
| T35 Local Movers | — | — | — | − 97 | − 85 |
| T43 Distribution, Service | − 43 | − 44 | − 70 | — | — |
| **4. HOUSING AND ETHNICITY** | 4. | 4. | 1. | | |
| T21 Council Housing | 71 | 71 | − 78 | | |
| T04 Welsh | 44 | 44 | − 33 | | |
| T08 Female Ratio | 38 | 36 | — | Not Found | |
| T20 Owner Occupied | − 44 | − 43 | 52 | | |
| T05 Born Overseas | − 61 | − 60 | 50 | | |
| T16 No Bath | − 66 | − 65 | 53 | | |
| TOTAL EXPLANATION | 67.0% | | | 91.5% | 91.5% |

It is impossible to map the scores for all 541 areas at the scale needed to reproduce at a page size so isopleths have been drawn to show the distribution of values. In this way, perhaps, a better visual impression of the 'social topography' of Cardiff's areas can be obtained, which is, presumably, the main reason for producing maps of component scores. In addition, a summary table of the highest values of the factor scores for each axis and the final set of cluster groups is provided in Table 16. This ensures that subsequent investigators wishing to sample in these areas can immediately identify the places with the most typical characteristics of the axis.

The results show that there are comparatively few substantive differences between the two rotation solutions — except for the tendency of the varimax axes to have more minor loadings. Similarly, the Image and Principal Axes loadings are very comparable for four of the six axes; it is in the smallest axes that differences occur. The Image vector of the fifth axis is only a poor reflection of the fifth Principal Axes vector, whilst the sixth Principal Axes vector could not be identified by the Image solution. This discrepancy immediately raises the problem of which solution is the most appropriate to use, since it is apparent that there is some variation by technique between the two solutions. The decision was made to use the Principal Axes solution because the Image Analysis had very low communalities for the variables that identified the fifth and sixth axes. It must be remembered that the images, or common parts of the variance of variables, are predicted from all other variables. In cases where highly localized indicators are found, the images are so low that much of the variance is treated as error by the common factor method. Given these circumstances and the fact that the study is also concerned with describing the specific patterns of variation, the Principal Axes results were used as the basis for the description of the dimensions. However, the fifth and sixth vectors must be recognized as being technique dependent dimensions.

(i) Component I is a familiar axis to factorial ecologists. It is one that separates high and low socio-economic status and is measured by the variables that relate to occupations, housing conditions and content. Table 9 shows that in this case the axis also has an ethnic association, for the largest loading variables on either side of this axis are those relating to people born in either England or Wales, the former associated with the high status characteristics, the latter with low status. Obviously one must not exaggerate this point by assuming very high percentages of English born are found in certain areas, since the correlations input into the factor analysis are calculated on standard scores so the absolute sizes of variables are eradicated. Thus the percentage of the population born in England as opposed to Wales is 12% for the former and 78% for the latter. Nevertheless the relatively higher proportions of English born people in the high status areas testify to the way in which immigration to this part of Wales has been at the managerial, high income level, providing a further illustration of the importance of the mobility of the 'spiralists' in society (Bell, 1968). The axis is, therefore, described as *Socio-Economic Status.*

Figure 15 shows that the pattern of component scores for this axis displays some quite strong sectoral associations with particular parts of the city, but that these sectors are rarely the type of continuous zones extending from the central city out to the suburbs suggested by Hoyt's original sector hypothesis (1939). Instead, the continuity of the various sectors is broken, and each is often replaced by areas of different status; the result is the production of a much more complex and variegated pattern compared to many comparable British cities. In terms of specific areas the most important zone of high status starts in the vicinity of Roath Park and extends northward as a ridge through Cyncoed and Penylan to Llanishen, with less intense high status values found in the vicinity of Heath. Far less continuous is a sector following the axis of the river Taff, one that is split into three nodes by parkland. This is associated with the areas preserved from early development by the policies of the Bute estate, and by the location of high status residential areas on land above the Taff flood plain. This discontinuous sector begins on the western edge of the Central Business District on either side of the Taff in the Cathays Park-Cathedral Road area. The second node is in Llandaff, the cathedral centre

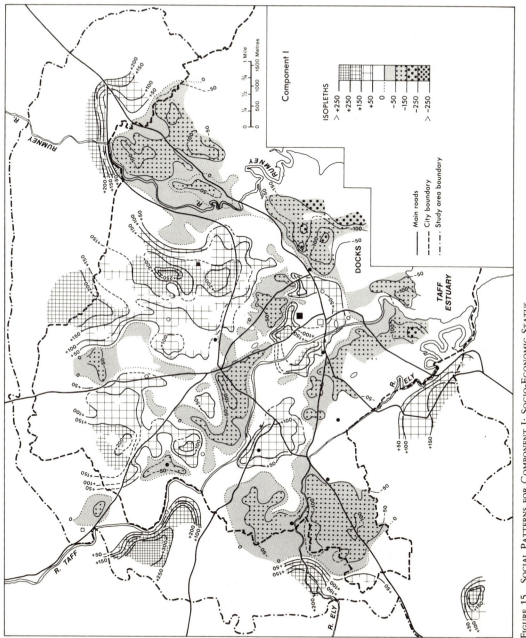

FIGURE 15   SOCIAL PATTERNS FOR COMPONENT I: SOCIO-ECONOMIC STATUS

of Cardiff, the third node is in Radyr, outside the city boundary. Apart from these two sectors another extensive area of high status can be recognized running from Whitchurch to Rhiwbina. In its eastward extension this area almost forms a continuous link to the main ridge of high status in the Cyncoed area. Outside these places peripheral high status areas are linked to small villages on the edge of the city, places that have been virtually brought into the continuous urban land use area, such as Llandough, St. Fagans, Radyr, Lisvane and St. Mellons.

Similar patterns of discontinuity in the pattern of low status scores can be recognized. The core is found in the docks area south of the commercial centre. One sector starts in the Butetown-Grangetown area and extends through Canton, is broken by the industrial area and flood plain of the Ely, but re-emerges in the Fairwater-Caerau area of the city. Further westward expansion is blocked by the high status area of St. Fagans outside the city boundary. The second sector has its core in the working class areas of Adamstown, Splott and Tremorfa, north-east of the Docks, and has two branches to the north-west and to the northeast. The former is the most discontinuous, since the Newport Road-Roath higher status area interrupts its continuity with the community of Cathays. The medium status characteristics of Maindy interrupts its north-western extension through Llandaff North and Gabalfa, although it can be considered to re-emerge again in Tongwynlais, outside the city proper. Finally, the extensive low status area in the Rumney area to the east of the city is virtually separated from the Adamstown-Tremorfa core by the flood plain of the Rumney valley. This area is mainly composed of council houses and is bounded by the high status area of St. Mellons, providing a rather comparable situation to that found on the west of the city.

(ii) Component III, described as the *Life Cycle and Tenure* axis, represents a familiar factorial axis in terms of comparable studies of British towns. Positive loadings are associated with children and family characteristics, whereas negative loadings are linked to the variables measuring old age and non family features. However, the presence of tenure variables, albeit with minor loadings, means that the axis confirms the close association between age and family characteristics and tenure found in other studies of British towns (Evans, 1973; Davies and Lewis, 1973).

The same comparability for this axis does not, however, extend to the distribution of component scores, since Figure 16 does not display the classical concentric zonation with old age in the city centre gradually decreasing outwards to the family orientated suburbs. Instead, the zone of old age-non family status occupies most of the northern part of the inner and middle areas of the city, in the area bounded by Llandaff, Whitchurch and South Rhiwbina, Heath, and Roath as far as the Newport Road-Cowbridge Road axis, and the city centre. The highest scores in this zone are found in Roath, the city centre, Llandaff, and along the Pontypridd Road axis through Whitchurch. The North Llandaff and Cathays area provide exceptions in this zone as their positive scores indicate the presence of family conditions.

The pattern of negative, or family orientated, scores shows a less coherent distribution. Apart from the exceptions already mentioned it is associated with the old

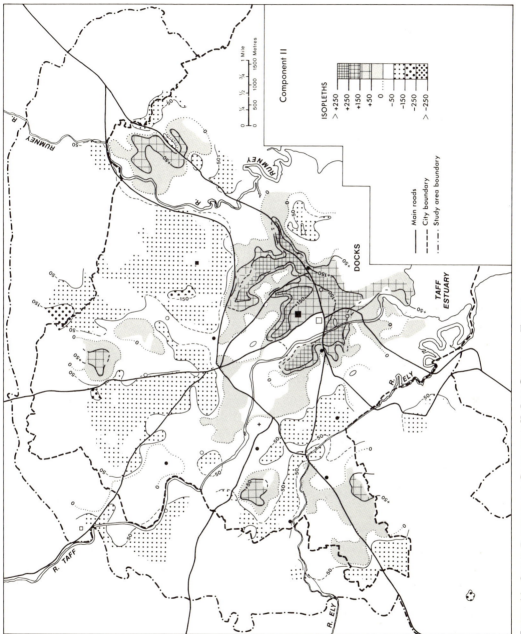

FIGURE 16 SOCIAL PATTERNS FOR COMPONENT II: LIFE CYCLE AND TENURE

87

peripheral villages, from Llandough to St. Mellons, and the outer suburbs, the Fairwater-Caerau communities on the west, Rhiwbina and Llanishen to the north, Cyncoed, Penylan and Rumney to the north-east. In addition to these areas of young, affluent suburbs and council estates, high family characteristics are found in the southern belt around the central area from Canton, through Grangetown and Butetown to Adamstown and Splott. Since it has already been shown that the area is basically of low status it is apparent that Figure 16 has identified an inner city area of working class character retaining strong family associations.

(iii) Component II has been labelled a *Young Adult/Non Family* vector because the positive loadings dominate the axis and are linked to people in the 15-24 years of age group and to non-family characteristics. Minor ethnic associations are also found, with foreign born people linked to the young adult side of the vector, whilst the Welsh born and children indicators have negative loadings that reinforce the highest, but still only medium value negative loading of the owner occupation variable. To some extent the axis is comparable with the Mobile Young Adult axis of Leicester (Davies and Lewis, 1973) and the inverse association with owner occupation means that it indexes the opposite of stable community life, or 'residentialism' in the city. As such it may be thought of as measuring the extent to which young adults leave home to find higher education or job opportunities in the service economy of central areas, and therefore, increasingly locate themselves in the immediate vicinity of the central city. Figure 17 confirms the explanation, since the highest positive (or non-family) scores are found in the central city. Specifically, the map shows the base of the axis runs through the Canton-Arms Park-North Butetown-Newport Road area, extending northward as three prongs: firstly, along Cathedral Road and East Canton; secondly, Cathays; and thirdly from Roath to Roath Park. This distribution, therefore, identifies the classic 'bed sitter' zones around the central business district and the university colleges in Cardiff. Elsewhere, scattered concentrations of young adult character are found in some of the older council estates in, for example, Caerau-Ely, and in Rumney. The rest of the city has practically all low positive scores, illustrating higher levels of owner occupation or low concentrations of young adult and non-family character.

(iv) Component IV is also a very distinct axis, this time indexing *Housing and Ethnicity* variables, and is described as such. Positive loadings are linked to council housing, the Welsh born population and marginally with a high female to male ratio, whereas the negative loadings apply to substandard housing, the foreign born population and owner occupation. Figure 18 shows a marked spatial separation in the high positive and negative loadings; the former picking out the major council estates in Cardiff which are found in a discontinuous zone in the outer edge of the city running from Caerau-Ely and Fairwater in the west, through Llandaff North, Whitchurch-Llanishen, Llanedeyrn, Llanrumney, Rumney and Tremorfa. By contrast, the high negative scores, which identify substandard housing and foreign born population, are found principally in two belts on either side of the city centre: the western one running from Butetown across

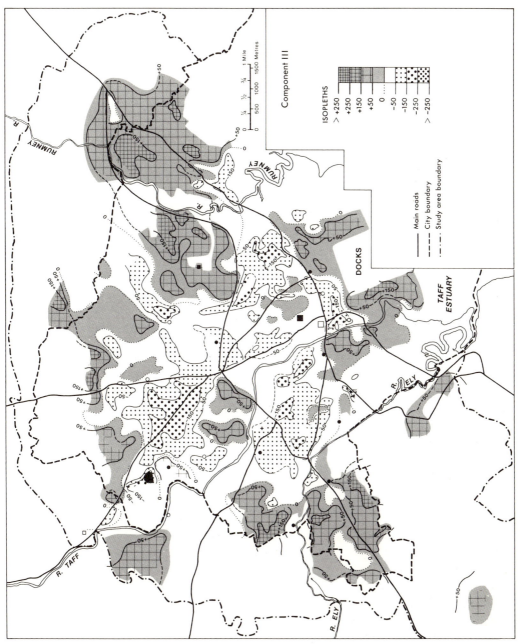

FIGURE 17 SOCIAL PATTERNS FOR COMPONENT III: YOUNG ADULT AND NON-FAMILY

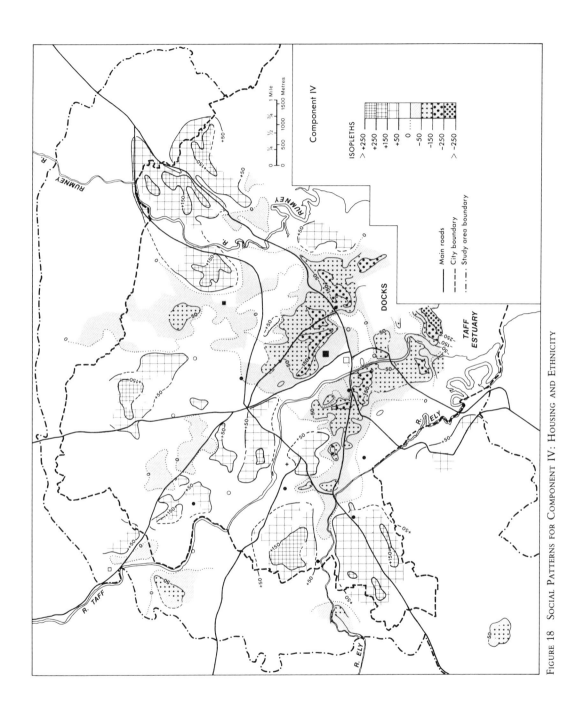

FIGURE 18 SOCIAL PATTERNS FOR COMPONENT IV: HOUSING AND ETHNICITY

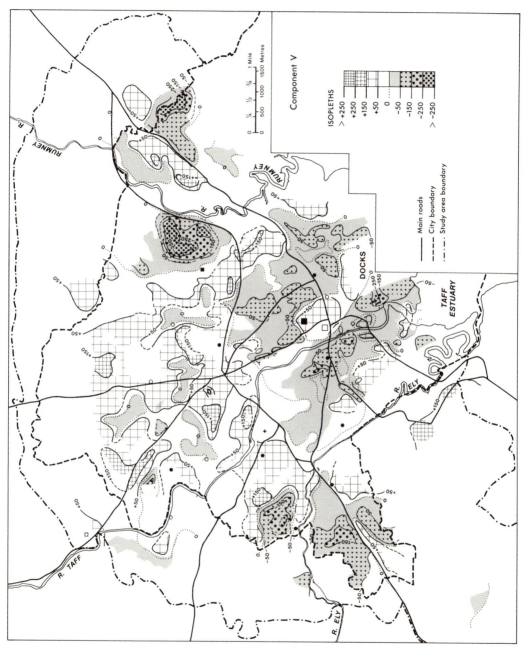

FIGURE 19  SOCIAL PATTERNS FOR COMPONENT V: LATE FAMILY/MOBILITY

91

Grangetown and Canton through to Ely; the eastern one from Maindy through Cathays to Adamstown. Apart from the historic ethnic concentration in Butetown, the famed Tiger Bay of the Cardiff's coal port days, the highest ethnic values are found immediately outside the central city in east Canton, North Adamstown and west of the universities. Isolated concentrations of older housing in areas on the fringe of the city also have negative scores greater than 0.5, whilst the larger areas of negative scores shown in Figure 18 are only marginally above the 0.0 level. Judging from the values on the original variables they are principally in this category because of above average concentrations of owner occupation.

Despite the clarity of the dimension in separating the decaying inner city areas with foreign born populations from the new council estates the axis has not been found in many previous factorial studies of British towns, apart from Leicester (Davies and Lewis, 1973). However, it does appear to have some similarities with axes identified in previous studies of Cardiff, namely, Evans's 'Residential Quality' axis (1973) and Herbert's 'Ethnic' axis (1970).

(v) The fifth component, described in Table 9 as *Late Family/Mobility*, does not have very high loadings and is certainly indistinct in the Image Analysis. However, it does separate the characteristics of a middle aged population with higher levels of economically active females, from those of high migration and the families. Figure 19 shows that the axis separates the older, stable residential areas of positive scores from those with negative scores where mobility and high family characteristics are found. In the case of the latter, namely, mobility and family character, two very different spatial patterns can be identified; firstly, those areas surrounding the central area as far out as 1½ miles from the centre, with the highest scores nearest the commercial centre and in Butetown, Cardiff's original 'skid row'; secondly, a discontinuous belt of high mobility characteristics is linked to the newest peripheral council estates, particularly Fairwater, Llanedeyrn Estate and Rumney. By contrast, the stable, late family areas are found mainly in the middle city, one on the inner edge of this area approximately (1½ to 2 miles from the city centre) in a belt extending from S. Grangetown, Llandaff, Gabalfa and Heath to Roath. Another set of areas with the same late family, non mobile characteristics is found in another broken belt approximately 3 miles from the city centre in Fairwater, Rhiwbina, Llanishen and South Rumney, all areas of older public and private housing estates. In general, therefore, the axis is close to a *Residentialism* construct, since it picks out the older, stable residential areas that separate the inner city areas of change, transition and mobility, from the new peripheral council estates. As such the axis identifies the process of aging and mobility in the city and displays the doughnut or hollow ring pattern found in axes identified in North American cities such as Edmonton (Davies, 1978).

(vi) The final axis picked out by the Principal Axes procedure at the enumeration district level is a more familiar construct and isolates *Urban Fringe* characteristics. It is similar to vectors identified in other studies of British cities (Davies, 1975) when the built-up area and its surrounding rural fringe was used in the analysis instead of just the political city. The only high positive scores are those in the largely agricultural areas located outside the city boundary, so they are not worth mapping separately.

## 3. Higher Order Axes and Relationship to Postulated Axes

### Table 10
### Higher Order Loadings

#### (a) Cardiff Enumeration Districts, 1971

|  | Higher Order Loadings | | | Communalities |
|---|---|---|---|---|
|  | I | II | III |  |
| 1. Economic Status | 71 | | | 54 |
| 4. Late Family | 62 | | | 44 |
| 2. Age | − 59 | − 37 | 37 | 63 |
| 3. Non Family | | 60 | | 59 |
| 6. Ethnicity and Tenure | | − 77 | | 64 |
| 5. Fringe | | | 87 | 76 |

Variance Explanation: 3 axes = 60.0%

#### (b) Cardiff Wards, 1971

|  | Higher Order Loadings | | | Communalities |
|---|---|---|---|---|
|  | I | II | III |  |
| 1. Economic Status | 66 | 37 | | 65 |
| 4. Non Family | − 86 | 37 | | 83 |
| 2. Age | | 93 | | 85 |
| 3. Late Family | | | 89 | 83 |
| 5. Fringe | | | 68 | 67 |

Variance Explanation: 3 axes = 76.6%

Table 10 shows the results of the higher order analysis of the correlations between the factors in relation to the original six first order vectors. These are compared to previous factorial results obtained for Cardiff, and Leicester, a similar sized city, in Table 11. The

93

## Table 11

## Comparison of Factorial Studies for Cardiff and Leicester

| City Date (Pop.) Author | LEICESTER 1966 (283,260) (Davies and Lewis, 1973) | | CARDIFF 1971 (278,221) a. Results b. Postulated Axes (Davies, 1980) | | | CARDIFF 1966 (253,000) (Evans, 1973; Herbert & Evans, 1973) | CARDIFF 1961 (256,682) (Herbert, 1970) |
|---|---|---|---|---|---|---|---|
| | Higher Order | First Order | Higher Order | First Order | b. Postulated Axes | First Order | First Order |
| | I SOCIAL STATUS | 4. Substandardness | I NON-URBAN | N.F. (part of 4) | 1. Substandardness | 4. Tenure and Life Cycle (Residential Quality)* | 2. (Ethnic, Residential Quality)* |
| | | −61 ⎰ +76 — 8. Urban Fringe | | 87 — 5. Urban Fringe | 2. Urban Fringe | N.F. | N.F. |
| | | +69 — 1. Socio-Economic Status | | 37 — 3. Life Cycle and Tenure | 3. Socio-Economic Status | — | — |
| | | 3. Life Cycle/Tenure | | 3. Life Cycle and Tenure | 4. Life Cycle | 2. Tenure and Life Cycle | 1. (Tenure/Age)** |
| | II FAMILY STATUS | +74 | II FAMILY AND SOCIAL STATUS | −59 ⎰ +62 — 5. Late Family/Mobility | 5. Late Family | N.F. | N.F. |
| | | −64 — 7. Economic Participation and Late Family | | +71 — 1. Socio-Economic Status | | 1. Social Status | ?N.F. |
| | | +54 (Socio-Economic Status) | | | 6. Young Adult/Pre-Family | | |
| | III ETHNICITY-MIGRANTS | 5. Young Adult (Mobile) | III ETHNICITY-NON FAMILY | 2. Young Adult/Non Family | 7. Ethnicity | 5. Urbanization (Young Adult)* | 4. (Non Family/Children)* |
| | | +50 ⎰ +87 — 6. Ethnicity | | 60 ⎰ 77 — 4. Housing and Ethnicity | 8. Mobility | 3. Residential Quality (Ethnic, Housing)* | 3. (Ethnic)* |
| | | +66 2. Mobility | | −37 ?N.F. (Part of 7.) | 9. Females | — | 5. Not shown |
| | | (Females) | | (Life Cycle and Tenure) | 10. Tenure | | |
| | | | | | 11. Economy | | |

*Titles in brackets represent either a re-naming of axes, on the basis of the loadings, or the addition of titles when they were absent in original study.

| Model: | Component | Component and Factor | Component | Component |
|---|---|---|---|---|
| Techniques: | Principal Axes | Principal Axes, Image | Principal Axes | Principal Axes |
| Rotation: | Oblique; Varimax | Oblique, Varimax | Varimax | None |
| Variables: | 56 | 27 | 40 | 26 |
| Areas: | 143 | 541 | 119 | 334 |
| Axes: | 9 | 6 | 5 | 5 |
| Variance: | 72.2% | 67.0% | 70.6% | 73.0% |

higher order solution was obtained by the application of the same methodology used in the derivation of the first order axes, with the same care being taken over the number of axes abstracted. The higher order Cardiff results do not show the simple hierarchical pattern of first order axes collapsing to three higher order axes as previously identified for British cities such as Leicester, namely, Social Status, Life Cycle, and Ethnic and Migrant status. Instead, this Cardiff study shows: firstly, a general axis accounting for most of the variance of the first order Socio-economic Status, Age and Tenure and Late Family vectors; a second one somewhat similar to the Ethnicity-Migrant higher order axis, linked primarily to the inner city axes of Young Adult-Non Family and Housing and Ethnicity; and a third axis associated with the Urban Fringe, a vector measuring conditions outside the continuously built up area of Cardiff, although the first order Age and Tenure axis has minor associations with both the third and second vectors. This intimate association between the Social Status and Life Cycle axes means that this study provides additional evidence for one of the ideas expressed at the beginning of this study. This is that the largest city in Wales deviates more from the standard Shevky-Bell model than the evidence from comparable sized English cities at this second order of generality would lead one to suspect. When this finding is compared to the overlap of parallel axes in the analysis of the Welsh urban system (Davies, 1977), it suggests that these Welsh towns show rather different structural patterns of social differentiation from at least the more prosperous English cities that have been studied by factorial ecologists. Whether this result is a function of the type of society found in Wales, even in English speaking South Wales, or is a characteristic of all areas with lower degrees of economic prosperity and modernization must remain a moot point, and the object of further study. The latter explanation would seem to be the most reasonable.

These results mean that at the first order level few of the eleven postulated axes were found as the distinct dimensions that could be expected in post-industrial society, although elements of seven of the postulated dimensions could be identified. For example, Social Status is clearly indexed, but it is a more general axis than expected since it is associated with ethnic, economic and mobility variables. Similarly, Life Cycle is an important dimension, but is mixed up with tenure and female characteristics, whilst Urban Fringe is associated with economic differentials. Separate Substandardness and Ethnicity dimensions were not identified; instead, a Housing and Ethnicity axis picks up elements of both potential structures, and even this is also associated with tenure. Two other postulated axes are also found to co-exist, in the Late Family/Mobility axis. Neither characteristic was strong enough to form separate dimensions in the Principal Axes results, and they proved elusive in the Image Analysis solution. In relation to the other expected family related axis, namely, the Pre-Family (or Young Adult) vector, a much clearer source of differentiation was found. Again it was not only linked to the postulated variables, rather it was associated with variables identifying ethnicity, housing tenure, and housing condition. These results mean that the first order axes do not form simple vectors unequivocally related to a small number of variables; more general dimensions are found that have elements, the word is used advisedly, of the expected structures. Finally, separate tenure, female or economy vectors were not found in the Principal Axes solution, although the identification of a minor female vector in place of the Late Family/Mobility axis in the Image results must be noted.

It is difficult to rigorously compare this set of Cardiff results with previous factorial studies of the city since there are variations between the variable sets and techniques used, whilst different scales of analysis, as shown by the number of units analyzed, were employed. Nevertheless, at a descriptive level the first order results show much greater similarity with the Leicester axes (Davies and Lewis, 1973) than the other studies, despite the failure to find separate substandardness and mobility axes in Cardiff and the presence of a rather indistinct late family vector. Table 11 shows the comparison at a descriptive level with the addition of appropriate component names to the vectors identified by Herbert (1970). Some of the component labels used by Evans (1973) were not particularly satisfactory in view of the distribution of loadings. Hence revised component labels are added to the original proposals (Table 11) in an attempt to clarify the relationships involved. Despite the problems in comparison noted above many of the major axes of differentiation do seem to be common to all three studies, with the obvious exception of the absence of a separate Social Status axis for Cardiff in 1960 (Herbert, 1970). The 1971 study, however, produces more detailed axes of differentiation. Although the studies of Cardiff span the period from 1960, through 1966 to 1971, it is not profitable to argue that the differences provide evidence of the temporal unfolding of more specialized axes by 1971; the more general axes identified by Herbert and Evans (1973) are more likely to be product of the fact that the investigators had access to less powerful factoring techniques than those used here. In other words the differences are attributed to technical progress from the earlier studies, based only on the use of unrotated or only varimax solutions, and, perhaps, to a less comprehensive data source than that available before 1971. Where this study really shows an improvement, however, is in investigating the degree of technical invariance and using higher order analysis to uncover the relationships between the first order axes. This leads to the identification of a less specialized or overlapping social structure for the largest city in Wales.

To some extent, of course, the same argument of technical variation could be used to explain the differences between the postulated and derived axes. Hence it is worth emphasizing that the more general axes derived here were not, however, a function of the factorial solution; the extraction of more axes added little extra variance and did not produce vectors any more closely related to the postulated dimensions. Hence the dimensionality of the data set was considered to represent a structural characteristic of Cardiff, rather than a statistical artifact of the choice of factor solution.

## 4. The Ward Scale Analysis

The whole factorial analysis of 28 variables carried out on the 541 enumeration areas was repeated using 20 areas, in an attempt to further test the invariance of the solution, this time a scale invariance. These areas consisted of the nineteen wards of the city and an additional unit composed of all the urban fringe areas outside the political city proper (Figure 14). Exactly the same methodology was followed in relation to the extraction of axes, but this time a five vector solution was used. The reasons were: first, there was a break of slope at the fifth axis in the distribution of eigenvalues; second, all the variables had communalities greater than 0.7 in this solution; and, third, the sixth and subsequent components produced vectors which contained an axis without a single variable having its largest loading on the axis, in other words one that offered little in substantive interpretation. In addition, this sixth axis had the disadvantage of having very high correlations with the axes previously extracted.

### Table 12

### Congruence Coefficients (c.c.) between the Results at Two Scales

| Enumeration Districts | | Wards | |
|---|---|---|---|
| 1. Socio-Economic Status | + 0.88 | 1. Socio-Economic Status | |
| 3. Life Cycle and Tenure | − 0.81 | 2. Life Cycle *and Tenure* | |
| 2. Young Adult | + 0.94 | 4. Young Adult | |
| 6. Urban Fringe | + 0.63 | 6. Urban Fringe and *Mobility* | |
| 5. Late Family/Mobility | − 0.56 | 3. *Females* | |
| 4. Housing and Ethnicity | | Not Found | |

Table 9 shows that the ward results accounted for a much higher level of variance at this coarser scale of analysis. This confirms the findings of most workers who have compared solutions at different scales (Perle, 1977). However, Table 9 shows that the axes of differentiation themselves were also more general, in the sense that far more minor loadings were found on each vector. This is a consequence of the fact that the 20 wards contain a much greater range of social variation than the 541 enumeration districts. However, in spite of the drastic change in scale and the addition of these minor loadings, Table 9 illustrates that the results are quite comparable. The major difference is that a separate Housing and Ethnic vector is not found at the ward scale; instead, the tenure variables are linked to Age and Tenure, whilst the ethnic indicators load on either the Economic Status or the Young Adult vectors. Yet this should not be an unexpected result. The separate ecological effects of both the inner city ethnic areas and many of the peripheral council estates are lost at the ward scale because places with these characteristics are incorporated into a series of geographical units which overlap these areas, thereby losing the distinctive character of these specialized regions. In the case of the other varimax vectors, the Socio-Economic Status, Life Cycle and Tenure, and Young Adult/Non Family axes are very similar with congruence coefficients (Harman,

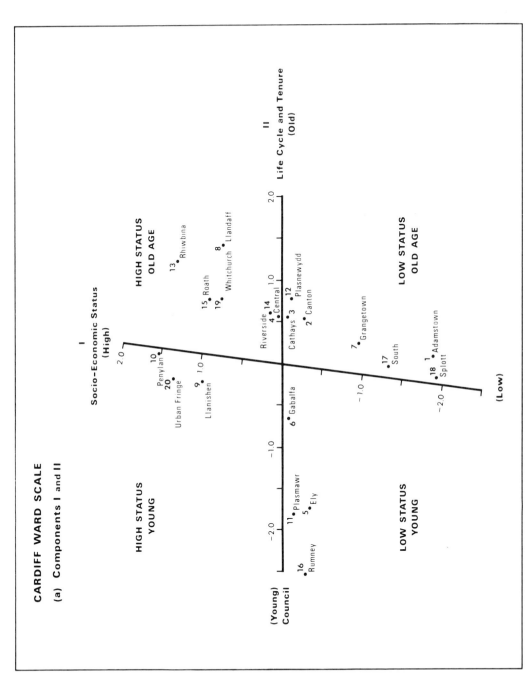

FIGURE 20 SOCIAL STRUCTURE SPACES FOR WARD SCALE ANALYSIS

98

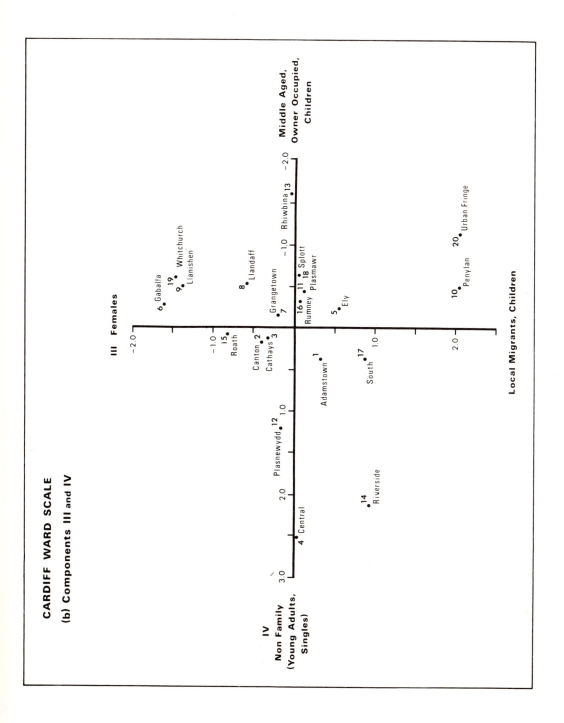

**CARDIFF WARD SCALE**

**(b) Components III and IV**

III  Females

IV
Non Family
(Young Adults,
Singles)

Middle Aged,
Owner Occupied,
Children

Local Migrants, Children

6 • Gabalfa

19 • Whitchurch
9 • Llanishen

8 • Llandaff

Rhiwbina 13 •

-2.0

-1.0

Grangetown
7 •

11 • Splott
18 • Plasmawr
16 • Rumney

5 • Ely

10 • Penylan

20 • Urban Fringe

-2.0

-1.0

15 • Roath
Canton 2 •
Cathays • 3

Adamstown • 1

South • 17
1.0

Plasnewydd 12 • 1.0

2.0

14 • Riverside

4 • Central

3.0

2.0

1976) greater than 0.8. The other two axes are less similar with coefficients of 0.63 for the Urban Fringe axis and $-0.56$ for the Late Family vector (Table 12). Two of these factors have some modifications in the pattern of negative loadings by reason of the loss of single variables. For example, the Urban Fringe vector is negatively associated with local movers, not with distribution and service workers, and the Young Adult axis is negatively related to the middle aged population and to a range of minor household and family variables. It is, therefore, in the Late Family/Mobility vector that the greatest differences between the ward and enumeration district data can be seen and, not surprisingly, the lowest congruence coefficient of $-0.56$ is recorded. Since the positive loadings of the ward analysis measure female characteristics rather than the very distinct middle aged-mobility character of the E.D. study it may be more appropriate to re-label this vector *Female Characteristics* at the ward scale. With these exceptions, therefore, the ward analysis is very similar to the enumeration district results for four of the axes, even though these are more general in the sense that more variables load on the dimensions. The major differences lie in the loss of a separate Housing-Ethnicity vector and the modification of the Late Family-Mobility axis. The conclusion must be, therefore, that the scale of analysis does make some difference to the factorial description of urban differentiation. However, despite the greater difference in the scales of the analysis, 541 to 20 areas, the variations are far less divergent than previous studies of single cities at different geographical scales (Romsa et al, 1972; Perle, 1977) have shown.

Figure 20 shows the classification of the twenty areas, using two diagrams to array the component scores according to their position on each pair of vectors. Figure 20 clearly parallels the patterns produced by the enumeration area maps. Rhiwbina, Llandaff, Roath and Whitchurch fall into the high status — old age sector, whereas Penylan, Llanishen and the urban fringe have high status, but are much younger in age structure. By contrast the biggest differentiation for middle status communities runs from the old areas of Plasnewydd and Canton through to the young areas of Rumney, Plasmawr and Ely. In addition, Splott, Adamstown, South, and Grangetown are the lowest in status with their middle ranking values on the age scale commensurate with their role as working class communities located near the docks and industrial areas. Figure 20b, by contrast, classifies each ward into sectors on the basis of the Young Adult-Non Family axis and the Female vector. The basic contrast shown is between areas such as Gabalfa, Llanishen and Whitchurch, from those such as Penylan and Urban Fringe. Both are linked to stable, middle aged, owner occupied housing characteristics rather than young adults, but the former have high levels of female participation and more females; the latter have low values on these characteristics. Similarly, Central has high non-family character whereas Rhiwbina has the opposite characteristics. Although both communities are in the middle size range of female component scores, Riverside has high non-family values, but is low in female participation.

## 5. Classification of the Enumeration Areas

Like most factorial ecologies the primary substantive objective of this paper has been to disentangle the very different sources of social differentiation and their associated patterns within the complex social mosaic found in the study area. The results of this essentially analytical approach have been displayed in Table 9 and Figures 15 to 20. However, it is possible to go one stage further and synthesize the results of the individual distribution maps in order to produce a final classification of the sub-areas of the city. The most usual approach adopted is to apply a cluster analysis solution to the similarity matrix calculated between each pair of areas on the basis of the component scores. This method was adopted as the preliminary grouping procedure, with Ward's hierarchical clustering technique applied to the Euclidean distances between the scores (Wishart, 1975). The fusion summary statistics revealed a major change of slope in the distribution of values after nine groups (Table 13) and the members of each cluster were subjected to a Discriminant Analysis test of the adequacy of the group membership. The first test revealed that many of the individual areas were misclassified. This is not a surprising conclusion since it is well known that hierarchical clustering methods have the disadvantage of keeping taxonomic units within the cluster they join, even though at subsequent grouping stages individuals may be closer to some other cluster (Sokal and Sneath, 1973). A re-allocation of enumeration areas into the groups was made on the basis of these Discriminant Analysis solutions until a stable solution was reached.

## Table 13
### Grouping of Cardiff Enumeration Districts: Cluster Analysis Statistics

| Grouping Stage | Fusion Summary (Difference) | |
|:---:|:---:|:---:|
| 3 | 27.5 | |
| 4 | 25.0 | (2.5) |
| 5 | 24.3 | (0.7) |
| 6 | 19.6 | (4.7) |
| 7 | 16.3 | (3.3) |
| 8 | 15.5 | (0.8) |
| 9 | 9.9 | (5.6) |
| 10 | 9.2 | (0.7) |
| 11 | 8.0 | (1.2) |
| 12 | 7.8 | (0.2) |
| 13 | 7.4 | (0.4) |

## Table 14
## Group Means for the Component Scores: Cardiff, 1971

| Titles | Groups (Cases) | Components | | | | | |
|---|---|---|---|---|---|---|---|
| | | 1 | 2 | 3 | 4 | 5 | 6 |
| 1. Inner City: Decay and Immigrant | (107) | −0.80(.47)* | +0.05(.57) | +0.21(.57) | −1.34(.60) | −0.20(.63) | −0.07(.67) |
| 2. Inner City: Non Family and Transient | (29) | +0.53(.57) | +2.48(1.00) | −0.29(.74) | −0.92(.67) | −0.79(.69) | −0.04(.85) |
| 3. Inner City: Public Housing | (49) | −0.66(.59) | +0.21(.38) | −0.31(.80) | +0.78(.51) | +0.08(.85) | +0.12(.71) |
| 4. Middle City: Established | (126) | +0.12(.52) | −0.42(.51) | −0.80(.66) | −0.07(.33) | +0.23(.58) | −0.30(.72) |
| 5. New Peripheral Estates (Public Housing) | (59) | −0.66(.39) | −0.17(.56) | +1.23(.74) | +1.24(.48) | −1.53(1.16) | −0.01(.54) |
| 6. Middle City: Public Housing and Mixed Family | (48) | −0.60(.34) | +0.44(.40) | +1.01(.77) | +1.37(.33) | +1.00(.57) | −0.13(.66) |
| 7. New Peripheral, High Status | (85) | +1.23(.65) | −0.94(.43) | +0.03(.63) | +0.00(.31) | +0.68(.69) | −0.03(.75) |
| 8. Inner City: Aging Status and Non Family | (14) | +2.52(1.57) | −0.81(.47) | +0.60(.67) | −0.09(.60) | +0.23(.84) | +3.93(2.02) |
| 9. Family | (24) | +0.67(.48) | +1.71(.87) | −1.35(.79) | +0.21(.42) | −0.25(.57) | −0.29(.72) |

*Standard deviations in brackets.

**Table 15**

**Cluster Groups: Postulated Types and Empirical Evidence**

| Short Title of Cluster | Importance of Individual Dimensions to each Group | | | 2. Postulated Types |
|---|---|---|---|---|
| | Very High Scores (> ± 1.5) | High Scores (± 1.5 to 1.0) | Fairly High Scores (± 0.99 to 0.5) | |
| 1. Inner City: Decay and Immigrant | | (4) Substandard Housing and Immigrant | + (1) Low Status (includes Manuf. and Welsh Born) | Inner City: (a) Decay (b) Immigrant |
| 2. Inner City: Non Family and Transient | (2) Young Adult and Non Family | | + (4) Substandard Housing and Immigrant + (5) Migrants + (1) Low Status | Inner City: Transient |
| 3. Inner City: Public Housing | | | (4) Public Housing + (1) Low Status | Inner City: Old Public Housing |
| 9. Inner City: Aging Status and Non Family | (3) Young Adult and Non Family | + Old Aged Females (2) | (1) + High Status (includes English Born and Tertiary workers) | Inner: Aging Status |
| 4. Middle City Areas | | | Old Aged and Females (3) | Middle City: Established Middle Status |
| 6. Public Housing & Mixed Family, Middle City | | (4) Public Housing (5) + Late Family (3) + Young Family | + Low Status (1) | Middle City: Established Public Housing |
| 7. High Status, Established Family Areas | | (1) High Status | + Old Aged and Females (2) + (5) Late Family | Middle City: Established High Status |
| 8. New, Peripheral High Status Areas | (6) Urban Fringe + (1) High Status | | + Owner Occupied (2) | Outer City: (a) New High Status (b) Rural Urban Fringe |
| 5. New, Peripheral, Public Housing Estates | (5) Migrants | + (3) Young Family + (4) Public Housing | + Low Status (1) | Outer City: (a) New Public Housing; Outer City: New Middle Status |

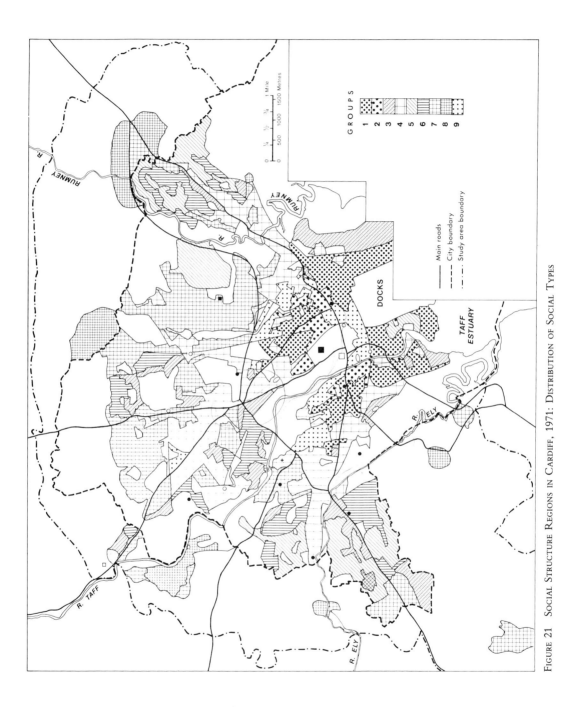

GROUPS
1 2 3 4 5 6 7 8 9

Main roads
City boundary
Study area boundary

RUMNEY

R. TAFF

R. ELY

R. ELY

TAFF ESTUARY

DOCKS

Figure 21   Social Structure Regions in Cardiff, 1971: Distribution of Social Types

Nine groups of areas ranging from 107 (Group 1) to 14 enumeration districts (Group 8) in size were derived, numbered according to their derivation by the analysis. The average component scores for these groups are shown in Table 14 and the distribution of the clusters is shown in Figure 21. In Table 16 sets of sample areas for the individual components and cluster groups are identified, areas which could be used for a more detailed study of behavioural characteristics. In relation to the clusters these areas are the closest to the mean values for the group; the sample areas identified on the individual components are the areas with the highest values on each axis.

Four very different types of cluster groups can be identified: the first is composed of Groups 1, 2 and 9, all inner city areas within 1½ miles of the city centre; the second, composed of Groups 7 and 8, pick out the highest status parts of the study area in two different zones; the third separates the middle suburbs as Group 4; the fourth picks out Groups 3, 5 and 6, all representing areas with high concentrations of council (or public) housing.

Before describing each of these zones in detail it is worth emphasizing that a quantitative comparison of those results with the postulated typology could not be made since not all the axes of differentiation used in the postulated typology were identified in the factor analysis. Moreover, the axes that were found in the solution were more general than expected. So the comparison can only be made at the descriptive level. Despite these limitations, Table 15 shows that the findings are in general accord with the original expectations since nine of the types of social areas empirically identified are very similar to those proposed.

(i) Group 1, with 107 enumeration districts, is the largest cluster of areas and is principally associated with areas of substandard housing, immigrants and the low status axis which is linked to high proportions of Welsh born, manufacturing workers and foreign born people. In essence the areas identified are those of the classic zones of *Inner City: Decay and Immigration,* and the type is described as such. Figure 21 shows that these areas are the inner city terrace houses built in the nineteenth century. However, the age statistics show that this zone is not characterized by the very old population found in areas of extreme decay, since families with children are found in the region. So part of the original Inner city-Decay postulate must be modified. In more general terms it is obvious the results do not separate the postulated types of decay and immigration into distinct entities. Part of this can be explained by the fact that the general level of new Commonwealth immigration into Cardiff is low compared to equivalent sized British cities. But it is also a function of the limitations of the data set, in the sense that variables measuring colour, or ethnic origin beyond birth place, cannot be obtained from the census. This means that the old immigrant areas of Cardiff (Butetown) are not identified as a separate group. A similar association between substandardness and immigrant characteristics was found by Herbert (1973) in his classification of Cardiff using 1966 data for 119 areas.

(ii) The 29 cases of Group 2 are found in a more central city location, being located between the city centre and the Group 1 districts, in Canton, Cathays Park, and Roath.

They are similar to Group 1 in terms of their low status character, substandard property and immigrant populations. However, they differ in a very important way, namely, in the high proportions of young adult, and single or non family people, as well as the association with mobility, in addition to being slightly higher in social status. These areas are really the inner city 'transient' or 'bed sitter' areas, and may best be described as *Inner City: Non Family and Transient*. Compared to the postulated typology, the group is very similar to the expectations, although the absence of separate female and service sector vectors does mean some discrepancy is found. However, the presence of a high loading female variable on the young adult vector partially compensates for the difference. In Herbert's classification (1973), Group 6 appears to provide the closest parallel to this type of area.

(iii) The 24 enumeration areas of Group 9 are located on the outer, rather than inner, edge of Group 1 districts in two sectors: firstly, along the Cathedral Road axis from Canton to Llandaff; secondly, on the edge of Cathays in Roath. The two areas are linked together by the rather large enumeration districts comprising the central business district which has a small number of residential apartments. The principal characteristics found in these areas are young, single person households and old age, with higher proportions of English born people, and high status households. These seem to be the areas in the inner city that were formerly of high status, but now have a residual old population, and a young adult one from invading 'bed sit' activities. As a result they are called *Inner City: Aging Status Areas*. This type closely parallels the postulated type although there is much greater emphasis upon the young adult, pre-family character, rather than the female association. In part, the group is similar to Herbert's (1973, pp. 41-4) Group 5 category with the exceptions of a much wider zone in the east and a narrower one in the eastern Pontcanna area, presumably a function of the greater detail produced by the enumeration areas used in this study.

(iv) Group 7 areas, of which 85 were identified, represent the high status areas in the city which were also characterized by high levels of owner occupation and a middle aged population. An important feature of these areas is the higher proportions of English born in the population providing an additional type of ethnic differentiation. The most extensive zone of these areas, already identified in Figure 21, is found in Cyncoed, with Rhiwbina, Llanishen, and Llandaff also having concentrations of these characteristics. Small outliers are found in places such as Llandough and around Culver House Cross. These are the areas called *High Status, Established Family Areas*. The group compares very well with the postulated type with the exception that a rather older character seems to have been found. The type is similar to Herbert's Group 9 areas, but Herbert's grouping failed to separate these established families from the young, high status people identified in this study as Group 7.

(v) The largest group of 126 enumeration districts comprises Group 4. This occupies a very extensive zone in the middle area of the city between 1.5 and 2.5 miles from the city centre. The area represents the housing estates of the city primarily built before

World War II. Only old age and female character were picked out by the high component scores, but the fact that so many of the scores are near 0.0 means an older and middle aged population with high levels of owner occupation and medium social status is identified, paralleling the postulated structure by its average values rather than by the extremes. The principal regions occupied by this group are on the outer edges of Canton, in the Llandaff to Ely area, as well as between Maindy and South Rhiwbina and the Roath to South Rumney area. These places comprise the *Middle City* areas and seem to have some correspondence with Herbert's Group 2 areas.

(vi) The 14 Group 8 areas are also high status areas, in actual fact the highest status areas of all. Without exception they are found on the fringes of the city, principally in the old villages or new private estates added to these centres at St. Fagans, Radyr, Lisvane, St. Mellons and Leckwith. Unlike the Group 7 areas, these places are identified by: commuting across political boundaries, in this case to Cardiff itself; the presence of agricultural workers; as well as by the high percentages of children that are found in the communities. Hence, these areas have been described as the *New, Peripheral High Status* areas and represent the two postulated types of similar family and status character, one on the periphery of the city, and the other in the rural-urban fringe proper where new high status estates have been built on the edge of older villages.

(vii) Group 3 consists of 49 areas, all with high levels of council ownership and low status, but distinguished from the other areas by an older population and more females. The group is found mainly in Tremorfa, Llandaff North, and South Grangetown, and the places are described as *Older Council Estates*. As such the group confirms the postulated type but without the expected age character. Again it is difficult to find a close relationship with Herbert's grouping since his areas are so much larger, but there are parallels with his Group 3 (a mixed group of housing estates).

(viii) There are 59 areas in Group 5, again with low status and council housing, but this time with high proportions of children, large households, and movers. The distribution map, Figure 21, shows that these districts are located in the Fairwater, Llanedeyrn Estate and Ely areas. Since they clearly represent the newest suburban council estates, it is appropriate to describe them as *New Peripheral Council Estates*. As such they are very close to Herbert's Group 8 when allowance is made for the different age of the study.

(ix) Finally, Figure 21 shows that the 48 areas comprising Group 6 are found in Caerau, Llandaff North, Gabalfa, and Rumney. Again they are low status in character with high proportions of council housing, but since they contain a mixture of young families with children and a middle aged population, and high levels of economic activity among females, they have been labelled *Public Housing*. They identify most, but not all, of the communities picked out in Herbert's Group 7. It is possible that the rather different family types found in the area could be a statistical anomaly due to the mixing of areas with very different characters into one enumeration district. However, a detailed study of the enumeration districts involved showed that this group was composed of a

Table 16

## Sample Areas for Clusters and Components: Cardiff, 1971

### (a) Enumeration Districts (E.D.) for the Cluster Groups (31 areas)

| Cluster 1 (107 cases) | Cluster 2 (29 cases) | Cluster 3 (24 cases) |
|---|---|---|
| A)  E.D. 78 | A)  E.D. 377 | A)  E.D. 411 (410) |
| B)  E.D. 4 | B)  E.D. 91 | B)  E.D. 186 |
| C)  E.D. 371 | C)  E.D. 375 (376) | C)  E.D. 271 |
| D)  E.D. 379 | | |
| E)  E.D. 87 | | |
| | | |
| Cluster 4 (126 cases) | Cluster 7 (85 cases) | Cluster 8 (14 cases) |
| A)  E.D. 47 | A)  E.D. 243 | A)  E.D. 539 |
| B)  E.D. 39 | B)  E.D. 217 | B)  E.D. 532 (534) |
| C)  E.D. 415 | C)  E.D. 355 | |
| D)  E.D. 48 | D)  E.D. 178 | |
| E)  E.D. 66 | | |
| | | |
| Cluster 3 (49 cases) | Cluster 5 (59 cases) | Cluster 6 (48 cases) |
| A)  E.D. 280 | A)  E.D. 109 | A)  E.D. 443 |
| B)  E.D. 145 | B)  E.D. 127 | B)  E.D. 103 |
| C)  E.D. 210 | C)  E.D. 450 | C)  E.D. 206 |

Numbers: (a) Minimum of per two cluster. Under 35 cases – 2 areas; 36 to 70 cases – 3 areas; 71 to 100 cases – 4 areas; 101 to 130 cases – 5 areas.

(b) Total 31 areas.

### (b) Enumeration District Scores on the Individual Axes (33 areas)

| Component 1 | | Component 2 | | Component 3 | |
|---|---|---|---|---|---|
| E.D. 545 (546) | + 4.51 | E.D.  74 | + 4.83 | E.D. 301 | + 3.16 |
| 537 | + 3.81 | 90 | + 4.47 | 451 | + 2.88 |
| 252 | + 3.07 | 322 | + 3.46 | 247 | + 1.93 |
| E.D. 470 | − 1.64 | E.D. 339 | − 1.68 | E.D.  93 | − 2.61 |
| 489 | − 1.76 | 256 | − 1.73 | 512 | − 2.67 |
| 491 (497) | − 1.87 | 115 | − 1.88 | 387 | − 2.79 |
| | | | | | |
| Component 4 | | Component 5 | | Component 6 | |
| E.D. 298 | + 2.97 | E.D. 507 (509) | + 2.73 | E.D. 554 | + 7.10 |
| 457 | + 1.94 | 444 | + 2.36 | 535 | + 6.09 |
| 264 | + 1.85 | 149 | + 2.29 | 552 | + 4.79 |
| E.D. 493 | − 2.53 | E.D. 460 | − 3.26 | | |
| 367 | − 2.68 | 425 | − 3.65 | | |
| 459 (466) | − 3.64 | 249 | − 4.73 | | |

The three largest scores for the negative and positive sides of the components are identified. Component 6 does not have any negative values.

particular type of balanced family status area with low status character, not the postulated type of late family public housing estates.

Table 16 lists the E.D. areas shown to be the most closely associated with each of the cluster groups by the Discriminant Analysis and the highest scoring area on the six components. These sample areas could be used as places in which to carry out behavioural investigations.

Although it has *not* been possible quantitatively to measure the degree of relationship between the postulated and empirically derived typology, Table 15 shows that the findings are in general accord with the original expectations, since many of the social area types found in the area are very similar to those proposed. The major exception in the inner city lies in the absence of separate substandard and immigrant areas; they are combined into one group. Presumably this is a function of the fact that the level of New Commonwealth immigration to Cardiff is low compared to many equivalent sized British cities. However, the failure of the census data source to measure ethnic variations does influence this finding. The older immigrant communities in the Butetown area are not separated out from the other inner city, substandard, blue collar areas. In other words, the inner city ethnic/non-ethnic areas of Cardiff cannot be distinguished in this study by reason of the limitations of the data source. So these results should not be used as support for combining the two postulated types of inner city area.

In the outer city and urban fringe, there is another combination of two of the zones originally hypothesized; this time the high status areas, such as those on the edge of the city, and those in small villages outside the city. Finally, it must be noted that the postulated outer city-new middle status zone cannot be identified. This is probably a function of two features: first, the high levels of council house occupation in Britain and the polarization of the housing market between the public and private sectors; and, second, the fact that many people who work in Cardiff live beyond the city in the older industrial towns of the South Wales coalfield to the north, ensuring that middle status estates are located outside the boundaries of this study.

## Conclusion

Any review of the factorial evidence on the social structures of cities makes it increasingly obvious that the standard model of Western urban social structure originally proposed by Shevky and Bell (1955) and modified by McElrath (1968) and Timms (1971) is in need of revision. Far too many specialized axes have been identified in recent factorial ecologies, and these axes cannot be related simply to unique or local peculiarities of cities. This study of Cardiff has attempted to provide empirical evidence for such a revision, in which it is also postulated that Western cities do not form an undifferentiated set; rather Western cities display important variations from one another that go beyond the city specific differences. The approach chosen to test this idea in the present chapter was to explore the relevance of an eleven axis model of intra-urban dimensions to the city of Cardiff. These eleven constructs were those identified from previous empirical studies and from the post-industrial societal postulates of Daniel Bell (1974). The results have shown that the first order dimensions of Cardiff cannot be summarized as either the eleven axis model or the classical, but simplistic three or four axis model of Shevky-Bell or McElrath and Timms. Rather, the evidence points to the presence of six axes of differentiation at the enumeration district level. These six, rather complex, axes contain elements of the missing five vectors. There are some similarities with previous oblique factorial studies of equivalent regional centres in Britain and Canada but the axes identified in Cardiff seem to be more general than might be expected. For example, the traditional Socio-Economic status axis contains an English-Welsh differential; Life Cycle is linked to tenure; Ethnicity is combined with housing conditions; and Mobility is inversely associated with Late Family characteristics. The simplest axes, by contrast, are the minor ones, those described as Urban Fringe and Young Adults/Non Family status. Of the rest of the original set of postulated axes, separate or distinct Substandardness, Female, Tenure and Economy axes could not be identified. The conclusion of the first order factor analysis of Cardiff must be that despite similarities to the results of equivalent sized British cities — Davies (1975) showed that Leicester and Southampton both have equivalent levels of variance explanation — the social dimensions of Cardiff lie between the postulated eleven axis model and the simplistic three or four axis model.

At the second order of analysis even bigger differences occur. The most important is that the Life Cycle and Socio-Economic status vectors coalesce to form a single higher order axis, leaving Urban Fringe as another second order dimension and the Young Adult and Housing-Ethnicity vectors as a third component. Some minor associations between the Life Cycle vector and both the other second order axes qualify the simplistic hierarchical structure, but the results mean that the overlap between largest vectors — Life Cycle and Social Status — is much more pronounced in Cardiff than in equivalent studies of other British cities (Davies, 1975). Insofar as the city of Cardiff is typical of other large centres it provides support for the initial hypothesis that a city in Wales is likely to show less separation between the major axes of differentiation than comparable sized English cities, whilst these, in turn, are but transitional states to the axial separation found in the prosperous North American regional capitals. Finally, it might be noted that these results also show that there must be differences between the inter-and intra-urban models of urban structure, since separate Economy axes could not be identified at this intra-city scale.

In technical terms the alternative analyses that were employed also show some important results. Two different factor techniques were used to test the stability of the interpreted solutions and there are some differences in the resulting structures. For example, the Image Analysis provides a much more general solution and only isolates the four largest axes; the more specific variables linked to the smaller axes are not identified because their communalities are so low in this type of common factor solution. So some technical dependence appears to be present. Yet even accepting the lower levels of explanation of the common factor model, it is apparent that the variations are not enough to modify the major conclusions of this study of Cardiff, namely, the greater generality of the axes in this city in Wales and the greater overlap of the major social dimensions that were found. At the other scale level, namely, the analysis of wards, even more general dimensions are produced. Again, however, only four of the axes can be considered to be comparable at the ward and enumeration area scales. Thus the separate 'Housing and Ethnicity' axis found at the enumeration level of analysis is not identified at the coarser ward scale, whilst what appears to be a 'Female' axis is substituted for the 'Late Family-Mobility' dimension. The conclusion from this study must be that technical and scale differences do occur in factorial ecologies but they influence the minor, rather than the major, sources of variation, paralleling Bourne's conclusions (1972) obtained from studies of Toronto.

The evidence in this chapter provides support for the modification of the traditional ideas of the social dimensional character of Western cities. These findings can be paralleled by the results obtained by the analysis of the spatial patterns of the axes of differentiation where a very complex mosaic of social areas has been identified. Inevitably some of these variations are city specific, since the urban area of Cardiff is discontinuous and is truncated by the docks and its associated industrial area to the south. Yet certain standard spatial patterns are found in Cardiff, such as the sectoral pattern of high status areas, the inner city concentrations of immigrants and mobility, etc., and the suburban associations of child rearing groups. By contrast, the presence of inner city working class family areas prevents the definition of a simplistic concentric variation for the Family Status source of differentiation. Perhaps of more importance than these individual patterns is the identification of nine clusters of socially differentiated areas, each of which have specific locational features. This led to the derivation of a new spatial model of social variation explicitly linked to factorial dimensions (Figure 33). For example, the inner city areas are characterized as either being 'in decay', or as 'mobile-transient' areas, or as 'aging status' regions. By contrast, the high status areas form distinct sectors in the city, or are found in tracts peripheral to the urban area. More geographically diffuse are the council estates which cover a range of different locations in the city and re-emphasize the dominant role played by the public housing sector in the British city. No single pattern is likely to be able to accommodate this source of variation; the unique housing policies of cities are likely to display quite different locational characteristics.

These results lead one to suggest that the public housing sector in British cities accounts for the uniqueness or specialization of some of the spatial patterns, whereas in terms of the dimensions of societal variation it hinders the specialization, the axial separation of the largest axes that might be otherwise expected since they are Western cities. The role of the public sector, therefore, when combined with the lower level of modernization found in Wales (a product of the heritage of economic depression) may be the critical factors lying behind the greater generality and overlap of the major axes of differentiation identified in Cardiff. Obviously this type of structural, single city, study cannot provide an explanation of the *causes* of these patterns. But such reasons seem more plausible than alternative ideas, such as those based on the cultural differentiation of

Welsh society — especially in a city with such a small Welsh speaking population. A complete explanation of the differentiation takes one beyond the scope of this study which has been to measure the differentiation of sub-areas in Cardiff within the context of ideas of homogeneous model of Western cities. It is clear from these results that the homogeneity thesis cannot be upheld; this city differs considerably from the standard model. If Cardiff is typical in Wales it provides additional support for the idea that the social structures of the cities of Wales differ somewhat from those in other parts of the Western world. It remains to explore this thesis at another scale of analysis.

## CHAPTER 5

## SOCIAL DIFFERENTIATION AT THE REGIONAL SCALE:
## CARDIFF CITY-REGION IN 1971

The second case study area can be conveniently described as Cardiff City-Region since it consists of the agricultural and industrial areas of Mid and South Glamorgan. Before dealing with the specific objectives of this study it is worth emphasizing that the application of factor and cluster analysis procedures have transformed the field of regional and community description in the last decade. Instead of subjective interpretations of the differentiation of places, or of single variable quantitative statements, it is now possible to obtain *precise* multivariate measurements of the degree of differentiation of one region or settlement from another. Also, rigorous syntheses of the similarity of settlements and regions have been obtained by the definition of groups or types of places, and these can have planning applications. But of more lasting impact than these quantitative advances, which, on their own, only provide more precise idiographic statements, has been the identification of the sources or dimensions of variation among variables that are analyzed. This has opened the way to the possibility of obtaining precise comparative statements about the differentiation of regions or cities, as well as providing tests of the applicability of existing theoretical ideas of urban and regional differentiation which primarily apply to intra-urban or urban system scales. Unfortunately, these nomothetic objectives have rarely been pursued by students of regional character, unlike those parallel endeavours in the study of urban social variations which have been described in previous chapters. This means that a primary objective of this chapter is to interpret the dimensionality of a large urbanized region, using the same methodology as that applied at the intra-urban scale. This will provide another case study of the way in which factorial dimensions vary — this time at the regional scale. Also, it is hoped to bridge the glaring gap between descriptions of the region produced by subjective and quantitative methods.

Since the philosophical values held by exponents of these approaches are so different there is rarely any debate about the utility of results produced by these alternative approaches. So another goal of this study must be to interlink our existing knowledge of the study area with quantitative information. In this way it can be shown how a systematically related body of literature on urban and regional differentiation can be obtained, as well as one which will test the utility of existing regional divisions used for planning policy statements in Mid and South Glamorgan.

This case study of the socio-economic structure of Cardiff City-Region in Wales uses a similar variable set to the case study of intra-urban structure in Cardiff and follows the same methodology in identifying the social dimensions and classifying the settlements of the area. Within the context of the goals already described two specific and interlinked objectives can be identified:

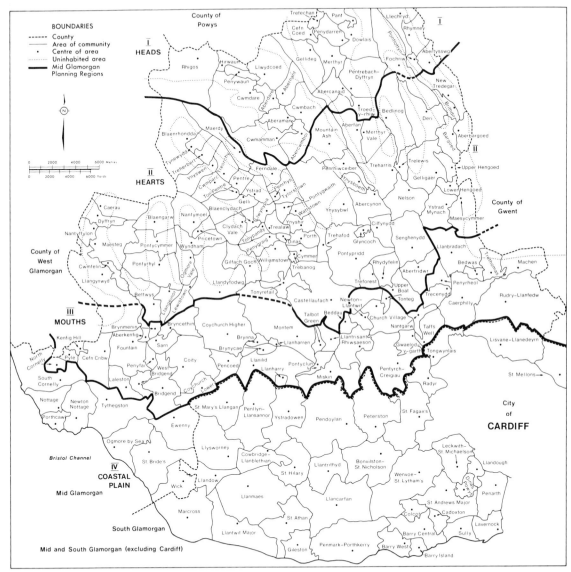

BOUNDARIES
- - - - County
——— Area of community
· Centre of area
······· Uninhabited area
━━━ Mid Glamorgan
Planning Regions

N

0    2000   4000   6000 Metres
0    2000   4000   6000 Yards

County of
Powys

I
HEADS

II
HEARTS

County of
West
Glamorgan

III
MOUTHS

Bristol Channel

IV
COASTAL
PLAIN

Mid Glamorgan

South Glamorgan

Mid and South Glamorgan (excluding Cardiff)

I

II

County of
Gwent

City
of
CARDIFF

FIGURE 22    COMMUNITIES IN CARDIFF CITY-REGION

114

**(i)** First, the study identifies the extent to which the dimensions of socio-economic differentiation, as defined by factor analysis, conforms to the set of eleven postulated axes of differentiation described in Chapter 3, namely, Socio-Economic Status, Life Cycle, Mobility, Ethnicity, Young Adult, Late Family, Substandardness, Tenure, Urban Fringe, Female and Economy. If the social dimensions of urban places really are 'scale free', as originally proposed by Shevky and Bell (1955), then the dimensions at this regional scale should be the same as those obtained at the intra-city scale of Cardiff (Chapter 4). Since Carter (1974), in a study of twenty-seven administrative units in the Glamorgan area, has already maintained that parallel results between regional and intra-urban scales *can* be obtained, the study represents a further example of this work at a more detailed scale.

**(ii)** Second, the study evaluates the degree of correspondence between a typology of settlements produced from existing qualitative descriptions of the regional differentiation of the area derived from geographical and planning studies with one obtained from a multivariate grouping of the scores on the dimensions of socio-economic variation. Unlike the preceding study it is unlikely that any postulated regional structure can be derived from theoretical considerations, or from descriptions of other regions as in the intra-urban case. Hence the postulated structure was obtained from existing regional descriptions, or planning policy documents.

To achieve these dual objectives, part of the same general programme of describing the community structure of the region, the discussion is divided into four sections. The first part provides a descriptive background to the study area and the reasons for the differentiation of settlements in the area. This leads to a postulated typology of community types, and its relationship to the regional divisions in the area. The second section only summarizes the data and techniques used in the study since Chapter 3 has already described these issues. The third section describes the results of the factorial analysis. The usual care is taken to document the degree of invariance of these solutions, by using alternative factor methods, before the results are related to the postulated set of axes. The fourth section takes the scores of the factor analysis and produces a taxonomy of settlements whose characteristics can be related back to the hypothesized typology and regional divisions. In this way, the study fulfils the goals originally described. Firstly it achieves the ideographic objective of providing a multivariate description of the socio-economic variations in the settlements of the area and its relationship to regional differentiation. Secondly, it achieves a nomothetic goal by relating the dimensionality of settlements at a regional scale to previous studies of intra-urban variation, thereby measuring the extent of 'scale-dependence' in studies of community differentiation. Obviously the results relate to the situation in 1971. Although dated, this is the latest year for which a comprehensive data set is available for a small area basis.

## 1. Regional Differentiation of Settlements in Cardiff City-Region

The area shown in Figure 22, described as Cardiff City-Region, contains all the settlements of the South Wales industrial region found in Mid and South Glamorgan (with a 1971 population of 651,000) excluding the city of Cardiff itself. In general terms this is the industrial area of South Wales that has closer functional connections with Cardiff than with its neighbouring large centres, Newport to the east, or Swansea to the west (Davies, 1972; Davies and Musson, 1978). Geographically the area is dominated by the physical contrast between the upland region of the South Wales coalfield to the north (part of Blaenau Morgannwg) and the Vale of Glamorgan (or Bro Morgannwg) to the south, although Carter (1958, p. 406) pointed to the presence of a third region which he described as 'The Border Vale' fringing 'The Vale of Glamorgan proper'. Throughout history, the variations in the agricultural economy and settlement of the whole area have reinforced the basic physicial contrast between these regions, but the effects of the Industrial Revolution and its aftermath have provided as great a differentiation between the towns of the areas as that imparted by physique and resource endowment. The development of first iron, then coal mining in the coalfield gave rise to an additional set of coalfield settlements, initially located on the north and south outcrops but gradually sited on the areas in which the deeper coal reserves of the central areas are found. Throughout most of the early industrial period the Vale of Glamorgan remained untouched by industrialization, except either for the expansion of coastal settlements serving the coalfield as ports, resorts or commercial centres, or for the occasional mining centre located to exploit a particular mineral (Manners, 1965; Humphrys, 1973).

From the 1920s onwards, however, the coalfield settlements or 'the Valleys' have lost population, the most catastrophic being the decline in the population of the Rhondda Valleys from 163,000 in 1921 to 89,000 in 1971, with a decrease in the number of mines in this area from 60 in 1913 to 3 in 1979. The result has been a heritage of more than fifty years of decay within the coalfield although in recent years the population has stabilized. Since the inter-war depression, however, attempts have been made to bring industry to the inhabitants of the coalfield valleys (Mid Glamorgan Structure Plan 1978). The main regional strategy has been the development of industrial estates and zones on the fringes of the area, whether at the open northern heads of the valleys, in Hirwaun or Merthyr, or more importantly, in the south, either in the lower reaches of the major valleys, or on the fringes of the Vale, as in Bridgend, Llantrisant, Treforest and Caerphilly (Humphrys, 1973). The result has been that most of the new growth of settlements has taken place in the vicinity of those new estates, many of them overlapping the coalfield border. The only exceptions have been in the development of new council housing estates in the coalfield, in areas not settled during the major mining booms, and a more limited scatter of small private housing developments. In the Vale of Glamorgan the major coastal settlements have expanded their commercial and industrial base and have also grown in population. The availability of private transport has enabled many people who work in these larger places to commute from new housing estates in the smaller agricultural centres, many of which have now been transformed into commuter villages. These changes have had a differential spatial impact as is recognized

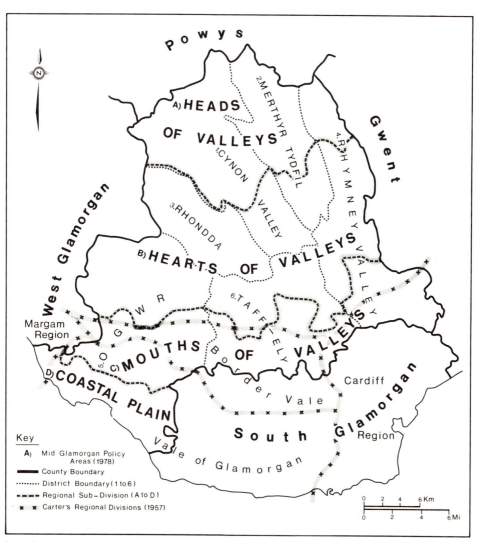

FIGURE 23   REGIONAL DIVISIONS IN THE STUDY AREA: (A) MID-GLAMORGAN PLANNERS (1978); (B) CARTER (1957)

in Mid Glamorgan's Stucture Plan (Mid Glamorgan, 1978) by the division of this part of the study area into four policy areas described as: Heads of the Valleys; Hearts of Valleys; Mouths of Valleys; Coastal Plain. To some extent the last two areal types relate to Carter's (1957) Border Vale/Vale distinction, although Figure 23 shows that the regions are far from coincident. The differentiation of the Valley Heads and Hearts reflects the similar way in which new growth in the north has been associated with the open reaches in the north of the coalfield valleys, the original focus of early metallurgical developments.

In many ways these two sets of regional divisions are based on the physical differentiation of the area, one which is not entirely useful for a classification of settlements since it implies a co-incidence of social and spatial character. Intuitively, therefore, it seems more appropriate to suggest a community typology based on the differentiating processes that have operated within the region. Inevitably some association with the physical or ecological characteristics of areas is involved since the processes of spatial differentiation are quite strongly linked to, but not dominated by, these regional variations. Seven basic types are postulated, three in the coalfield area, one on the border of the Coalfield and Vale, another three in the Vale of Glamorgan.

(i) In the Valleys a three-fold division among the coalfield settlements can be expected:
    (a) the older, decayed mining and industrial settlements;
    (b) those settlements that have experienced renewal because of proximity to the new manufacturing plants;
    (c) the new post-war communities built by public authorities and private developers, providing two sub-types.

The differentiation between these types, although primarily based upon economic and housing variables, should also be reflected in demographic differences, with the extremes represented by the older population in the decayed mining settlements and a very young population in the newer estates.

(ii) In the Border area or Southern Valley Mouths, an area which overlaps the edge of the Vale of Glamorgan and the southern Coalfield valleys, it is expected that a zone of settlements with rather different characteristics will be found, given its recent growth and the planning policy related to these areas. They should have high proportions of manufacturing employment, youthful age structures, and new, rather than substandard, housing.

(iii) In the Vale of Glamorgan a three-fold division is postulated from the processes of differentiation already described:
    (a) the growing commercial-industrial centres;
    (b) the commuter villages;
    (c) the rural areas, still largely agricultural in economy, that have not been seriously affected by industrialization and commercialization.

Like all verbal descriptions of community types, this categorization lacks precision in identifying the range of characteristics by which the settlements differ from one another, and fails to provide any method for allocating the settlements to the various categories. Fortunately, the Multivariate-Structural approach can solve both these problems and, in addition, provides links to the standard theories of urban social differentiation. However, it must be noted that this study does not adopt a completely rigorous hypothesis testing approach; to achieve this, the group membership of each settlement would have to be determined initially and the final set of results compared to the postulated membership. An initial assignment based on the processes that have caused change would have to be carried out subjectively and this was not considered to be a very profitable method. Perhaps the regional division in the Mid-Glamorgan Stucture plan (Figure 23) could be used as the basis for assignment but it only covers part of the study area. In any case the adoption of this regional division runs into a problem already mentioned. The typology would have to retain an exact geographical arrangement. These problems mean that it is much more appropriate to empirically derive the community typology *from* the data set and then compare it with the regional divisions in the area.

## 2. Data and Techniques

The initial choice of data to be used in the multivariate analysis is, of course, critical to any quantitative study of the differentiation of settlements since they define the bounds of the urban character to be analyzed. It must be emphasized, again, that the variables were not chosen on any *ad hoc* basis, but were deliberately derived from the existing theories on urban social differentiation and previous empirical studies of community differentiation at a structural level (Table 1). At first sight, Friedman's (1972) 'core-periphery' concepts would seem to be a satisfactory basis for organizing a study of regional variation as Davies (1972) has shown for the Greater Swansea area. But although these ideas can be related to the 'growth pole' concepts through the ideas of 'urban polarization and spinoffs', they only describe the spatial incidence of the differences, not the variations in urban social character. More comprehensive are the sets of generalizations originally proposed by the Social Area theorists (Shevky and Bell, 1955) which have been modified and extended in recent years by McElrath (1968) and Timms (1971). Here it is enough to note that twenty-eight variables were used in the analysis, each related to one of the eleven postulated axes, namely, Socio-Economic Status, Life Cycle, Mobility, Ethnicity, Young Adult, Late Family, Substandardness, Tenure, Urban Fringe, Females and Economy. This is the same variable set used in the study of Cardiff — with one exception. Mining employment has been added to the economic group of variables since it is an important occupational type in the Cardiff City-Region, although not in the city of Cardiff itself. Although the results of the Cardiff study in Chapter 4 differed from the postulated dimensions of Chapter 3, it is important, in a comparative sense, to maintain the same standard of comparison represented by the variables so that the effect of the *scale differences* of intra-urban and regional studies can be measured.

119

All the variables were measured for the 193 areas shown in Figure 22. As such the study provides a much finer mesh of differentiation than a previous factorial study of the twenty-seven administrative units of the area by Carter (1974). As far as possible the areas were chosen by adopting two procedures: first, separating out those settlements with an identifiable community or area name; second, isolating those places which were separated from other centres by either some discontinuity in the built-up area, or a spatial barrier such as a rail line or river. The enumeration districts comprising these areas were aggregated to provide the required data for these areas. A minimum number of two enumeration districts was needed before a place was defined as a settlement for the purposes of this analysis. Despite the almost continuous urban sprawl in the industrial valleys comparatively few problems were experienced in defining the units or settlements used in this analysis, although the non-inhabited portions of the enumeration districts were excluded from the maps to aid in the overall comprehension of the spatial patterns. In the Vale of Glamorgan problems of areal definition were more serious since the enumeration districts were often based on the ancient parishes, and these were not always co-incident with the centres of population. All that could be done in this area was to amalgamate the enumeration districts so as to avoid splitting existing settlements or villages within this region.

The result of these initial decisions was to derive a data set of one hundred and ninety three areas which are called settlements or communities in the subsequent discussion. The size of some of the larger places — Penarth, Barry, Pontypridd and Bridgend — was the subject of some initial concern. Such centres were difficult to break down into smaller areas on the basis of settlement discontinuities in order to make their size range comparable with other cities. However, a test of the effect of these larger places was carried out in the early stages of the analysis. The factorial results of the sub-divisions shown in Figure 22 were compared with those obtained by re-running the analysis using the total figures for the large places (Barry, Bridgend, Pontypridd, etc.). There was no deviation of substance in the pattern of loadings or the position of the places in the array of component scores. So this additional 'scale' problem was not considered to be important enough to produce any distortion in the results of this analysis.

## 3. The Factorial Results

In theory, the most appropriate methodology to adopt to test the validity of the postulated regional dimensionality is one of the common factor methods. As has been noted many of the inferential requirements of the method are breached in regional analysis, not the least being the independence of samples; here, the complete population of places is needed to produce the regional classification. In addition it is difficult to provide useful estimates of the size of the communality values. In these circumstances it was considered to be more useful to adopt the exploratory approach of the component model, given the final objective of regional description, so as not to lose specific variance associated with individual variables, and then to compare the results with those from common factor methods, producing a substantive not a statistical comparison.

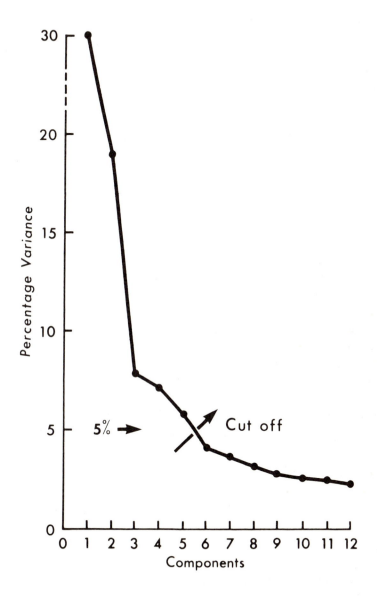

FIGURE 24   VARIANCE DISTRIBUTION IN COMPONENT SOLUTION: CARDIFF CITY-REGION, 1971

121

A series of Principal Axes component solutions followed by Direct Oblimin rotation, with gamma at 0.0, were obtained from the correlation matrix between the 192 areas and 28 variables in the initial search for a satisfactory solution. Figure 24 shows that a major break in the distribution of eigenvalues occurred between the fifth and sixth axes and this corresponded to a variance cut-off value of 5%. In addition, Table 17 shows that by the sixth axis all but one of the variables had more than half of their variance explained by the solution. But at this level one of the component axes had only one first ranking loading, meaning that it was primarily related to only one variable, hardly a result of much generality. These features, together with the fact that the rotated sixth axis proved to be quite highly correlated ( – .34) with another vector, led to the decision to use a five component model. This accounted for 69.4% of the variance of the similarity matrix.

**Table 17**

**Communality Tipping Points: Cardiff City-Region, 1971**

| Number of Communalities with loadings | Number of Axes in Solution | | |
|---|---|---|---|
| | 5 | 6 | 7 |
| > 0.7 | 13 | 17 | 21 |
| < 0.5 | 3 | 1 | 0 |
| Axes without first ranking loadings | 0 | 1 | 1 |

As a test of the stability of the results two varimax rotations were carried out on the five axis Principal Axes solution, using first the component, then the common factor methods. In addition, a third five axis varimax solution was derived from an Image Analysis of the co-variance matrix between the 28 variables. All four results are shown in Table 18. Even though the directions of the signs are sometimes reversed, and there are small variations in the size of loading or in the minor loadings, the general pattern is one of similarity, meaning that the same substantive interpretation can be given to all the axes. Hence these minor variations are not enough to alter the basic structure of the pattern of relationships in this data set. In other words, the dimensional structure is strong enough to be considered invariant by factor technique. Although all four solutions could just as easily be used in the final description, the oblique axes of the Principal Axes component results were used, primarily because they allow a higher order analysis of the correlations between the axes.

(i) Component I has been described as an *Ethnicity and Economy* axis in Table 18. Its largest positive loadings are associated with variables measuring people born overseas, or in England, and those employed in government service and defence, with smaller values

Table 18

# Factor Loadings for Various Methods: Cardiff City-Region, 1971

| Short Titles of Variables | Principal Axes | | | Image |
|---|---|---|---|---|
| | Component | | Factor | |
| I. ETHNICITY (and Economy) | Oblique 1* | Varimax 3 | Varimax 3 | Varimax 3 |
| T05  Born Overseas | 76 | 77 | 74 | 72 |
| T45  Government Employees | 72 | 73 | 61 | 62 |
| T03  Born in England | 68 | 71 | 75 | 72 |
| T18  Small Dwellings | 65 | 54 | 43 | 53 |
| T36  Distant Migrants | 41 | 49 | 49 | 46 |
| T14  Single Adults | — | − 33 | − 34 | — |
| T16  No Bath | — | − 36 | − 35 | − 34 |
| T33  Unskilled | − 33 | — | — | — |
| T40  Manufacturing | − 34 | − 39 | − 38 | − 33 |
| T39  Mining | − 52 | − 50 | − 44 | − 41 |
| T04  Welsh | − 74 | − 76 | − 81 | − 77 |
| **II. TENURE AND AGE** | 2 | 1 | 1 | 1 |
| T20  Owner Occupied | 90 | − 88 | − 87 | − 83 |
| T13  Old Aged | 62 | − 60 | − 61 | − 67 |
| T08  Females | 37 | − 41 | − 35 | − 42 |
| T16  No Bath | 35 | − 31 | − 30 | − 32 |
| T29  High Employment Status | 32 | − 34 | − 31 | − 30 |
| T17  One Person Households | — | — | − 30 | − 40 |
| T43  Distribution-Service | — | — | — | − 32 |
| T14  Single Adults | — | 33 | 33 | — |
| T40  Manufacturing | − 32 | 30 | — | — |
| T18  Small Dwellings | − 37 | 33 | — | — |
| T33  Unskilled | − 43 | 42 | 38 | 35 |
| T35  Local Migrants | − 52 | 48 | 45 | 43 |
| T10  Children | − 55 | 54 | 54 | 63 |
| T25  Large Households | − 71 | 73 | 70 | 76 |
| T11  Young Adult | − 82 | 80 | 75 | 73 |
| T21  Council Housing | − 88 | 84 | 84 | 81 |

*Order of axes abstracted.

123

**Table 18** (*continued*)

| Short Title of Variables | Principal Axes | | | Image |
|---|---|---|---|---|
| | Component | | Factor | |
| | Oblique | Varimax | Varimax | Varimax |
| **III. NON FAMILY** | 3 | 2 | 2 | 2 |
| T46 Single, Widowed, Divorced Females | 87 | 86 | 83 | 88 |
| T14 Single Adults | 86 | 79 | 81 | 84 |
| T17 One Person Households | 61 | 74 | 71 | 60 |
| T13 Old Aged | 56 | 68 | 67 | 60 |
| T12 Middle Aged | 39 | — | — | — |
| T18 Small Dwellings | 37 | 32 | | — |
| T16 No Bath | 36 | 48 | 44 | 37 |
| T29 High Employment Status | — | − 34 | − 33 | − 30 |
| T37 Commuters | − 30 | − 40 | − 31 | — |
| T36 Distant Migrants | − 46 | − 55 | − 53 | − 51 |
| T10 Children | − 69 | − 73 | − 72 | − 67 |
| **IV. RURAL AND INDUSTRIAL** | 4 | 4 | 4 | |
| T40 Manufacturing | 54 | − 60 | − 55 | 60 |
| T08 Female | 49 | − 38 | − 30 | — |
| T35 Local Movers | 43 | − 53 | − 46 | 45 |
| T17 One Person Households | 43 | − 39 | − 41 | 39 |
| T27 Economically Active Females | 38 | — | — | — |
| T33 Unskilled | 30 | − 40 | − 36 | 37 |
| T04 Welsh | — | − 43 | − 43 | 41 |
| T36 Distant Migrants | — | 32 | 32 | − 31 |
| T29 High Employment Status | — | 37 | 39 | − 34 |
| T03 English | − 32 | 45 | 45 | − 42 |
| T12 Middle Aged | − 44 | 56 | 47 | − 39 |
| T28 Two Car Households | − 58 | 72 | 74 | − 67 |
| T38 Agriculture | − 79 | 76 | 66 | − 81 |
| **V. ECONOMY AND STATUS** | 5 | 5 | 5 | 5 |
| T43 Distribution-Service | 66 | 72 | 71 | 75 |
| T27 Economically Active Females | 61 | 67 | 55 | 44 |
| T37 Commuters | 57 | 47 | 33 | 38 |
| T12 Middle Aged | 53 | 47 | 38 | 39 |
| T29 High Employment Status | 51 | 53 | 54 | 64 |

**Table 18** *(continued)*

| Short Titles of Variables | Principal Axes | | | Image |
| --- | --- | --- | --- | --- |
| | Component | | Factor | |
| | Oblique | Varimax | Varimax | Varimax |
| **V. ECONOMY AND STATUS** *(continued)* | 5 | 5 | 5 | 5 |
| T28 Two Car Households | 42 | 40 | 41 | 53 |
| T36 Distant Movers | 30 | 34 | 34 | 39 |
| T03 English | — | — | 30 | 39 |
| T04 Welsh | — | — | – 30 | – 37 |
| T25 Large Households | — | – 34 | – 34 | — |
| T45 Local Government | – 32 | — | — | — |
| T16 No Bath | – 44 | – 43 | – 41 | – 44 |
| T39 Mining | – 44 | – 54 | – 50 | – 46 |

for distant migrants and small dwellings. By contrast, the negative loadings index the born in Wales variable, those employed in mining and manufacturing, as well as those who are unskilled. Although there are some similarities with the variables found on the Socio-Economic Status axis identified in Cardiff (Table 9), this regional vector does not display the same status differentiation and is more closely identified with the ethnic and economic type variables. Not surprisingly, therefore, the congruence coefficient between the Cardiff and City-Region results is only +0.62.

Figure 25 shows that the characteristics identified by this axis display a strong north-south regional pattern. There is a much higher relative concentration of people born in Wales as well as those engaged in primary and secondary occupations north of a line from North Cornelly, Llanharry and Rhydyfelin, with a southward embayment in the Aberkenfig area, and outliers in the Caerphilly-Lisvane region. Within this coalfield region the highest scores are found in communities located in the blind ends of valleys, such as Caerau or Gilfach Goch, or in areas some distance away from the largest commercial centres in the region such as Abercynon and Treharris. Exceptions to this general trend appear in the new coalfield communities, for instance Penrhys, or in the oldest centres of all, such as Aberdare or Merthyr, where higher percentages of small dwellings are found, seemingly a product of the number of homes built for single or old adults. In the Vale of Glamorgan all the areas show the positive scores which are derived from relatively higher proportions of foreign born people, English, service and government workers, etc. The highest values are found in a coastal belt, with four cores in Sully, Barry Island, St. Athan and Merthyr Mawr. The continuity of this coastal zone is, however, broken by lower values in the Colcot-Cadoxton area of Barry and in Ewenny.

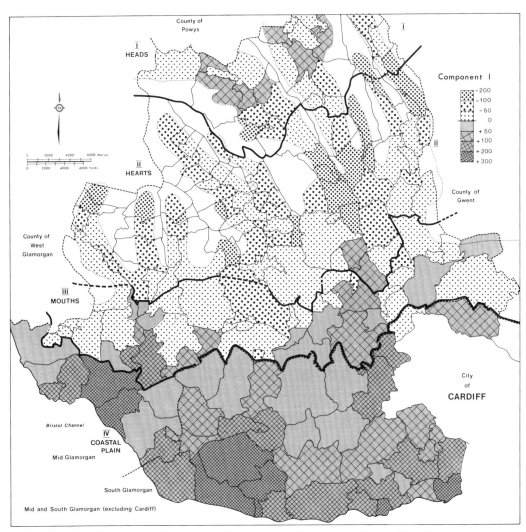

FIGURE 25   SOCIAL PATTERNS FOR COMPONENT I (ETHNICITY AND ECONOMY) IN CARDIFF CITY-REGION

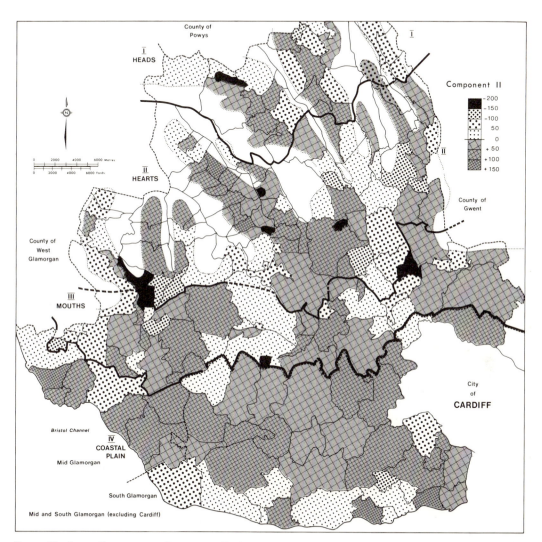

Figure 26   Social Patterns for Component II (Tenure and Age) in Cardiff City-Region

127

(ii) Component II displays elements of the other major differentiation feature found in previous studies of British towns, namely, tenure and age characteristics. Since the former achieve the highest saturations, it is labelled *Tenure and Age* in Table 18. The positive loadings are dominated by indicators measuring old age and owner occupation, with minor linkages to females, poor housing and high status. By contrast, the negative loadings are associated with council housing, younger people, large households and local migrants, with minor values for unskilled and manufacturing workers. Although there is some similarity with the Life Cycle and Tenure axis identified for Cardiff the congruence coefficient between the axes is only − 0.67 (Table 19). Most authorities (Harman, 1976) have suggested that values of over ±0.8 are needed if axes from different studies are considered to be very similar. The biggest difference between the two vectors is found in the more intimate links of the Glamorgan axis with housing tenure. But, in addition, the Glamorgan vector is less closely linked to the old age, single person household characteristics on the owner occupied side of the axis, and is much more related to the young adult and migrant indicators on the council housing — children side of the vector. These differences are a consequence of the young adult characteristics being separated on to an independent factor in the Cardiff study, whilst the single person indicators are found on a separate vector in the Glamorgan study.

Figure 26 does not provide as simple a regional pattern as many of the other maps of component scores; instead, the distribution is dominated by negative values greater than 1.50. These pick out the centres containing large proportions of post-war housing estates which have been identified as separate communities in this study. These are: Bettws, Llanharry, Dinas, Penrhys, Glyncoch, Penyrheol and Penywaun. Similar, but

## Table 19
## Comparison of Axes at Urban and City-Region Scales

| Axes in Cardiff | Congruence Coefficients | Axes in Cardiff City-Region |
|---|---|---|
| 1.  Socio-Economic Status | + 0.63<br>+ 0.62<br>(− 0.51) | 5.  Service Economy and Status<br>1.  Ethnicity and Economy<br>(4.  Rural and Industrial) |
| 2.  Young Adult | + 0.54 | 3.  Non Family |
| 3.  Life Cycle and Tenure | − 0.67 | 2.  Tenure and Age |
| 4.  Housing and Ethnicity | − 0.49 | (2.  Tenure and Age) |
| 5.  Late Family/Mobility | 0.48 | 5.  Service Economy and Status |
| 6.  Urban Fringe | − 0.32 | 4.  Rural and Industrial |

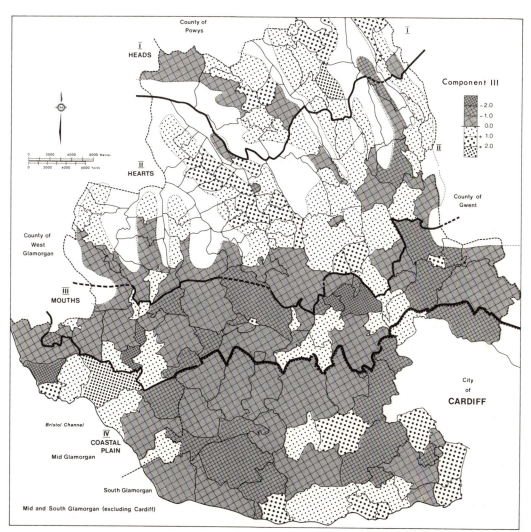

FIGURE 27   SOCIAL PATTERNS FOR COMPONENT III (NON-FAMILY) IN CARDIFF CITY-REGION

129

less intense, concentrations of negative scores are found throughout the area, but principally in five locations which had the dual advantage of having the undeveloped land necessary for residential expansion, as well as proximity to the job opportunities in the new industrial estates. The first area consists of the upper reaches of the coalfield valleys, especially those areas around the larger centres, where many of the communities around Merthyr show high relative concentrations of council housing and a younger population. The second is in a group of communities around Bridgend, from North and South Cornelly to Lewistown. These places reflect the post-war growth of employment in both Port Talbot to the west, and the expansion of the Bridgend estates, as well as the extensive re-housing of population from the Llynfi, Ogmore and Garw Valleys. The third has its core in the Gilfach Goch-Tonyrefail-Trebanog area. It is associated with the growth of centres in the upper Ely Valley connecting to the Rhondda Valleys, and extends down to St. Mary's in the Vale of Glamorgan because of links with the Bridgend industrial belt. The fourth area overlaps the lower Cynon, Taff and Rumney valleys, with cores in: Ynysboeth in the lower Cynon; the Gelligaer, Lower Hengoed, Aberbargoed area around Bargoed; Rhydyfelin and Nantgarw on either side of the Treforest Trading Estate; the Senghenydd to Trecenydd area on the west side of the Caerphilly basin and Bedwas-Trethomas to the east. The fifth area occupies a discontinuous coastal belt from Marcross to Sully, with an outlier at Leckwith, all associated with the growth of the larger coastal communities and the suburbanization of the small villages near the coast.

(iii) Component III is another family related axis that is more specifically dominated by *Non Family* characteristics than the Tenure and Age vector. The highest loadings are those of the non-family or single person variables with less important associations with the older age groups, substandard and small dwellings. Contrasting with these positive values are the medium negative loadings for the children and distant migrant indicators. This means that the axis is not the same as the second family related axis found in the intra-urban Cardiff study. Called *Young Adult-Non Family* the variables identifying Young Adult and Single Person household characteristics in Cardiff were the primary sources of differentiation. It has a low congruence coefficient of only 0.54 with the old age, non-family vector in the Cardiff City-Region.

Figure 27 shows that a broad north-south regional division can again be recognized in the area, with old age, non-family characteristics dominating the area north of a Maesteg-Gilfach Goch-Treforest-Hengoed axis. The highest scores, signifying the most intense concentrations of single and elderly persons, are found in some of the older coalfield communities such as: Penydarren, Dowlais and Pentrebach in Merthyr; Aberdare and Aberaman in the Cynon Valley; Rumney in the Rumney Valley; and the central Rhondda from Ynyswen-Trehafod. In addition, the Treforest-Rhydyfelin area falls into this category, although the cause here is more than a product of what can be described as the natural process of aging; it is a product of the extensive re-housing of older, single person households in new blocks of old people's flats in these communities. In this northern area of the coalfield the negative scores which identify concentrations of older people and non-family characteristics are found in two types of communities; those with higher percentages of council housing estates, or the more isolated communities where younger families have remained because mining was still an important employer in centres such as Maerdy, Ynysboeth, Trelewis and Fochriw in 1971.

South of this zone, in the Border Vale and the lower reaches of the coalfield, particularly in the Caerphilly basin and the middle Rumney valley, the opposite characteristics are found, namely, many children, fewer older people and migrants. The largest negative component scores, identifying the communities with the most intense of these features, are scattered through the area, although there are concentrations in three areas: the peripheries of the larger towns such as Bridgend, Cardiff; growing centres such as Cowbridge, Llantwit Major; or places near the industrial estates such as in the Llantrisant-Treforest Trading Estate-Caerphilly zone.

Figure 27 shows the exceptions to this general north-south differentiation for Component III. Old age character can be identified in the central areas of the older centres in the Vale, such as Bridgend itself, Barry and Penarth, or places which have been popular as retirement centres along the coast, either in the Porthcawl-Newton-Ogmore-by-Sea area or the Gileston to Barry and Lavernock belt, as well as in smaller villages such as Llantrithyd, Bonvilston, and Leckwith.

(iv) Component IV, labelled as *Rural and Industrial,* is quite unlike any of the other intra-urban axes of differentiation, and distinguishes some of the very different economies found in the region. The largest loadings are associated with the economic variables of manufacturing and agriculture, on the positive and negative side of the vector respectively. Also linked to the industrial (or positive) side of the vector are comparatively small loadings for female characteristics, local movers and one person households, whereas the rural (or negative) side of the component is associated with the relative higher values of the higher status households, English born and middle aged populations. Figure 28 shows that a basic north-south division can again be recognized. The agricultural and higher status characteristics are found in the Vale of Glamorgan where the non-urban parishes attain the highest negative scores, whilst the industrial features are found to the north, the highest values being found around the major manufacturing centres, for example, in the Merthyr and Treforest Trading Estate areas. There are four major exceptions to this trend. Firstly, the coastal belt from Penmark eastwards to Penarth and Llandough displays the positive scores associated with manufacturing, females and local migration, etc. Secondly, the same features are found in an urbanized area around Porthcawl and this extends northward to the residential zone around Pyle, an area occupied by workers employed in the Port Talbot and Bridgend industrial zones. Thirdly, a northern embayment of the agriculturally related negative scores can be seen in the coalfield area between the Bridgend and Llantrisant industrial estates, whilst a similar pattern occurs in the Lisvane-Rudry area north of Cardiff. Fourthly, a scatter of negative values is found throughout the coalfield, often near the working coalmines because these communities have low percentages of people employed in manufacturing. However, most of these scores are quite small, for example,

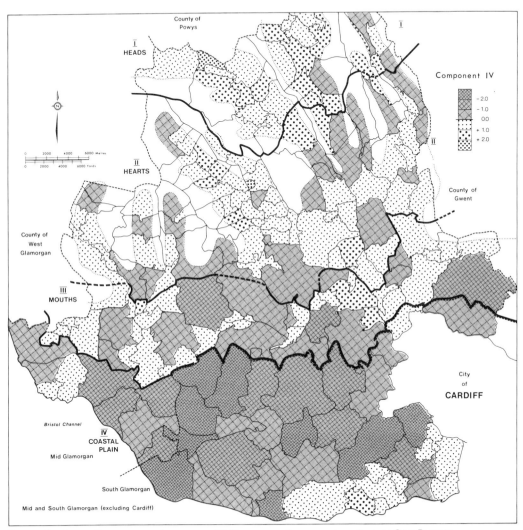

FIGURE 28   SOCIAL PATTERNS FOR COMPONENT IV (RURAL AND INDUSTRIAL) IN CARDIFF CITY-REGION

the scores for Treharris and Nelson are $-0.07$ and $-0.05$ respectively, and are barely over the 0.0 cut-off point for the shading patterns used in Figure 28.

(v) Component V is also an unique vector. It is linked to differences in the economic structure of the communities but the medium loadings show it is not a very strong axis of differentiation. In this case the small negative values of the mining employment and substandard housing variables are outweighed by a set of indicators identifying the service sector of the economy, the economically active, middle aged population, commuters and higher status people. Given the growth of service employment in the economy and its importance vis-a-vis mining, the vector can be visualized as identifying the relative extent of modernization in the economy and is, therefore, described as *Economy and Status.* This link with social status probably explains the fact that the axis has its closest association with the Socio-Economic vector in Cardiff — but the congruence coefficient is only 0.63 so the degree of comparability must be considered to be rather small.

The north-south difference present in many of the preceding distributions is not found in Figure 29. Instead, the positive scores indexing service economy and status are found in two zones, one peripheral to Cardiff, the dominant commercial centre of the region, the other in the western coastal belt south of Bridgend. The first zone, the one around Cardiff, extends as far as fourteen miles from the centre of the city and reflects the way in which higher status people, and those in the service sector of the economy, commute from the various towns and villages within half an hour's travel from Cardiff. The largest scores, and hence the strongest service-status character, are found in the commuter villages nearest to the city, namely, Lisvane, Radyr, St. Andrews Major, etc. However, the extension of these positive scores into the lower Taff and Rumney valleys is worthy of note. The influence of Cardiff, therefore, eradicates the traditional regional division based on the physical resources of the area. In the west the second zone of positive values stretches from North Cornelly to Llysworney, where it links up with the Cardiff based region. In this zone the highest scores are found in Laleston and Llysworney, where the suburbanization of villages has reached its greatest intensity. The existence of this separate western area would appear to be a by-product of two features in the local economy, the commercial importance of Bridgend and also the large number of service-distribution establishments found in the industrial estates east of the town.

Contrasting with these positive scores linked to the service economy and high social status, are the negative values which are found in most of the rest of the coalfield areas. The largest negative scores, identifying a mining economy and housing substandardness, are obviously found in the areas of active coal mining, namely, in a broken belt trending north-eastwards from the heads of the Garw, Ogmore, and Rhondda valleys through the lower Cynon and middle Taff valleys to areas such as Deri and Brithdir in the middle Rumney valley or its tributaries. This zone of continuous negative values is not restricted to the coalfield; it extends out of the coalfield into the St. Mary's and Penllyn areas of the Vale of Glamorgan simply because the presence of quarrying in the region. Outside this area Figure 29 shows two outliers of importance. The first, in the

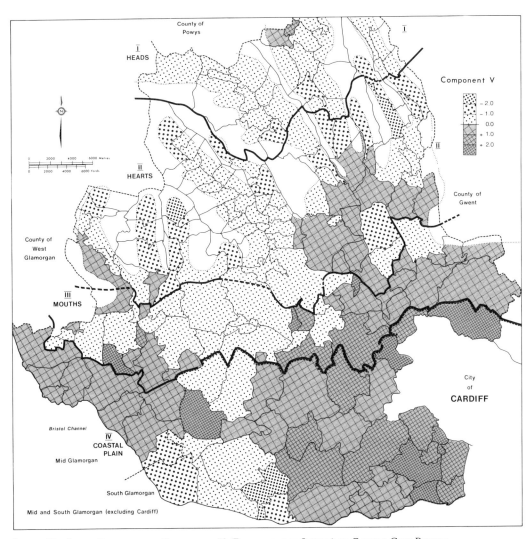

FIGURE 29   SOCIAL PATTERNS FOR COMPONENT V (ECONOMY AND STATUS) IN CARDIFF CITY-REGION

Senghenydd-Llanbradach area, identifies a zone with higher concentrations of miners in 1971, in other words, older mining centres whose inhabitants were still not absorbed into the emerging service based economy in 1971. The second area extends from Wick to St. Athan. Here, a major Air Force base ensures that the local communities have high percentages in the Local Government and Defence category, and this, in the Principal Axes solution, is linked to the negative side of the axis. This certainly produces a more complex vector than initially expected. Technically it represents one of the rare situations where the last vector extracted carries some additional variable weights, in this case Local Government and Defence, linked to some unique characteristics. In this case it did not prove possible to separate this source of variation from the other characteristics found on the axis by the usual procedure of rotating one more axis than is to be interpreted.

Before generalizing these axes of differentiation even further (by carrying out a higher order analysis on the factor correlation matrix) these results have to be compared to the initial expectations. It is apparent that there is little relationship between the postulated axes and those actually found in this region. The observed regional dimensions are much more general than expected, even when compared to axes derived from the same variable set for the city of Cardiff (Chapter 4), and seem to be more clearly related to ecological variations that are a product of the unique resource endowment and historical development of the area. Thus, three of the axes identified for Cardiff City-Region are linked to economic differences (Economy and Ethnicity, Service Economic and Status, Rural and Industrial) although the English-Welsh born and social status variations are inextricably mixed up with these characteristics. The two others are primarily associated with familial and life cycle differences (Tenure and Age, Non-Family) with the addition of tenure to the age axis.

The degree of similarity between the intra-urban and city regional axes was measured by congruence coefficients (Harman, 1976). Table 19 shows that all the values were too low to argue for parallelism in the axes at the two scales although some similarity can be identified between the largest axes. For example, Life Cycle and Tenure (Cardiff) has some degree of similarity (−0.67) with the Tenure and Age (City-Region) axis. (The negative sign is simply a product of the fact that the signs on the two axes were reversed.) The Socio-Economic Status (Cardiff) axis has similarities (0.63 and 0.62) with both city-regional axes that link social status, economic differences and the English-Welsh born division. Although these results demonstrate a *partial* relationship at the two scales for the largest axes, on balance the differences demonstrate that changes occur in the axes of differentiation as one moves from the intra-urban to the city-regional scale of analysis. Different ecological processes are at work and it seems that the economic variations between settlements provide the major mechanism for this differentiation by providing quite different degrees of concentration of people in various social categories.

This conclusion would appear to be confirmed by the loadings shown in Table 20, the two axis higher order solution produced by applying the same factorial methodology used at the first order. In this example the two axes accounted for 73.0% of the variance

135

of the $5 \times 5$ first order matrix. Table 20 shows that all the variables (that is, first order axes) have communalities greater than 0.60. Extraction of a third axis produced two vectors with a correlation of $-0.49$ which was considered to be too oblique to be identified as a separate axis. However, even the two axis solution had a correlation of 0.21 so the higher order axes are not completely orthogonal.

### Table 20
### Higher Order Loadings: Cardiff City-Region, 1971

|  | Second Order Axes | | Communality |
|---|---|---|---|
| First Order Axes | I | II |  |
| 1. Ethnicity and Economy | + 86 |  | 71 |
| 5. Economy and Status | + 78 |  | 61 |
| 3. Non-Family | − 83 |  | 67 |
| 4. Rural and Industrial | − 61 | − 50 | 74 |
| 2. Tenure and Age |  | 97 | 91 |
| Correlation | I and II = 0.21 | | Variance 73.0% |

The results of the higher order analysis show that four of the five first order axes have their highest values on one component. The direction of the signs indicates that this higher order axis separates the characteristics of English and Foreign born, Service Economy, Children and Agriculture from those of Welsh born, Mining, Single and Old People and Manufacturing, in other words, a basic Coalfield/Vale split. Contrasting with this, the Tenure and Age axis is also negatively associated with the minor part of Component IV, the Rural and Industrial axis, meaning that the Owner Occupation and Old Age indicators are linked to the Agriculture-High Status side of the vector, whilst the Council housing and Young Adult features are associated with Manufacturing and Female Character. This confirms that it is the economic differences between the Vale and the Coalfield which lie at the heart of the regional differentiation in the area, although tenure and age would appear to represent a separate, but not completely independent, source of variation.

## 4. Settlement Taxonomy

The results of the factor analysis of the twenty eight variables are sufficient to solve the first problem of this case study, the identification of the dimensionality of the communities. However, further analysis is needed before we can resolve the issues raised by the second problem, the utility of the postulated community typology and its relationship to the regional divisions in the study area. To answer these questions the

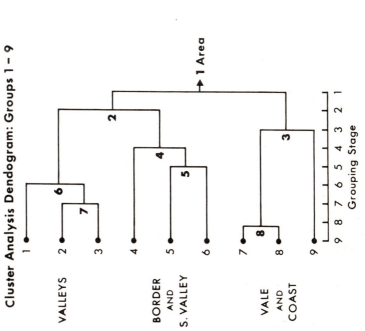

FIGURE 30   CLUSTER DIAGNOSTICS: CARDIFF CITY-REGION, 1971

137

results of the factor analysis that relate to the spatial variations of the various factors or sources of differentiation have to be integrated. In other words, a community typology or summary description of the five sources of variation over the one hundred and ninety three areas has to be produced to identify the structures in social space. Such a typology is of obvious interest in its own right, since the description of a limited number of categories complements the individual factor score maps. But it has additional advantages: firstly, it provides the empirical evidence upon which the postulated typology can be evaluated, and, secondly, it enables investigators to assess the relationship between community or settlement differentiation and the basic regional divisions.

A two-fold procedure was employed to determine the most appropriate typology or set of community types. The first stage consisted of the application of Ward's (1962) hierarchical clustering technique to the matrix of Euclidean distances between the five sets of component scores for the settlements. In theory, of course, the fact that these scores are obliquely related to one another did cause some concern, but since the varimax loadings and scores were so similar this problem was not considered to provide distortions in the results. Tests using the varimax instead of the oblique scores confirmed the similarity in structure so there seemed little point in pursuing the matter. A more important technical problem lay in the advisability of weighting the factor scores before using them in the cluster analysis. In this example the decision was taken to use the original scores. These scores represented different sources of variation and the relative sizes were primarily influenced by the number of variables of each type in the analysis. Indeed, it is possible that another set of variables may have produced different weights in terms of the sizes of the eigenvalues. Nevertheless, the theory of factor analysis suggests that these sources of variation should remain relatively stable if the underlying dimensionality of the data has been captured by the scores. In the strictest sense this theory is not applicable to the component approach adopted here; nevertheless, the similarity between common factor and component loadings meant that there seemed little point in weighting the scores in this study.

Figure 30 shows the results of the fusion summary from Ward's method, often considered to be one of the most useful hierarchical procedures. Unfortunately there is no rigorous statistical test to determine the most appropriate 'cut off' since Ward's method produces minimum variance clusters at each grouping stage; instead, investigators search for the breaks of slope in the fusion summary (Sokal and Sneath, 1973). Figure 30 shows that the first major break of slope in the distribution of values occurs after the ninth group with a further change of slope after the three group level. These breaks were used as the initial determination of group membership with a preference for the nine cluster rather than the very general three group solution.

Although Ward's method is not subject to the chaining problem of some of the other cluster methods, like all hierarchical methods it is very rigid with respect to group membership. In other words the hierarchical methods work by sequentially combining the most similar pair of taxonomic units at each state in the grouping process, and once

# Table 21

## Mean Component Scores for Nine and Three Group Solutions: Cardiff City-Region, 1971

| Groups | Mean Component Scores | | | | |
|---|---|---|---|---|---|
| | 1 | 2 | 3 | 4 | 5 |
| 1 | − 0.95 | + 0.17 | + 0.10 | − 0.20 | − 1.18 |
| 2 | − 0.27 | + 0.84 | + 0.89 | + 0.92 | − 0.29 |
| 3 | − 0.36 | − 0.31 | + 0.28 | + 0.33 | + 0.07 |
| 4 | − 0.30 | − 2.02 | − 0.48 | + 0.20 | − 0.21 |
| 5 | + 0.07 | + 0.18 | − 1.79 | + 0.33 | + 0.45 |
| 6 | + 6.48 | − 0.30 | − 3.48 | − 0.32 | − 3.84 |
| 7 | + 0.83 | + 0.46 | − 0.38 | − 1.82 | + 0.15 |
| 8 | + 0.68 | + 0.66 | − 0.37 | − 0.83 | + 1.99 |
| 9 | + 1.87 | + 0.02 | + 1.18 | + 0.48 | + 0.70 |
| I | − 0.48 | + 0.18 | + 0.43 | + 0.38 | − 0.34 |
| II | + 0.04 | − 1.01 | − 1.13 | + 0.24 | − 0.01 |
| III | + 1.01 | + 0.42 | − 0.04 | − 1.04 | + 0.77 |

an individual is allocated to a particular group it remains fixed within that cluster. Intuitively, we can imagine situations in which an individual unit may be closer to some other cluster at the highest level of grouping, than the one to which it has been joined by reason of its initial pattern of associations. Hence some method of testing the utility of the group membership is needed. This constituted the second stage of the taxonomic analysis. A Discriminant Analysis (Nie, Brent et al, 1976) of the cluster groups as produced by the hierarchical analysis was carried out with Mahalonobis's $D^2$ as the measure of similarity. As expected, several settlements proved to be misclassified and the analysis indicated the most appropriate group to which they should belong. Once these settlements were re-allocated to groups with which they were most similar the analysis was repeated until all of the cases were correctly classified. The same approach was adopted at the three group level and seemed more efficient than using non-hierarchial methods.

The settlements associated with each group are mapped in Figure 31 and the most typical members of each category as revealed by the lowest $D^2$ values in the Discriminant Analysis are listed in Table 24. The average component scores, which represent a weighted summary of several original variables, are shown in Table 21. In Table 22 the average values of the original variables are also provided for each group and this information provides the basis for the descriptive survey of the characteristics of the various groups and their relationship to the postulated community typology. A short descriptive title has been given to each group to ease the overall comprehension of the

## Table 22

## Mean Values for Variables for Social Types in Cardiff City-Region, 1971

### (a) Nine Groups

| T01/ Var 11 | Population | Regional Mean | Groups | | | | | | | | |
|---|---|---|---|---|---|---|---|---|---|---|---|
| | | | 1 | 2 | 3 | 4 | 5 | 6 | 7 | 8 | 9 |
| | Population | | 2498.54 | 4331.09 | 3030.42 | 3889.32 | 3784.12 | 4266.00 | 1049.58 | 1300.00 | 8330.10 |
| T03 | English | 10.38 | 5.04 | 5.49 | 7.58 | 7.44 | 12.53 | 42.59 | 19.07 | 20.51 | 18.94 |
| T04 | Welsh | 85.58 | 92.47 | 91.80 | 89.46 | 89.65 | 83.20 | 40.08 | 74.52 | 72.99 | 72.05 |
| T05 | Born Overseas | 0.95 | 0.49 | .55 | .72 | .78 | 1.07 | 7.23 | 1.65 | 1.39 | 1.89 |
| T08 | Female Ratio | 1.04 | 1.01 | 1.09 | 1.03 | 1.01 | 1.05 | 1.02 | 1.01 | 1.06 | 1.08 |
| T09 | Infants | | 8.12 | 6.98 | 7.98 | 10.56 | 11.20 | 13.36 | 8.92 | 7.06 | 7.03 |
| T10 | Children | 24.83 | 24.53 | 20.74 | 23.92 | 30.50 | 28.80 | 39.35 | 25.85 | 23.66 | 21.58 |
| T11 | Young Adult | 13.81 | 13.96 | 12.58 | 14.29 | 17.23 | 13.47 | 10.54 | 12.30 | 12.19 | 14.71 |
| T12 | Middle Aged | 13.18 | 12.30 | 13.22 | 13.13 | 12.55 | 12.05 | 11.13 | 14.06 | 15.96 | 13.56 |
| T13 | Old Aged | 11.78 | 12.62 | 15.93 | 12.25 | 7.16 | 8.07 | 3.38 | 10.53 | 11.24 | 14.49 |
| T14 | Single Adults | 17.13 | 18.33 | 18.03 | 18.03 | 17.81 | 12.35 | 9.16 | 16.25 | 15.99 | 18.01 |
| T16 | No Bath | 17.75 | 36.18 | 33.56 | 15.57 | 6.21 | 6.05 | 2.71 | 7.71 | 4.23 | 10.85 |
| T17 | One Person Households | 13.69 | 14.50 | 18.11 | 14.56 | 10.95 | 9.07 | 6.37 | 10.75 | 10.72 | 18.45 |
| T18 | Small Dwellings | 5.07 | 2.70 | 4.28 | 4.36 | 6.96 | 3.18 | 5.34 | 4.52 | 4.18 | 19.05 |
| T20 | Owner Occupied | 56.17 | 62.78 | 71.22 | 49.11 | 20.88 | 65.34 | 14.56 | 61.70 | 69.21 | 53.02 |
| T21 | Council | 25.71 | 12.71 | 11.34 | 35.95 | 69.73 | 23.00 | 10.08 | 15.24 | 15.09 | 14.59 |
| T25 | Large Households | 6.78 | 7.74 | 4.75 | 6.94 | 11.03 | 5.75 | 62.65 | 6.40 | 5.20 | 4.93 |
| T27 | E.A. Females | 36.28 | 31.37 | 38.97 | 37.75 | 33.35 | 38.25 | 31.21 | 34.29 | 40.58 | 38.13 |
| T28 | Two Car Households | 9.56 | 3.49 | 3.93 | 5.95 | 4.19 | 9.42 | 6.46 | 24.15 | 29.64 | 11.45 |
| T29 | High Employment Status | 14.52 | 6.46 | 9.27 | 9.40 | 6.26 | 20.88 | 2.68 | 25.56 | 43.21 | 22.40 |
| T33 | Unskilled | 6.54 | 7.27 | 7.61 | 8.48 | 10.38 | 4.06 | 4.46 | 2.50 | 2.32 | 4.09 |
| T35 | Local Migrants | 16.36 | 15.43 | 16.50 | 17.45 | 31.52 | 15.19 | 10.34 | 8.77 | 8.47 | 12.29 |
| T36 | Distant Migrants | 14.86 | 4.77 | 4.10 | 9.77 | 10.83 | 32.76 | 55.13 | 28.11 | 29.94 | 23.47 |
| T38 | Agriculture | 4.53 | 2.00 | .35 | 1.28 | .68 | 1.68 | 1.92 | 23.47 | 6.37 | 2.02 |
| T39 | Mining and Quarrying | 10.32 | 25.33 | 8.80 | 12.14 | 12.60 | 6.00 | 0 | 1.97 | 2.14 | .55 |
| T40 | Manufacturing | 29.05 | 28.42 | 35.18 | 33.75 | 37.92 | 30.61 | 10.90 | 13.95 | 18.52 | 21.38 |
| T43 | Distribution/Service | 33.78 | 26.07 | 33.22 | 31.93 | 26.94 | 35.20 | 19.23 | 37.26 | 52.49 | 47.81 |
| T45 | Government/Defence | 6.16 | 4.42 | 5.59 | 4.84 | 5.10 | 7.76 | 52.56 | 7.71 | 7.43 | 3.18 |
| T46 | S.W.D. Females | 18.48 | 18.88 | 20.87 | 19.07 | 18.07 | 13.74 | 9.10 | 17.16 | 18.04 | 20.66 |

## Table 22
## Mean Values for Variables for Social Types in Cardiff City-Region (1971)

### (b) Three Groups

| | Valleys | Growth | Vale | |
| Variables | I<br>Mean | III<br>Mean | II<br>Mean | Regional<br>Mean |
|---|---|---|---|---|
| T03 English | 6.28 | 9.27 | 19.87 | 10.38 |
| T04 Welsh | 90.98 | 87.25 | 72.94 | 85.58 |
| T05 Born Overseas | 0.60 | 0.90 | 1.74 | 0.95 |
| T08 Females | 104 | 102 | 104 | 104 |
| T10 Children | 23.05 | 29.29 | 24.72 | 24.83 |
| T11 Young Adult | 13.60 | 15.27 | 12.73 | 13.81 |
| T12 Middle Aged | 12.95 | 12.36 | 14.36 | 13.18 |
| T13 Old Aged | 13.95 | 7.86 | 11.38 | 11.78 |
| T14 Single Adults | 18.09 | 15.67 | 16.40 | 17.13 |
| T16 No Bath | 27.11 | 7.08 | 7.40 | 17.75 |
| T17 One Person Households | 15.78 | 10.32 | 12.23 | 13.69 |
| T18 Small Dwelling | 3.90 | 5.18 | 7.42 | 5.07 |
| T20 Owner Occupied | 59.60 | 42.42 | 60.80 | 56.17 |
| T21 Council | 22.01 | 46.84 | 15.31 | 25.71 |
| T25 Large Households | 6.39 | 8.68 | 5.88 | 6.78 |
| T27 E.A. Females | 36.63 | 35.11 | 36.55 | 36.28 |
| T28 Two Car Households | 4.70 | 6.21 | 22.54 | 9.56 |
| T29 High Employment Status | 8.61 | 12.26 | 28.78 | 14.52 |
| T33 Unskilled | 7.83 | 7.75 | 2.82 | 6.54 |
| T35 Local Migrants | 16.63 | 23.79 | 5.44 | 16.36 |
| T36 Distant Movers | 6.62 | 19.35 | 28.16 | 14.86 |
| T37 Commuters | 40.48 | 49.24 | 47.23 | 45.61 |
| T38 Agriculture | 1.21 | 1.04 | 14.47 | 4.53 |
| T39 Mining | 14.27 | 10.81 | 1.68 | 10.32 |
| T40 Manufacturing | 32.78 | 34.64 | 16.52 | 29.05 |
| T43 Distribution/Service | 30.91 | 30.25 | 42.78 | 33.78 |
| T45 Government/Defence | 5.01 | 6.05 | 8.65 | 6.16 |
| T46 Single Females | 19.62 | 16.38 | 17.98 | 18.48 |
| Mean Population | 3326 | 3767 | 2662 | |

characteristics involved, but it must be emphasized that this title is a shorthand statement, a general summary of many individual features. To avoid misunderstanding it is worth noting that the descriptions are based on the relative rather than the absolute variation in the values. To deal adequately with the issue of absolute differentiation is beyond the scope of this internal study of Mid and South Glamorgan since it would involve a comparison between the local values and either British or Welsh trends. This would take one into the type of study recommended by Webber (1978), namely, a cluster analysis of variables to measure the degree of community deviation from the national trends.

(1) The twenty-five *Group 1* places are distinguished by very high negative values on Components I and V. This means they have very high proportions of Welsh born inhabitants (92.5%), relatively higher values than the regional norm for Mining Employment (25.3%), Substandardness (36.2%, as measured by the absence of a bath), and lower values for: Distant Migrants (4.8%); Employment in Service-Distribution (26.1%); Economically Active Females (31.4%) and High Status Employment (6.5%). Many of these variables can be considered as representing low measures of modernization in many different contexts, whether in the physical fabric of the area, the 'mix' of the economy or in the sociological contexts of limited mobility and lower status. Yet the fact that these characteristics are relative ones must be noted, as can be illustrated by the fact that the percentages in both Manufacturing and Distribution-Service Employment are larger than those employed in the Mining work force.

The distinctiveness of socio-economic character is paralleled by a uniqueness in terms of location. These settlements are found in three types of area: firstly, the blind ends of minor valleys such as Caerau, Blaengarw, Bedlinog, Cwmamman, Senghenydd and Gilfach Goch; secondly, in those settlements in the central areas of valleys which never developed as major commercial places because of either a lack of concentration of demand or competition from other places, such as New Tredegar, Tylorstown or Merthyr Vale; thirdly, in the interstices of the major settlement areas, such as the sparsely populated area described as Castellau-fach, between Pontypridd and Tonyrefail. To a very large degree all these areas are locationally remote from the main industrial areas and communication axes. This suggests that a vital part in the ecological differentiation of this type of settlement is played by the influence of relative location and continuing mining activity in the preservation of this distinctive group of settlements. The group is, therefore, described as *Relict Communities,* the designation 'relict' applying to the relative lack of modernization as much as mining employment *per se.*

(2) The thirty-five *Group 2* settlements can be described as *Old Industrial Settlements* because they have high positive scores on Components II, III and IV. This means they have relatively higher proportions of: Old Age (15.9%), Owner Occupation (71.2%), Substandardness (33.6%), and Non Family Characteristics (18% for Single Adults; a 109:100 Female to Male ratio, and 18.1% for One Person Households). Less intense levels of differentiation are a consequence of high levels of Manufacturing employment (35.2%) and lower economic status (for example, 3.9% for Two Car Households).

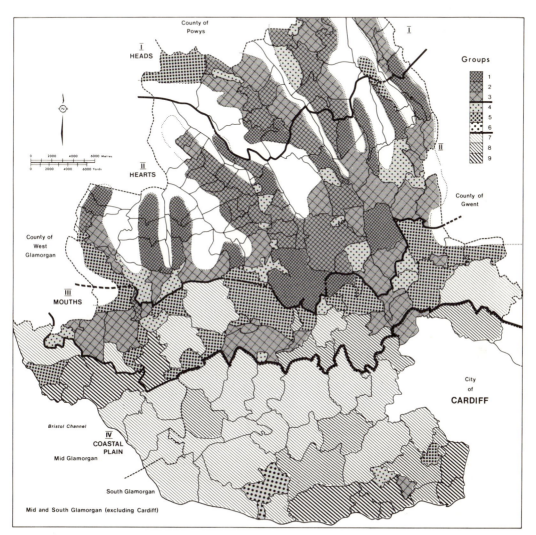

FIGURE 31   SOCIAL STRUCTURE REGIONS FOR CARDIFF CITY-REGION, 1971

143

Figure 31 demonstrates that most of the settlements in this category are located in the central part of the Coalfield, particularly in the Rhondda-Pontypridd area, Aberdare and Merthyr, with outliers at Nantyffyllon and Aberkenfig. In many ways these places resemble the categories of places originally postulated, but the differentiation of the Group II places from those of Group I reveals that the initial typology was not sensitive to the differences in the coalfield settlements revealed by the component scores and even the original values. Although Group I and Group II places have very similar characteristics for many variables, it is the higher proportions in Manufacturing and Service-Distribution employment rather than Mining, and the older population (with relatively low percentages of children) that separate the two groups.

(3) The forty *Group 3* settlements have rather similar profiles to Group 2 places albeit with less intense old age character by reason of more children and young adults (38.2% compared to 33.3%) and lower levels of substandardness (15.6%). Council house ownership is quite high (35.9%) and there are also slightly higher levels of migrant status. Figure 31 shows that this group has a much more discontinuous pattern. They are located on the fringes of Group 1 and 2 places, such as Maesteg in the Llynfi valley, Williamstown on the edge of the Rhondda, Ynysybwl and Cilfynydd around Pontypridd, Penydarren and Pentrebach near Merthyr, as well as Llwydcoed and Cwmbach near Aberdare. However, the cores of the group are found in four areas: firstly, the Kenfig Hill to Llangeinor area; secondly, the Abertridwr to Tongwynlais area; thirdly, Bryncae to Pontyclun; fourthly, eastwards from Treharris to Maesycymmer and Aberbargoed. The characteristics of the type indicate higher levels of renewal in the industrial areas of the Coalfield and a suitable summary title would appear to be *Renewing Industrial Settlements.* These are the places which correspond most closely to the characteristics of the hypothesized Type 1(b) category.

(4) The *Group 4* places are dominated by high negative scores on Component 2, meaning that they are linked to Council Housing (69.7%), Local Migrants (31.5%), Large Households (11.0%), Unskilled Workers (10.4%) and youthful populations (30.5% Children) with slightly lower proportions than the previous groups for the Welsh born population (89.7%) and the Female ratio (101) together with relatively higher percentages for Manufacturing (37.9%) and Mining (12.6%) compared to Distribution-Services (26.9%). These twenty-three settlements form the most discontinuous distribution of all, and are scattered throughout the 'valleys' and the southern edges of the Coalfield. However, a coalfield location in not essential to the community type since places in the Border Vale and even on the edge of one of the larger towns, namely, Colcot in Barry, are found in the category at this scale of analysis. The type parallels the 1(c) category and is called *New Council Settlements* although it is obvious that the type is not restricted to the Coalfield location, as originally postulated, and does not imply that all council house estates are picked out. The scale of ecological generality means that they are only identified if one of the 193 settlements is dominated by these features.

(5) The nineteen *Group 5* settlements are principally associated with negative scores on Component III. This means they are typified by youthful age structures (28.8%) and Migrants from outside the local authority area (32.8%) as well as lower levels of Substandardness (6%) and Old Age (98%), than communities previously described. In addition they are indexed by higher proportions of Economically Active Females (38.3%) and Distribution-Service employees (35.2%). With the exception of places such as Dinas Powys the settlements comprising this type are all located in a belt on the junction of the Vale of Glamorgan and the Southern extremity of the Coalfield from Nottage to the Caerphilly basin. These are the settlements that have experienced some of the largest population growth in the last generation, a growth that is linked to the creation of the new industrial estates in the vicinity of the growth areas (from Bridgend to Caerphilly) that have long been part of the industrial strategy for South Wales (Mid Glamorgan Report, 1978). As such they resemble the 2(a) category of places originally postulated and are described as *New Growth Communities* although it must be emphasized that they form a discontinuous and quite limited spatial pattern within the general area normally described as the Mouths of the Valleys.

(6) *Group 6* has only one representative, the community area of St. Athan, which contains a major national Air Force base with its inevitably youthful population and high degree of mobility. Not surprisingly, therefore, the community is dominated by high positive values for Component I and high negative scores for Component III. This means that the largest distinguishing percentages shown in Table 7a are English born (42.6%), Distant Migrants (55.1%), Children (39.4%), Employment in Defence and Government (52.8%). By contrast the area has low percentages of Old Aged (3.4%), Single Adults (9.2%), Owner Occupation (14.5%) as well as Council Housing (10.1%) because of high proportions of rented accommodation. Given the uniqueness of the area it is called *National Defence Community*. The area was not, of course, one of the postulated community types, but it might be noted that the very differentiation of this category does demonstrate the way in which really individual settlements can be distinguished by this type of analysis.

(7) The twenty-six *Group 7* areas are primarily located in a contiguous area occupying the Vale of Glamorgan with outliers at North Cornelly, Coity, Coychurch and Rudry. The high negative scores for Component IV are the main distinguishing feature, in addition to medium-high positive scores on Component I. This means that the area has significantly higher proportions of: Agricultural employment (23.5%); Two Car Households (24.2%); High Employment Status (25.6%); Distant Migrants (28.1%) and English born (19.1%). These are complemented by low levels of Housing Standardness (7.7%) and Council Housing (15.2%). These areas clearly form the agricultural core of the Vale of Glamorgan and are similar to the postulated 3(c) category of communities. However, the individual values show that these areas are not completely dominated by agricultural activities for suburbanization (with the presence of high status people commuting to the largest centres) has also obviously affected these places. Nevertheless, they can still be labelled as *Rural Communities*. A final point of warning must be

introduced at this stage, one related to the way these areas in the Vale of Glamorgan were constructed. Since the enumeration areas were based on parishes which now bear little relationship to the settlement pattern of the region, care must be taken over the interpretation of the attributes of members of this group.

(8) The fourteen *Group 8* places are very similar to those of Group 7 in many respects but have lower negative scores on Component IV and higher positive scores on Component V. These less intensive associations with the rural sector can be seen by lower percentages for the Agricultural occupation variable (6.4%) and more emphasis upon the tertiary sector, as shown by higher proportions in Distribution-Service (52.5%) and people in High Employment Status (43.2%). These characteristics, together with the high levels of Commuting (47.2%), Distant Migrants (29.9%) and Economically Active Females (40.6%), identify the areas which have developed the largest concentrations of high status commuter estates in the last twenty years. Although they are scattered throughout the Vale of Glamorgan there are large concentrations near Cardiff, the largest commercial centre: firstly, from Llandough to Sully; secondly from Radyr to Miskin; and thirdly, from Bonvilston to Llancarfan. The identification of this category provides empirical evidence for the postulated 3(b) type and it is convenient to summarize the group as *High Status Commuter Settlements.*

(9) *Group 9* represents the last distinctive cluster, this time of ten settlements in the Vale of Glamorgan distinguished by high positive scores on Components I and III. They are similar to the settlements of Groups 7 and 8 in many ways, particularly in their emphasis upon Distribution-Service employment (47.8%), high levels of Distant Migrants (23.5%) and lower levels of Welsh born population (72.1%). However, they differ from these other lowland types by reason of lower levels of affluence or status as measured by the average values for Two Car Households (11.5%) and High Employment Status (22.4%), and higher proportions of Females (108:100), One Person Households (18.5%) and Small Dwellings (19.1%). Two zones of concentration can be identified, one from Porthcawl to Bridgend, the other from Porthkerry and Barry through to Penarth, with a gap at Sully. These settlements are the largest urban places on the coast and lowland and their immediate peripheries. They have expanded very rapidly in the 1951-71 period, but many of them contain underdeveloped older areas with higher levels of substandard property (10.9% of houses are without a bath) and older average ages (14.5% of the population are over 65 years) than the averages for settlements of the Vale — although these are still far below the values for the Coalfield settlements. Also many places have continued to attract sizeable retired populations, all of which helps explain the relatively high levels of non-family character. The short title of *Lowland Urban Settlements* is given to the group.

To concentrate only upon the nine group solution ignores the fact that another break of slope in the distribution of the error sum of squares can be identified in Figure 30 at the three group level — in other words, the nine groups can be arranged into a set of more generalized or higher order clusters, which are called categories in this study. Two of these categories have a close association with the traditional geographical distinction in the area, namely, between the Coalfield and the Vale. The first of these is labelled *Category I,* or *Valleys* Type, and is composed of Relict, Mining Communities (Group 1), Old Industrial Settlements (Group 2) and Renewing Industrial Settlements (Group 3). All are similar enough to coalesce at this higher level of grouping. Table 22 shows that on average they are characterized by a primarily Welsh born population (90.9%), have approximately similar proportions in the Under 15 age category (23%) to the Over 45 age category (26%), but are also distinguished by high levels of One Person Dwellings (15.8%) and Substandard Housing (27.1%), a relatively Unskilled population (7.8%) with low percentages in the High Employment Status category (8.6%). Economically, employment in Manufacturing is larger than in any of the other groups (33%), although Mining has shrunk to 14%. Apart from age characteristics, very different features are found in the three first order groups that form the second higher order group or *Category II.* This is called *Vale* since there is a very close relationship with geographical area. The three groups composing the category are found primarily in the Vale of Glamorgan and have been described as Rural Communities (Group 6), High Status Commuter Settlements (Group 8) and Lowland Urban Centres (Group 9). Table 22 shows that the dominant characteristics of these centres are those of high proportions of English born (19.1%) and Distant Migrants with Two Car Households (22.5%), High Employment status (28.8%) and a relatively high Agricultural sector (14.5%) together with large percentages of Single Person and Owner-Occupied Dwellings.

The third general cluster of community types (Category III) does not have such a strong relationship with geographical area. The core of the category is Group 5, the New Growth Settlements. They are found primarily in the Border Vale and Valley Mouths, but this higher order group also includes the St. Athan National Defence Community (Group 6), as well as the New Council Settlements (Group 4) which are found throughout the region. As a result the generic title, *Growth,* rather than a locational or geographical title, has been given to the category. In view of the previous discussion of the cluster group which make up the type it is not surprising to find that, on average, 45 per cent of the population is under 25 years of age and that a similar proportion of the housing stock is publicly owned. High levels of commuting (49%) across local administrative boundaries, and larger percentages of local (23.8%) and distant migrants (19.3%) contribute to the relatively mobile character of the population in this category.

Now that the synthesis of the one hundred and ninety three areas into nine community types and three higher order categories has been completed, it remains to evaluate two relationships: firstly, the correspondence between these groupings and the initial descriptive typology; secondly, the relationship between the sociological character of the places as revealed in their socio-economic structures and their geographical location.

In terms of the first problem the most significant point is that the vague descriptive generalizations about community character are replaced by precise quantitative evidence of the differentiation of places. Obviously it is difficult to equate subjective descriptions with quantitative categories. Insofar as this is possible it can be seen that the multivariate taxonomy has a very high level of similarity with the postulated set of types — although the fact that communities are associated with each of these types must be noted. The most important difference is that the seven postulates are replaced by nine empirical categories. One of the two extra types, Group 6, is simply a highly specialized or unique case whose distinctiveness from other areas was underestimated in the original hypothesis. The second deviation is a consequence of the identification of an additional category (Group 1). The expected Coalfield settlement type associated with old age and decay proved to be too general; instead, two clusters were identified, separating the Relict, Mining Communities (that actually have younger age profiles and high levels of mining activity) from the Old, Industrial Communities of the Coalfield, which have lost their mining heritage and have experienced low levels of renewal.

In many ways the second problem, the relationship between social structure and location, is more difficult to resolve since two scales of grouping, the nine clusters and three categories, have been identified. At the most general level two of the three categories have a close relationship to geographical location. Table 23 shows that of the ninety-nine places in Category I (Clusters 1, 2 and 3) all but fifteen are found in the Coalfield areas designated 'Hearts' and 'Heads' in Mid Glamorgan Structure Plan. Similarly, of the fifty communities in Category III (Clusters 7, 8, 9), forty-one are found in South Glamorgan and the Coastal Plain of Mid Glamorgan. The third one, called Growth or Category II (Clusters 4, 5, 6), has been shown to have less consistent relationships to geographical location. Of the forty-three places in the category only twenty-two are found in the Valley Mouths region, demonstrating that the social structure characteristics of this type extend beyond a single geographical region.

Discussion of the problem at the threefold category, or general cluster, level does not, however, produce a satisfactory resolution of the issues involved. The nine cluster result was, after all, the preferred solution. Hence the question of the relationship between the four areas — five if South Glamorgan is treated as a separate unit from Mid Glamorgan — and the nine cluster types must be looked at in more detail.

In the Vale (South Glamorgan and the Coastal Plain) forty-one of the forty-six areas are classified in one of the three lowland clusters forming Groups 7, 8 and 9: commuter villages, rural areas and lowland urban centres (Table 23). Although they have sufficiently similar characteristics to be identified as a separate category or higher order grouping, no sub-regions or specific locations for each of the three clusters at the nine group taxonomic level in this area can be found. Hence the generalization of a complete identity between area and social structure is seen to be a fairly superficial one. In addition it is worth noting the exceptions that are found within the area. Colcot (in Barry) is dominated by council estates and takes on the character of the Group 4 places found in the Valleys and Valley Mouths; Dinas Powys is a typical new growth community similar to those in Group 5, which are found primarily on the edge of the Vale and at the Valley

Mouths; Cadoxton (in Barry) and Tongwynlais are two of the Group 3 centres characterized by an older population but with higher levels of renewal — in other words, the sort of community that is typically found in the areas on the edge of the Coalfield that experienced industrialization in the last seventy years.

**Table 23**

**Relationships between Community Taxonomy and Planning Regions**

| County Areas and Regional Divisions | Number in Each Group | | | | | | | | | Total |
|---|---|---|---|---|---|---|---|---|---|---|
| | 1 | 2 | 3 | 4 | 5 | 6 | 7 | 8 | 9 | |
| 1. South Glamorgan | | | 2 | 1 | 1 | 1 | 17 | 9 | 6 | 37 |
| 2. Mid Glamorgan | | | | | | | | | | |
| (a) Coastal Plain | | | | | | 0 | 4 | 2 | 3 | 9 |
| (b) Valley 'Mouths' | 0 | 1 | 12 | 7 | 15 | 0 | 5 | 3 | 1 | 44 |
| (c) Valley 'Hearts' | 22 | 24 | 17 | 13 | | | | | | 76 |
| (d) Valley 'Heads' | 3 | 10 | 9 | 3 | 2 | | | | | 27 |
| Totals: 9 groups | 25 | 35 | 40 | 24 | 18 | 1 | 26 | 14 | 10 | 193 |
| Totals: 3 groups | | 99 | | | 43 | | | 50 | | 193 |

In the Coalfield two separate types of area — called 'Hearts' and 'Heads of the Valley' — have been identified in the Mid Glamorgan Structure Plan. At the general three category level the separate identity of the Coalfield area is confirmed, but within the area three very distinctive types of settlement cluster have been distinguished by the present study. All but eighteen of the one hundred and thirteen communities are in three clusters (Groups 1, 2, 3). Of these, sixteen were classified in the Group IV Council House Estate type — a finding that may be expected since renewal of the urban fabric has taken place in the Coalfield as well. The two other exceptions, Fochriw and Rhigos, were grouped in the New Growth area types, principally because of their higher proportions of young people, council housing, and manufacturing employment. Any scrutiny of the map of taxonomic structure reveals that there are no regional concentrations of these three types in particular areas of the Coalfield. Hence it is difficult to argue the case for separate 'Valley Heart' and 'Valley Head' categories on social structure grounds. Certainly, the areas described as Heads of the Valleys have more communities in the renewing, rather than in the relict community category, but overall the areas are similar in their social structures.

Given the comments already made about the presence of a third or Growth Centre category of community type — one which overlaps the Border Vale and Valley Mouths area — it cannot be expected that this region contains a single taxonomic structure.

Over half of the settlements in the area, twenty-two out of forty-four communities, are in two of the groups (Groups 4 and 5), whilst twelve others are in the Renewing, Industrial cluster, thereby showing similar structures to many of the centres found on the edge of the Coalfield. Another community, Aberkenfig, is typical of the Old Industrial Settlement type (Group 2), whilst five other places are classified in the Rural Cluster (Group 6) and represent areas left behind in the original nineteenth century industrialization and more recent growth phases. Three others on the edge of the region are classified in Group 8 as High Status Commuter Settlements (Miskin, Pentyrch and Talbot Green), whilst another, Bridgend, is one of the Lowland, Urban types (Group 9). Clearly the 'Valley Mouths' area contains a kaleidoscope of communities in which the typical settlement types to the north and south overlap into the area. The result is to produce a belt of very varied settlement types in the six mile wide zone running from Porthcawl to Caerphilly, a zone overlapping the Vale in its western extremities and extending into the Caerphilly basin in the east. This complex zone is identified on the north and south by communities from North Cornelly, to Tythegston, Tonyrefail to Beddau and Llanbradach to Caerphilly. Within it the exact social character of a settlement is determined by several features: the initial resource endowment which influenced its development in the coal era, its proximity to the new industrial estates, and its relative growth as a residential area for the employment centres to the north and south. Although it can be argued that over half of the communities in the area are of the typical growth type the presence of so many other categories destroys the relatively simplistic association of social types and geographical location found in other parts of the area. To use a geological analogy, the area is really a type of sociological shatter belt with no simple association between social typology and geographical area.

## 5. Utility of the Results

This case study of the social differentiation of settlements in Cardiff City-Region using census-based data has shown how the application of synthesizing quantitative methods — such as factor and cluster analysis — to regional description has provided geographers, sociologists and planners with the opportunity to produce precise measurements of the differential character of areas. These results go beyond the traditional regional analyses where areal differences are either subjectively identified, or where the areas are defined on the basis of a small number of statistical indicators. The multivariate approach allows investigators to simultaneously incorporate many variables in an analysis to produce generalized profiles of community character in which the separate sources of variation in the data set are identified. Obviously the degree of comprehensiveness of the results is dependent upon the scope of the data set. But the fact that the structural generalizations, the factors, or the sources of variation on the data, are *derived from* the information rather than being *imposed upon* the data by the choice of single indicators represents a major advantage. Moreover, the provision of precise figures for the social structures, patterns, and typologies represent another advantage over previous methodologies.

In terms of the social structure of the area the factor dimensions proved to be invariant over a range of alternative factor techniques. This degree of strength and stability in the structure of the data means that technical reasons cannot be used to overturn the general conclusion that the social dimensions of Cardiff City-Region are different from those obtained from the same variable set analyzed for Cardiff itself (Chapter 3). In other words, Shevky and Bell's assumption (1955) that social dimensions are invariant over urban and regional scales cannot be supported. At least for this area, the differences between the axes at the two scales demonstrate that the results of *social processes alone cannot explain the social structure of areas.* The differences mean that there must be some geographical, or area-specific effects, that influence the distribution of social types. In this area the very real differences in the economy and historical development of the communities can be proposed as accounting for these variations.

Although the basic geographical variation between the Coalfield and Vale frequently emerges in the analyses, the degree of coincidence of these patterns varies, and the communities vary in the relative strength of the patterns. For many axes the Border Vale and Valley Mouths take on the character of areas to the north or south, whilst the coastal belt of settlements frequently stands out as being different in type to the rural areas of the Vale. But not all the maps of social structures can be placed into this simplistic pattern. For example, the Tenure-Age axis does not conform to any major regional division, whilst the Service Economy and Status axis is more closely related to distance from the two major employment centres of the Cardiff-Barry zone and the Bridgend area. But despite these individual variations in social character and patterns, the summary typology of communities does provide support at the most general level for the idea of separate typologies linked to at least two of the traditional regional divisions in the area, the Coalfield and the Vale, with the third type overlapping the boundary between these areas and extending to new communities in both the other areas. Within each of the broad typologies at the three group level additional clusters of community types can be recognized. This demonstrates the important influence that geographical scale differences play in regional description. At the three group level there is a general Valleys-Vale distinction with the addition of the Growth type; at the more detailed nine-group scale these types 'break-up' into more specialized entities. The important point is that these additional types are not exclusively linked to one area within the overall region, so simple location-social structure relationships break down at this nine-group level. In addition, the complex nature of the area described as 'Valley Mouths' in the Mid Glamorgan Structure Plan must be noted. Most of the communities in the area conform to the Growth or New Council Estate types, but there are many other community types in the area. Hence it is difficult to argue the case for the area being identified as a separate geographical region — at least on the basis of the social criteria used in this study. Similarly, the 'Valley Heads' region cannot claim a sufficiently separate social structure to be identified as another homogeneous region in social geographical terms.

The basic orientation of this study has been towards two themes; firstly, to the

## Table 24
### Sample Areas in Mid and South Glamorgan

#### (a) 9 Groups

| *Group 1 (28)* | | *Group 2 (34)* | | *Group 3 (43)* | |
|---|---|---|---|---|---|
| 136 | New Tredegar | 125 | Troedyrhiw | 21 | Kenfig Hill |
| 9 | Pontrhyl | 77 | Ynyshir | 45 | Llanharran |
| 84 | Blaenrhondda & | | | | |
| | Blaencwm | 76 | Porth | 4 | Maesteg |
| 79 | Pontygwaith | 89 | Pentre | 112 | Llwydcoed |
| | | | | | |
| *Group 4 (22)* | | *Group 5 (17)* | | *Group 6 (1)* | |
| 13 | Sarn (Bryncoch) | 151 | Caerphilly | 170 | St. Athan |
| 22 | Pyle | 15 | Bryncethin | | |
| 16 | Lewistown | 37 | Penyfai | | |
| 142 | Gelligaer | 40 | Pencoed | | |
| | | | | | |
| *Group 7 (26)* | | *Group 8 (12)* | | *Group 9 (10)* | |
| 169 | Ystradowen | 172 | Llancarfan | 182 | Penarth |
| 170 | Pendoylan | 59 | Pentyrch (Creigiau) | 27 | Porthcawl |
| 174 | Peterston | 184 | Sully | 189 | Barry Island |
| 32 | Ewenny | 181 | St. Andrews Major | 28 | Newton Nottage |
| 108 | St. Hilary | | | | |

#### (b) 3 Groups

| *Group 1 (103)* | | *Group 2 (42)* | | *Group 3 (48)* | |
|---|---|---|---|---|---|
| 79 | Pontygwaith | 13 | Sarn (Bryncoch) | 168 | St. Hilary |
| 107 | Cwmbach | 40 | Pencoed | 174 | Peterston |
| 128 | Treharris | 153 | Trethomas | 184 | Sully |
| 78 | Wattstown | 16 | Lewistown | 156 | Wick |
| 86 | Treherbert | 11 | Bettws | 172 | Llancarfan |
| 116 | Cefncoed | 149 | Penyrheol | 161 | St. Mary—Llangan |

These areas are the places closest to the mean of the cluster groups.

development of social structure theory and measurement, and, secondly, to the quantification of regional description. Nevertheless, the utility of this study for planning purposes can be stressed. The analysis provides a quantified description of the relative position of each community on a wide range of social indicators. As such this contributes to the knowledge of social differentiation in the area. Inevitably the scaling of areas provides a sample basis for more community specific behavioural investigations, or for the identification of areas of social deprivation. Ideally, of course, the range of information used in the study should be extended to include non-census data and indicators more directly related to 'quality of life' considerations, problems that go beyond the scope of this analysis. Yet, of more immediate relevance to this study, is the finding that a considerable range of community types can be found in the area, and these areas cannot be identified solely on the basis of their geographical location such that a one-to-one relationship between social type and geographical area is found. This means that planning policies must be designed to take into account these differential community characters; blanket policies designed for each of the areas identified in the Mid Glamorgan Structure Plan — particularly in the complex 'Mouths of the Valleys' area — are likely to face serious problems because of the range of community structures found in the areas.

## CHAPTER 6

## CONCLUSION

The very different sets of values displayed by contemporary research workers in urban studies make it difficult to conceive of a single body of inter-related literature — even on a subject such as urban social differentiation. Even within each discipline there are several schools of scholars, each of which has its own sets of standards by which a particular piece of work is judged. For a radical geographer dedicated to removing the inequities in society the subjective, individualistic concern of those of phenomenological persuasion is, at best, regarded as irrelevant. For the humanist, the Marxist's dogmatic and single-minded identification of an economically determined path to understanding puts a strait-jacket on thought, and represents a denial of man's rich experience and creativity. For urban researchers concerned with solving immediate urban problems, or evaluating the effect of different urban planning policies, much of the elaborate theorizing or quantification practised by adherents to a modern scientific method indicates the presence of an ivory tower mentality of little immediate utility. Not surprisingly, therefore, it is difficult to see how any single study can simultaneously satisfy *all* points of view. Fortunately, the adoption of a pluralist approach helps mitigate this dilemma, for each type of study is regarded as an alternative and additional contribution to our understanding of the complex social mosaics that we recognize as cities.

This methodological discussion and the case studies of the social differentiation of settlements in parts of Wales have *not* been concerned directly with planning or policy issues. Instead, they lie within the generalizing, normative tradition used by many social scientists, rather than the individualistic or characterizing approach favoured by most humanists or urban historians. This means that the emphasis of the study has been upon the general description of the problems of a particular approach to urban social differentiation using a case study at one point in time, 1971, rather than with the identification of the uniqueness of towns. After setting the context within which the social scientific approach lies, the study has concentrated upon developing a conceptual rationale for the multivariate taxonomic approach. From this basis the case studies have produced specific dimensions of social variation and classifications of areas within a systematic body of literature — rather than upon the creation or testing of a theory of urban social differentiation. Nevertheless, it is hoped that the results will contribute to the development of such a theory in the future by identifying the structures or constructs upon which a theory can be based.

In many ways, therefore, the case studies have set themselves firmly within the empirical and scientific tradition first developed by Charles Booth in his Presidential Address to the Royal Statistical Society (Booth, 1895; Davies, 1978). For Booth the first office of the science of his day was to establish a solid factual base for his problem — in his case the measurement of what he called the 'social condition' of London in the late nineteenth century. To achieve this end he moved away from direct measures of poverty collected by laborious house-to-house survey methods. Instead, he combined variables derived from the census to obtain a general ranking of areas. Obviously Booth's techniques can be criticized today, whilst his idea that a single dimension of social variation represented an adequate basis for understanding the general social structure of cities was replaced by models with more axes — ranging from Shevky and Bell's (1955) three axis model of social area structure to the more complex arrangements identified here. Nevertheless, Booth was astute enough to recognize that his approach was only a first attempt at the problem, as the quotation on the very first page of this study illustrates. Yet it is worth re-quoting part of this statement to demonstrate that Booth thought his method:

> may be sufficiently interesting to tempt and revise the ingenuity of inquirers to the invention of further tests touching other springs and wider vistas.
>
> (Booth, 1893, p. 591.)

Unlike Booth, however, this study does not extend to the alternative approaches to community character — the subjective description of both the sights and sounds of areas or the summary of the life and work of the residents. Booth, after all, needed seventeen volumes to undertake his work! Instead, this study restricts itself to two points made in the quotation above: the application of procedures for defining urban social variation in a quantitative fashion; and the setting of these results within the 'vista' of societal and geographical forces, in the context of different scales of analysis and alternative methodologies.

Any review of the history of ideas in the study of urban social differentiation in the last twenty years will demonstrate that the application of more and more sophisticated techniques has focused attention upon the details of these specific procedures rather than upon the development of a systematic methodology or related body of generalizations in this field. This has probably contributed to the relative decline of interest in quantitative approaches. Yet such interest in the 'nuts and bolts' of the means whereby generalizations are produced *is* important; without a clear understanding of the quantitative procedures the utility of any sets of results cannot be judged. But in the last resort these techniques are the common property of all scientists. In any case the development of new procedures is likely to remain in the hands of the applied mathematicians and statisticians, since their particular skills make them best able to deal with these issues. This means that urban and social geographers should ultimately be more concerned with the substantive results produced by the application of these procedures rather than with the techniques themselves — although the technical problems are still important parts of the whole methodological debate. Given this interpretation, it seems appropriate to summarize the methodological and technical conclusions separately from the specific findings of the study.

## 1. Methodological and Technical Issues

(a) *Analytical Stages.* The summary review of the history of ideas in the field of urban social differentiation revealed that a variety of alternative methodologies have been used by investigators — even when the objective has been to isolate the generalities found between areas of towns rather then to provide unique characterizations. But despite this long history of endeavour in the field the various analytical stages of interest to the nomothetic urban geographer do not seem to have been clearly defined by investigators in this area. One of the first tasks of this study, therefore, was to develop a paradigm to clarify the difference between the analytical stages in any investigation, namely, social indicators, social structures, social patterns, social typologies and social regions, each of which could be applied at the individual scale or at various geographical scales.

(b) *The Multivariate-Structural Method.* Although the term 'factorial ecology' has been coined to describe the application of factor methods to the measurement of urban social variation the inadequacies of this description must be emphasized. The problems implicit in the quantitative approach require the application of additional techniques to those described as factorial, whilst it is clear that the approach can only deal with part of the problem of interpreting the social mosaic of urban areas. As a result it has been proposed that the term *Multivariate-Structural* is a more appropriate description of the methodology that has been followed in this study. The advantage of this new title is that it allows the use of multivariate techniques other than those of factor analysis — even those additional to the ones used here (Atkin, 1975; Johnston, 1979). In addition, the use of the term 'structural' in the sense of identifying, or describing, the uniformities in social patterns — rather than in the causal interpretation sense — provides both a context and limits for a study of this type. These issues have been explored in the first two chapters of this monograph.

(c) *Data and Techniques.* Given the scope of the field of multivariate analysis and the rate of development of new procedures, it is inevitable that many of the technical problems facing students of urban social differentiation are going to be of a technical rather than a substantive nature. Such technical problems have to be resolved before confidence can be placed in the conclusions. It would be arrogant to claim that all possible technical problems associated with this approach are dealt with in this study. Nevertheless, particular attention was paid to several basic sets of technical issues. One set consisted of the choice of variables used in the analysis. Rather than simply seeking as comprehensive a variable set as the data sources allowed the indicators were chosen as representative of a set of expected axes of differentiation, although variables from closed number systems or those that were badly skewed were excluded after preliminary analysis. However, this 'data grooming' and identification of 'expected' axes does not mean that the inferential methods of common factor analysis were followed. The 'expected' axes and areas were simply used as guides for the choice of variables and areas.

One useful by-product of all factor analyses of a data set is the derivation of a number of key or diagnostic indicators for each axis — indicators that come closest to identifying the constructs lying behind the factor dimensions. Table 25 shows the diagnostic indicators produced by this study, namely, the two highest loadings on each vector and

# Table 25
## Diagnostic or Key Variables at each Scale
*(Variables with loadings > ±0.7 and/or the two highest loadings on each axis latter shown by asterisk)*

| | Variables | Dimensions: Urban System | City Region | Intra-Urban |
|---|---|---|---|---|
| *Age, Family* | Old Age | Age & Economy | | Life Cycle |
| | Children | Age & Economy | Non Family* | Life Cycle |
| | Young Adult | College-Resort | Tenure/Age | Young Adult |
| | Middle Aged | — | — | Late Family/Mobility* |
| | Single Adult | — | — | Young Adult |
| *Housing* | Substandardness | Degree of Renewal | — | Housing/Ethnicity* |
| | Council Housing | Tenure | Tenure/Age | Housing/Ethnicity |
| | Owner Occupation | Tenure | Tenure/Age | — |
| | Persons/Room | Age & Economy | — | — |
| | Dense Occupation | — | Tenure/Age | Young Adult |
| *Mobility* | Distant Migrants | Degree of Renewal | — | — |
| | Local Movers | — | — | Late Family/Mobility* |
| | Commuters | — | — | Urban Fringe* |
| | Visitors | College-Resort | — | — |
| *Ethnicity* | English Born | N.U. | — | Socio-Economic Status |
| | Welsh Speakers | Welsh Centres | N.U. | N.U. |
| | Welsh Born | — | Ethnicity & Economy | Socio-Economic Status |
| | Overseas Born | — | Ethnicity & Economy | Socio-Economic Status |
| | Irish | Specialized Economy | N.U. | N.U. |
| *Economy* | Mining | — | Economy & Status* | — |
| | Agriculture | — | Rural-Industrial | Urban Fringe |
| | Manufacturing | — | Rural-Industrial* | Socio-Economic Status |
| | Service-Distribution | Age & Economy | Economy & Status* | — |
| | Government | — | Ethnicity & Economy | — |
| | Construction-Transport | Specialized Economy | — | — |
| *Social Status* | Two Car Households | — | — | Socio-Economic Status |
| | High Employment Status | — | — | Socio-Economic Status |
| *Size* | Population Size | Size | N.U. | N.U. |
| | Retail Turnover | Size | N.U. | N.U. |
| *Females* | Single, Widowed, Divorced Females | — | Non Family | Young Adult |
| | Economically Active Females | Welsh Centres? | Economy & Status | — |
| | Female Ratio | Age-Major Economy | — | — |

N.U. — Not used at this scale.

157

all variables with loadings over ±0.7. The results show that practically all the variables used in the analysis come into this diagnostic category at one or other scales; only two indicators on each side are missing. This would imply that the variable sets used in this study could not be further reduced in number without serious effects upon the quality of the results. Nevertheless, it is accepted that the restriction of the data to the information available from the latest census in 1971 must circumscribe the degree of comprehensiveness of the results. The restriction was made because of the necessity of obtaining a standard set of indicators for quite small areas for which other unpublished data cannot be obtained. Ideally, of course, one would like to go beyond the type of variables used here — indicators that measure the tangible structural characteristics of settlements — to those that more closely measure the elusive 'quality of life' variables (Liu, B-C., 1977). Although axes of differentiation linked to such 'quality' dimensions may be identified it is likely that many of the 'quality' variables will overlap with the axes derived from standard social indicators, as Davies and Tapper (1979) have shown in their study of the dimensionality of the urban system of the United States of America. Moreover, even if one moves into a new domain of variables, such as those dealing with values and perceptions of people, Knox and MacLaran (1978, p. 241) concluded after a study of Dundee that:

> for the purposes of generally describing or evaluating *ecological* disparities in well-being, conventional hard data are as good a surrogate as any.

The stress on 'ecological' made here is important since the authors go on to point out that the addition of information on values accentuates the extent of deprivation. This, however, takes one into the behavioural, value-attitudinal aspects that were described, in Chapter 2, as being beyond the scope of this enquiry. Nevertheless, it is encouraging for the integration of different sets of knowledge, to know that the objective variables used here have a relevance to more subjectively derived indicators. Yet it is important to ensure that the bounds of particular analyses are carefully delimited. Indeed, one of the doyens of factor analytical methods, Cattell (1978), has gone so far as to recommend that, in the early stages of factorial investigations, analyses should keep to particular *domains of variables* — for example, objective behavioural tests as opposed to attitudinal information derived from questionnaire — so that the axes relevant to particular domains can be clearly identified. Once this has been achieved, the mixing of domains will probably show overlap between axes derived from the different data sets. This study, therefore, has deliberately avoided the mixing of data sets and has followed Cattell's precept.

(d) *Scale of Taxonomic Units.* It was observed in Chapter 2 that there has been considerable debate in the research journals about the effect of different sized collecting units upon the results of any factorial study. The comparison between the ward and enumeration area results in Cardiff indicated that, in terms of the substantive interpretation of the axes, the distortion in the results was rather less than expected, given the scale of the differences between five hundred and forty one districts and twenty wards. Three axes, namely, Socio-Economic Status, Life Cycle and Young Adult, were very similar at all scales. Moreover, some rather typical results were obtained between the two levels of aggregation, for the ward level axes were more general and accounted for more variance than the detailed enumeration district results. The most important difference lay in the absence of the Housing-Ethnicity vector at the ward scale. Any study of the distribution of scores on the Housing-Ethnicity vector and the pattern of ward boundaries will reveal that the wards cut across the areas where ethnic groups and substandard housing are concentrated. In other words, the distinctiveness of the enumeration district structure is destroyed by the areal aggregation at the ward level so these axes cannot be expected. Such reasons also account for the relatively low congruence coefficients for the Urban Fringe and Late Family-Mobility axes which were different enough to be named Urban Fringe-Mobility and Female at the ward level. It is possible, of course, that this failure of the ward scale collecting cells to match the detail of the social distribution in cities accounts for the inability of other workers (Perle, 1977; Romsa et al, 1972) to identify similar structures at the different scales employed in their analyses. This leads to the next question, whether there are any distortions produced by the preferred scale of analysis: namely, the enumeration districts. In the last resort, of course, there is no easy answer to the problem. These districts represent the most detailed areal data scale made available by census authorities. Perhaps it is worth stressing that five hundred and forty one areas were used in the study, so it is difficult to see how a much finer scale of analysis can be employed. Indeed, it represents a much more detailed multivariate analysis of Cardiff when compared to previous work (Herbert, 1970; Herbert and Evans, 1974). However, the comparability between the results of the two scales demonstrates the need to relate the pattern of taxonomic units to the facts of social distributions within cities. Studies with high levels of aggregation cannot expect to pick out the detail of axes of differentiation if they fail to use appropriate collecting (or taxonomic) cells. In this context the problem of comparing urban areas in Cardiff with larger sets of rural enumeration areas in the Vale of Glamorgan must be reviewed. Purists can argue that comparisons cannot be made. However, the fact that similar results were obtained when various groupings of enumeration areas were used in test analyses provided useful evidence that the comparisons were worthwhile and could not be invalidated for technical scale-dependent reasons.

(e) *Stability*. One of the other technical problems looked at in detail concerns the degree of stability in the results — given the variety of alternative multivariate methods that are available. In all the factor analyses a deliberate attempt was made to explore these problems by using different rotations and factor methods. Again it would be foolish to deny that differences occurred between some of the procedures. But on balance the same substantive interpretation could be given to most axes. Some of the minor vectors, such as the 'Welsh Centre' factor (Table 2) in the urban system study described in Chapter 3, were not at all clear, so their identification must be queried, whilst certain other axes were given slightly different titles. Probably the biggest differences — although only with one of the axes in each of the studies — occurred with the results of the Image Analysis solutions. Checks revealed that the variables that should have been linked to these unstable Image axes had lower communalities, so the discrepancies were attributed to the failure of this method to incorporate areally specific sources of differentiation into the common factors — paralleling findings obtained elsewhere (Davies, 1978). Since the analysis reported here is concerned with summarizing the variable set, rather than identifying common axes that would ignore such localized distributions, more support for the choice of the component model is provided. Finally, it is worth noting that a deliberate attempt was made to avoid the imposition of hierarchical structures upon the social typologies in this study. The hierarchical cluster results were subjected to Discriminant Analysis to test the utility of the groups. Relatively minor re-adjustments to the membership of each group was needed to provide a revised grouping at both intra-urban and regional scales.

(f) *Problems of the Factor Analysis Approach.* Whether the multivariate methods used in this study will prove satisfactory for the foreseeable future must await the test of time. There is no doubt that certain requirements of these particular methods still cause considerable anguish to the exponents of the approach. For example, the factor and correlation methods used here assume there is linearity between the variables in the data set. This requirement may not always be satisfied so any investigator using Product Moment Correlation Coefficients will be working with measures which represent underestimates of the true relationships. But Cattell (1978) has reviewed evidence from many fields and has concluded that the factor approach is very robust so long as there are not significant departures from linearity. In any case it can be argued that if well over two-thirds of the variation in a twenty-seven variable data set can be accounted for by five or six axes, a very useful, albeit linear, interpretation of the structures involved has been made, although it is recognized that these may be minimum relationships. In the future it is likely that the application of non-linear factor methods (McDonald, 1974) may help resolve this problem. Similarly, the debate over the use of component or common factor models still rages. Most experienced workers in psychology (Cattell, 1978) — where factor analysis has been most widely employed — argue for the common factor model since it is pointed out that all studies will have some specific (or single) variable-associated variance as well as error variance. So the diagonal values in the factor matrix should contain values other than 1.0. In theoretical terms it is hard to disagree with this point. But it does not help one to solve the next problem which concerns the value to be used. Many suggestions have been made (Rummel, 1971; Cattell, 1978), but the most usual method is to use the squared multiple correlation of variables. When this standard value was adopted in this study the results of the common factor solutions were virtually identical to the component approach. Given this stability in interpretation there seemed little advantage in using the common factor results — given the descriptive orientation of this study.

Another major problem relates to the use of significance tests and the independence of samples. The objectives of regional and urban description necessitate the use of a complete population in this study. As a result the tests of significance associated with common factor models are not relevant. They assume that independently derived samples are used and calculate the probability that the result obtained could have arisen by chance because of the way the sample values estimate the true values. It can be proposed that the aggregation of information for areas at any scale can be made on any number of bases, so they are a sample in this sense. But this is not a strong argument. In any case the fact that one area is a neighbour of another probably means that the patterns and processes in one area can be found in the other, so independence — in a statistical sense — is hardly achieved, whilst the variables are bound to be autocorrelated. There seems little that geographers can do to avoid these problems in the multivariate case as the assumptions of the statisticians are breached, although the work of Cliff and Ord (1973) has demonstrated certain ways around the difficulties in bivariate situations. In any case, Cattell (1978) has pointed out that factor analysts should be wary of using tests designed for one type of mode — normally individuals — in other contexts, for example, variables in the Q mode or time in the P mode, since doubt must exist that the sampled observations are homogeneous. Similar reasoning would apply to the replacement of areas for individuals in the R mode approach used here, for it is obvious that the areas cannot be a homogeneous population.

Confronted with these problems it is easy to become despondent and to reject the use of factor, or indeed all, quantitative techniques. This would be unfortunate since the factor methods need not be used in a strictly inferential context; they are sufficiently comprehensive and stable enough to be used for synthesizing data sets without reference to the inferential tests. Indeed, Rummel (1971) has referred to the methods as the 'calculus' of social science. Yet we should, perhaps, work for the day when the whole apparatus of rigorous statistical methods can be applied. For the time being, however, we have to work with less rigorous procedures. Nevertheless, this should not lead to the conclusion that the results presented here are the product of arbitrary technical decisions. The stability of the results under different factoring methods help provide a great deal of confidence in the results. In addition, the use of cut-off procedures can be justified. For example, the $\pm 0.3$ level for the component loadings is increasingly recognized as an appropriate, if conservative, limit, since factor testing procedures (Pennal, 1974) have shown that such values are almost always significant. Moreover, the demonstration (Davies, 1978) that the use of scale-free multivariate procedures using cross-product (not correlation) matrices produced basically similar results in the interpretation of factors in the study of intra-urban variations is also encouraging. However, the issue of size differences in the inter-urban case does take one into a different problem area to this discussion of similarities between areas. Similarly, the question of the internal homogeneity of the areal units (Newton and Johnston, 1976) represents another type of problem that is not investigated here. As with all studies of the real world, decisions have to be made about the scope of an analysis; it is part of the reductionist problem described in Chapter 2. The conclusion must be, therefore, that the application of the multivariate procedures used here to the problems of this study still have a sufficiently strong rationale to allow their continued use in circumstances that may not be ideal in a purely statistical or inferential case. The technical problems that have been encountered should encourage investigators to find answers to these difficulties rather than to immediately proceed to alternative methods. This, of course, is not an argument for the perpetuation of out-moded procedures; rather it is a recognition of the very real difference between the practical concerns of those of a scientific disposition who are primarily interested in finding results that other investigators can accept as reasonable interpretations of the real world, and the theoretical circumstances in which most of the inferential tests associated with modern statistics are formulated. Cattell's (1978) arguments for the scientific as opposed to the mathematical use of factor analysis, and Harman's (1976, p. 351) discussion of the difference between statistical and psychological significance (we can use 'content area significance' to describe the broader application of the idea) provide recent demonstrations of this point. Thus, given the way in which factor analyses have improved the flexibility of the procedures, it was not proven at the time of the analysis that it is worth rejecting factorial methods for newer scaling devices, all of which have their own problems. Only when alternative methods have been *conclusively* shown to fulfil *all* the functions of factor analysis and *improve* on it can new methods be used with any confidence. Even then, of course, they only represent technical improvements in the general methodology of the Multivariate-Structural approach described here.

## 2. Social Structures, Patterns, Typologies, Regions and Models

The results of the various analyses seem sufficiently stable to have resolved one of the major problems of any systematic description, namely, that several independent investigators using the same data and investigating the same problem would have arrived at the same results — in this case social dimensions and clusters of areas. Now it is necessary to turn to the more substantive results. Figure 32 summarizes the results of the structural analyses by identifying the dimensions found at the city and city-regional scales of analysis, as well as those at the national system level. It was unfortunate that the intra-urban dimensions could not be directly measured against the others because an identical variable set was not available from the data source. Nevertheless, the fact that over half the indicators were identical between the inter and intra-urban scales meant that it seemed appropriate to add these results to Figure 32 to provide a further context for the interpretation of the results.

(a) No satisfactory theory of urban social differentiation has been formulated at the urban system or city-regional level. At the intra-urban scale Shevky and Bell's theory (1955) has been modified by McElrath (1968) and Timms (1971). The results of this study provide further proof of the inadequacy of these ideas since far more axes of differentiation than are proposed in these models have been identified. It is apparent that any new theory of social differentiation at the intra-urban scale should take into account at least the Late Family, Young Adult and Rural Fringe axes and probably a Sub-standardness dimension, in addition to the traditional Social Status, Age or Family, Ethnicity (or rather Ethnicities) and Migrant axes. The presence of a separate tenure

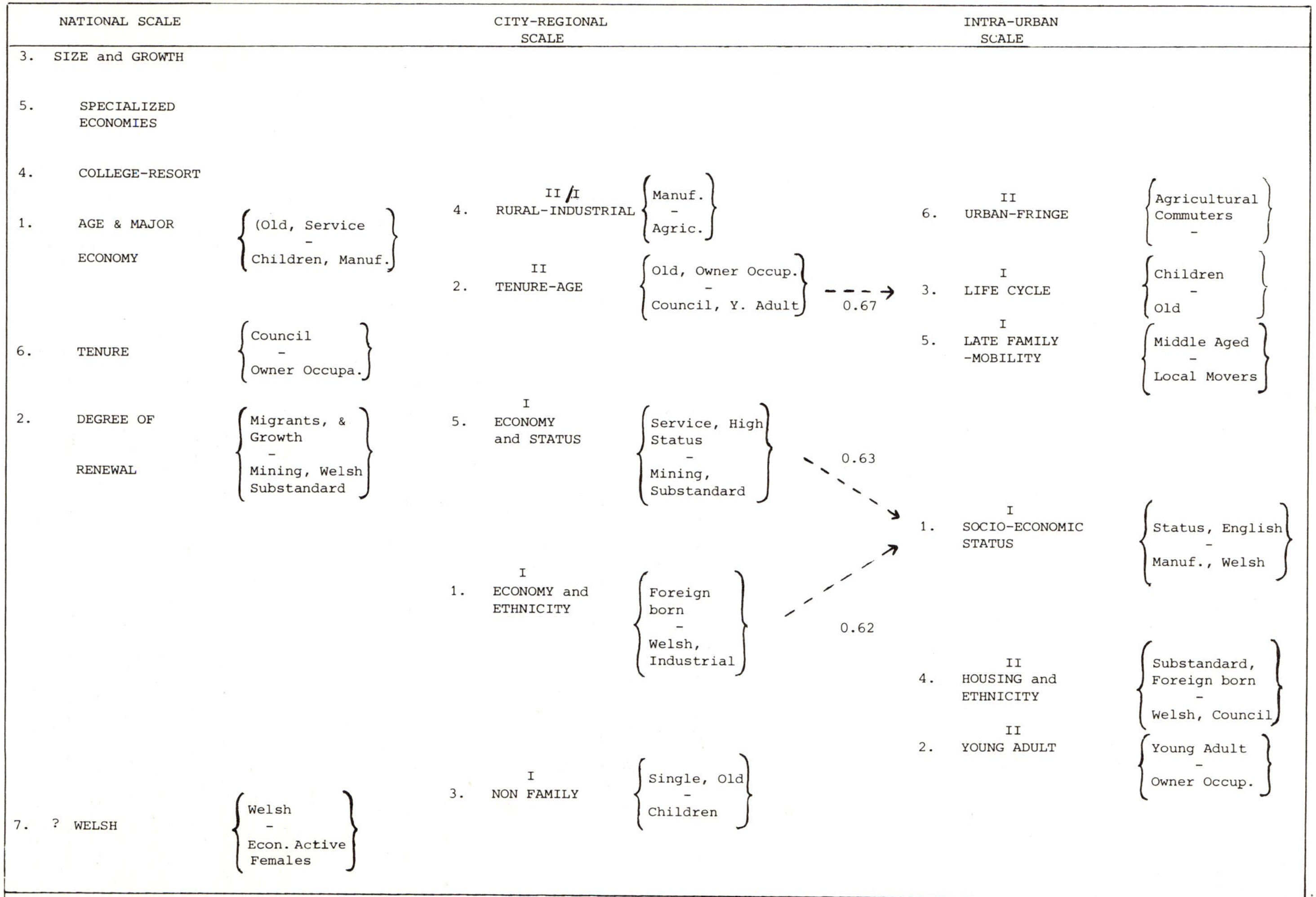

# Axes of Social Differentiation at the Three Scales

| NATIONAL SCALE | CITY-REGIONAL SCALE | INTRA-URBAN SCALE |
|---|---|---|
| 3. SIZE and GROWTH | | |
| 5. SPECIALIZED ECONOMIES | | |
| 4. COLLEGE-RESORT | | |
| 1. AGE & MAJOR ECONOMY { (Old, Service) – Children, Manuf. } | 4. RURAL-INDUSTRIAL (II/I) { Manuf. – Agric. } | 6. URBAN-FRINGE (II) { Agricultural Commuters } |
| | 2. TENURE-AGE (II) { Old, Owner Occup. – Council, Y. Adult } | 3. LIFE CYCLE (I) { Children – Old } |
| 6. TENURE { Council – Owner Occupa. } | | 5. LATE FAMILY –MOBILITY (I) { Middle Aged – Local Movers } |
| 2. DEGREE OF RENEWAL { Migrants, & Growth – Mining, Welsh Substandard } | 5. ECONOMY and STATUS (I) { Service, High Status – Mining, Substandard } | 1. SOCIO-ECONOMIC STATUS (I) { Status, English – Manuf., Welsh } |
| | 1. ECONOMY and ETHNICITY (I) { Foreign born – Welsh, Industrial } | 4. HOUSING and ETHNICITY (II) { Substandard, Foreign born – Welsh, Council } |
| 7. ? WELSH { Welsh – Econ. Active Females } | 3. NON FAMILY (I) { Single, Old – Children } | 2. YOUNG ADULT (II) { Young Adult – Owner Occup. } |

0.67   0.63   0.62

First order axes are shown by capital letters and numbers. Examples of the original variables are in brackets. Second order relationships are shown by Roman numerals.

FIGURE 32   AXES OF SOCIAL DIFFERENTIATION AT THE THREE SCALES

dimension is difficult to substantiate since it is so closely linked to other features. Moreover, no clear evidence could be found for the presence of female or economic variations, although one of the minor axes at the ward scale measured female differentiation. It is possible, of course, that the social area theories are more appropriate descriptions at the second, rather than the first order scale (as Davies and Lewis suggested in their study of Leicester (1973)) whilst some axes may be intermingled, as in this study. This still does not resolve the question of why these additional axes can be recognized — although it is recognized they are relatively minor dimensions. One possibility is that the transition into a post-industrial society (Bell, 1974) produces specialization in family and economic axes and this is reflected here.

The identification of these more specialized axes does not mean that they corresponded to the initial postulates. The axes in Cardiff were much more general than expected and some of the postulated dimensions were found on opposite sides of a single vector. The major examples were: the Housing-Ethnicity axis where the indicators of council tenants and the Welsh born were found in inverse relationship to the ethnic and substandardness variables; and the fifth axis where Late Family variables were opposed to the Migrant features. Perhaps of more importance for the development of ideas about the social characteristics of Welsh towns is the finding that these axes displayed significant degrees of overlap — particularly at the second order — between the Age and Status vectors. This must be added to the generality displayed by the urban system results where the two largest axes were called Age and Economy, and Degree of Renewal — the latter separating substandardness, Welsh born and declining economy variables from growth characteristics.

These results demonstrate that these Welsh towns have rather different dimensional structures to those found in many other cities of the Western world. It provides support for the basic proposition of the study that a single model of urban social differentiation is *not* applicable even in Western society. Obviously structural differences in Western society can be expected where there are variations in the ethnic composition of the population. But the results reported here go further, since they link together the Age and Status variations — axes that should be independent according to the tenets of the existing social area theory. It is always notoriously difficult to make the connection between empirical relationships — in this case the factor dimensions — and the theoretical principles they reflect. In this case study it can be suggested that two characteristics of society in Wales are influential in producing this age structure and economy overlap. One is the differential level of economic modernization in Wales, for service based economies are intimately linked to growing populations, whilst extractive industries are linked to declining, aging populations living in substandard urban fabrics. The other — a more general British characteristic — is related to the degree of government intervention in the housing market. Since council housing is allocated to low status people (principally the old and large families) it is likely that social status and age-family characteristics will overlap. These findings mean that any new theory of social differentiation must be flexible enough to take account of such society-specific effects if it is to be successfully applied to different areas. Yet to conclusively demonstrate the influence of specific causes upon dimensional structures requires an experimental approach, involving studies from different societies.

(b) The comparison of the three sets of results demonstrates that there is no single or simple relationship between the scales of analysis since congruence coefficients are relatively low. The argument for scale invariance made by Shevky and Bell (1955) and echoed by Carter (1974) must, therefore, be rejected. If social processes alone accounted for structural variations one might expect a great deal of comparability between the results. The fact that differences in the structures have been identified indicate that other processes must be at work to provide residential differentiation; processes that provide differential spatial concentrations of the social characteristics. These can be described as geographical or ecological features, since they affect spatial distributions and probably work within the general differentiating opportunities provided by social changes. In other words, Udry's suggestion (1964) that social areas are the product of two theories, one of social change, the other of sub-area differentiation, is supported by these results, although his diffusion analogy does not provide a satisfactory explanatory mechanism for the changes.

To investigate the theoretical implications of the two theory approach goes beyond the scope of this study. It is likely that societal changes produce the opportunity for societal differentiation, but these changes are only identified by a separate axis if some spatial concentration of this element of differentiation takes place. The definition of these ecological processes must await the elaboration of a complete theory of social structure differentiation. One example of the type of relationship operating can be provided. All people age and pass through the young adult stage — defined here as the 15-24 years of age group. Increasingly, however, individuals at this stage in life leave their homes, either to take up employment elsewhere, or to go for further education training. Limited financial resources for most members of the group mean limited housing choices. This restriction must be combined with the desire of individuals in the group to be close to educational, employment, and leisure time activities, for travel is also expensive. In an intra-urban context a location near the centres of large cities is preferred since these areas contain a high proportion of the employment and educational opportunities — whilst the aging of the older houses in the area leads to the subdivision of properties into flats or bedsitters. Locational preferences as well as locational constraints in terms of housing opportunities, lead to the differentiation of a separate axis of this type based on the concentrations of young adults in this area. In Wales, some of the smaller service centres — such as Aberystwyth and Bangor — also contain university colleges. The large numbers of students in these small towns is bound to affect the urban age structures, thereby producing the necessary element of spatial concentration of young adults at another scale, and the resultant isolation of a college town axis at the urban system level. Both examples demonstrate the need for some spatial or ecological differentiating features, in addition to societal conditions, before the axes of differentiation can be recognized. Indeed, the creation of societal changes cannot be the major cause for sub-area differentiation, otherwise axes would be invariant at different scales. Moreover, it is only when these changes produce *concentrations* in area — and hence imbalances in the spatial variations — that separate axes can be identified, and these concentrations have to be recognizable at the scale being employed. To go back to the young adult example, everybody passes through this stage, but there must be something different about modern society that provides the opportunity for these groups to cluster in area if it is only in this particular type of society that this dimension is found. So *it is the clustering forces, not the biological or societal aging processes, that are the key to differentiation.* Shevky and Bell's theory of social change provides another example. It is not the ethnic mixing in society that is the key feature — after all the ethnic groups could be equally distributed — rather it is the process of segregation that leads to ethnic concentrations in area. Each of the dimensions of variation are likely to have separate ecological forces affecting their patterning. Perhaps now that the primacy of ecological forces in this situation has been restored, and the social structures have been identified, it may be easier to derive a theory of social differentiation — at least at the intra-urban level. At the city-region and inter-urban level specific localized resource distributions are more likely to impart a strong element of individuality to the differentiation of the system.

(c) If the evidence of Figure 32 is typical, it shows that there are likely to be more specialized axes at the intra-urban scale than at other levels, for the city represents the area where greater social heterogeneity over several taxonomic units is found. At this point it is worth re-emphasizing that the generalizing nature of the analysis presented here means that unique characteristics associated with single areas will not be identified in the study; the variation will be treated as error variance. But of more importance is the fact that the domination of economic differentials at the city system and city-region scales is replaced by one associated with more specifically social considerations, namely, family based and ethnic variations. This means that the ecological (or geographical) arguments needed to explain the differentiation at the various scales will vary. For example, in Figure 32 the Age-Economy and Tenure axes at the national scale are replaced by Rural-Industrial and Tenure-Age vectors at the city-regional level. In part, perhaps, the rural side of the axis is reflected in the urban-rural division found in the Fringe axis at the urban scale. The Life-Cycle urban axis is a more specialized form of the Tenure-Age dimension found at the city-region scale, and the addition of the Late Family-Mobility factor provides a further element of differentiation identifiable only at the city scale. Similarly, the Degree of Renewal vector is represented by separate Service Economy-Status and Economy-Ethnicity axes at the city-regional scale, with the addition of a separate Old Age-Non Family type of vector. By the time the intra-urban scale is reached, separate Socio-Economic Status and Ethnicity vectors are found, whilst the Housing-Ethnicity and Young Adult axes identify further degrees of specialization. The Size vector in the urban system is, of course, excluded from the city-regional level results, since appropriate variables were not included because of the need to match the intra-urban variables. Size would not be expected at the intra-urban level unless commercial characteristics were included. Similarly, the Specialized Economies of the urban system find no echo at the city-regional level and are most unlikely to be identified at the city scale — although in many non-Western societies high concentrations of specialized craft workers can still be found. Intra-urban economic differentials may be expected in such circumstances.

(d) In any city or region the spatial patterns of the social structures are bound to display specific variations that are related to the peculiarities of place. These studies are no exceptions. In Cardiff the continuous urban area is divided into separate entities by the riverine park systems and the whole area is trunctuated to the south by the docks. The economy and history of the Coalfield and Vale are so different that many area-specific patterns can be found. Nevertheless, within the detailed patterns of the social structures that have been described, some rather general spatial features can be identified. In the Cardiff case, at least, they correspond to patterns that have been described elsewhere (Davies and Lewis, 1973). As a result they are worth re-emphasizing, although the danger of falling into the universalist fallacy must be noted.

   (i)   The Socio-Economic axis displays sectoral concentrations of high status, with high levels of low status in a semi-circle around the city centre as well as in sectors with above average concentrations of council houses.

   (ii)  Life Cycle characteristics have a rather shallow concentric zonation, with young families on the growing edges of the city and in the area close to the docks. Old age is found near the city centre, but is highest in some of the older middle city areas.

   (iii) Young Adults have their highest concentrations in the inner city, but particularly in areas immediately adjacent to the city centre where two university colleges are located.

   (iv)  High levels of Mobility are found in the areas close to the city centre and in the new estates on the edge of the city. By contrast, the most stable zones are found in a discontinuous girdle in the middle city, an area that is broken by the major arteries of movement.

   (v)   Ethnic variations are more difficult to generalize about, given the failure of the 1971 census to record religion or colour. Undoubtedly there is a new, inner city cluster of people who were born overseas. This is located principally to the west of the city centre and north of the traditional ethnic quarter of Cardiff — Tiger Bay. Added to this, however, is a higher proportion of people of English extraction in the outer, more affluent, suburbs. The minimal cultural differences — apart from language — between those born in Wales, compared to England, means that no *exclusive* ethnic areas of Welsh or English can be identified, in the sense of over half or two-thirds of people in an area coming from one background. To some extent the higher proportions of English in the commuter villages and small towns in the Vale provide the counterpart of this pattern at the city-region scale, but the fact that one is dealing with less than a quarter of the population in these areas should put the issue in perspective. Nevertheless, it is

167

possible to see a new phase of Anglicization in these areas, although the trend has not reached the stage of ethnic concentration usually identified with either ghettoes or completely exclusive elite areas.

(vi) Although Substandardness was linked to Overseas Ethnicity in the study the pattern of scores demonstrate its close association with the central city in a typical inner city zonal distribution around the core.

(vii) Finally, the Urban Fringe obviously identifies areas outside the continuously built-up area where new housing estates are intermingled with the still rural areas.

Similar generalized statements relating to spatial differentiation are difficult to derive from the city-regional study, given the complex nature of many of the axes. Much of the differentiation is associated with the typical Coalfield-Vale contrast and the growth communities. However, additional patterns to this basic division, such as those associated with the coastal belt, and with distance from the major centres of commercial and industrial activity in the lowland areas, can be recognized. These provide an additional degree of social complexity to the spatial patterns of the area.

**(e)** A final set of generalizations relates to the social regions, those that represent the areal grouping of the social typologies. It has already been shown (Chapter 2) that when communities or groups of enumeration areas have similar typological structures a socially homogeneous space is formed. If these units are adjacent to one another then social regions can be defined. Since the details of the social regions have already been described it remains to generalize these findings into models which crystallize the essential elements of these spatial patterns. These models are designed as summary frameworks derived from these areas, not as universal models of urban or regional form.

**(i)** In the case of Cardiff twelve separate types of area were identified. Additional types — namely, ethnic communities and inner city areas that have been privately renewed — can be added in the spatial model since they have been clearly identified in other centres. The relatively close association of these intra-urban types with distance from the city centre was used to construct a general spatial model of the urban social structure of British cities in which the community types are allocated to general locations (Figure 33). The tendency to misinterpret simplistic models of urban structure is fairly widespread, as can be seen by a comparison of Burgess's (1925) original, cautious, statements with the subsequent criticisms made of these ideas in most texts. It must be stressed that this model only provides a generalized interpretation of the social regions. In locational terms it goes beyond the specifics of Cardiff, yet the construction was primarily influenced by the findings of the case study. In any case no model is intended to incorporate the specific patterns of the real world city; there are always distortions caused by roads, rivers, parks, or trunctations caused by rivers, docks, industrial areas, etc. All such distortions are assumed away in this model. Obviously, this summary of social regions has similarities with the models posed by a long list of investigators, such as: Burgess (1925), Harris and Ullman (1945), Mann (1965), McGee (1969) and Robson

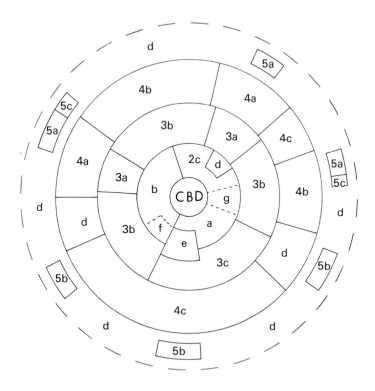

1. CENTRAL BUSINESS DISTRICT
   (RETAIL, OFFICES, WHOLESALING)

2. INNER CITY
a. SUBSTANDARD, WORKING CLASS
b. SUBSTANDARD, IMMIGRANT
c. BEDSIT, TRANSIENT
d. AGING STATUS
e. OLD COUNCIL
f. RENEWED : COUNCIL
g. RENEWED : GENTRIFICATION

3. MIDDLE CITY
   (LATE AND ESTABLISHED FAMILY)
a. HIGH STATUS
b. MIDDLE INCOME
c. COUNCIL HOUSING

4. OUTER CITY
a. HIGH STATUS
b. MIDDLE INCOME
c. COUNCIL HOUSING
d. UNDEVELOPED

5. FRINGE
a. HIGH STATUS
b. MIXED STATUS SATELLITES
c. OLDER VILLAGES
d. RURAL

FIGURE 33   A MODEL OF SOCIAL REGIONS IN BRITISH CITIES

(1975). The difference is that the model proposed here displays much more detailed social variations than those found in previous proposals and, more importantly, most of its areas are not implicitly assumed. They can be directly linked to the empirical evidence of the case study described here. Obviously this type of model cannot be applied to all cases. There is little doubt that larger British cities, for example, those of over a million population, or urban conurbations, will not have the same type of functional dependence upon a single central core. In such cases the city may not function as a single entity and alternative, or suburban, nuclei may be very important in the pattern of social differentiation. The result is that rather more complex regional patterns may be found in the city. Nevertheless, the model shown in Figure 33 and its associated community types may provide a useful summary description of the social regions of the size of city analyzed here, so long as the model is viewed as a hypothetical structure which gives approximate, not deterministic, directions for the various regional entities. In any real world situation the addition of area-specific distortions will complicate the model, and will reduce its use as a summary structure vis-a-vis the particular pattern of social regions. The advantage, however, of providing a summary statement of the social regions is to provide a framework for the spatial interpretation of the city, an introductory framework useful as a sampling or a descriptive tool.

(ii) At the city-regional level the community typologies do not fit so easily into a simple model with general geographical positions. Many of the community types that have been identified are scattered throughout the area rather than forming single homogeneous regions. This, of course, is not true at the most general scale of analysis — the three group level — where two of the community categories are found primarily in the traditional regional areas, 'Coalfield' and 'Vale'. But the 'Growth' communities cannot be described so simply. Although there is a concentration in the 'Valley Mouths' planning region, they can be found throughout the region. This result provides another illustration of the scale problem in geographical description. At the most general scale of description the broad regional division of 'Coalfield' and 'Vale' can be made — with the Growth communities overlapping these areas. At the more detailed scale the complexity of the social patterns found within each major region cannot be pinned down to a single geographical area. Social structure does not coincide neatly with geographical area. Yet it is possible to provide a diagrammatic representation of the various regional structures found in the area and their approximate relationships to one another in a community rather than a real world space. In this way the relationships between the various settlement type can be more easily identified. Figure 34 shows that the historical core of mining-iron working communities in the Coalfield is represented by relict, mining settlements. These are set within a general framework of old communities with continuing high levels of substandardness and a fringe of more rapidly renewing settlements near the new employment nodes. In the Vale the rural core is being changed by the transformations produced by commuter villages and housing estates, whilst the lowland urban centres have grown rapidly and show younger age profiles. Added to these basic patterns are the new growth areas — both privately and publicly developed

171

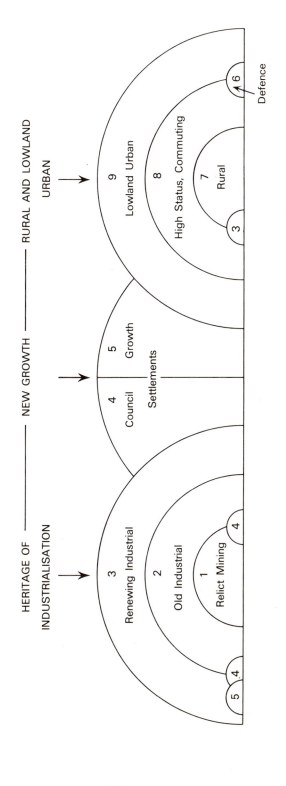

HERITAGE OF ——— NEW GROWTH ——— RURAL AND LOWLAND
INDUSTRIALISATION                                    URBAN

3
Renewing Industrial

2
Old Industrial

1
Relict Mining

4

4

5

5
Growth
Settlements

4
Council

9
Lowland Urban

8
High Status, Commuting

7
Rural

3

6

Defence

FIGURE 34   A MODEL OF COMMUNITY TYPES IN CARDIFF CITY-REGION

— areas which overlap the historical divisions and, especially in the case of the public council estates, are scattered throughout the region.

It must be emphasized, once again, that the question of how individual communities have attained the characteristics represented by these particular types can only be answered by reference to the complex variety of forces constantly at work changing the character of places — especially upon their resource bases, age of development, general location, and the effect of planning policy — in terms of industrial and residential rehabilitation. Only a detailed analysis of the historical development of each area would reveal which of these and other forces are of primary importance in accounting for any individual case. In addition, there is always the problem that the settlements as defined here represent aggregates of areas in which individual streets or zones may have more similar characteristics to some other type. These historical issues, as well as the more detailed scale changes, are outside the terms of reference of the analysis reported here. It has been enough to have defined the social differentiation of each settlement in terms of their aggregate characteristics as defined by a particular data set. Nevertheless, this data set does seem to have been sufficiently comprehensive to have identified far more dimensions of social variation than in previous analyses. Undoubtedly, more refined data will add to the list of characteristics, but on the basis of analogies with factorial work in psychology (Cattell, 1978), it is likely that these will be minor, additional, sources of variation, and that the axes revealed here will overlap with dimensions that more directly measure degrees of satisfaction, or quality of life, in the area.

The creation of these two models of social regions in the study area represents the final degree of abstraction and simplication in this study. The discussion has ranged from the identification of the problems of describing the character of urban places, through the definition of one particular approach to description (the Multivariate-Structural method), to a series of case studies illustrating this particular approach. Critics of the quantitative method in general can undoubtedly provide the usual arguments against the approach. In the last resort this boils down to the observation that counting is a substitute for thought, and that the generalizations provided could be obtained by simpler — perhaps intuitive — means. It is pointless denying that *any* generalization — whether the social regions produced or others — can be produced in a variety of different ways. Yet such a conclusion misses the main point of the study. The important issue is that measurements provide a common meaning about the nature of the phenomena among groups of people. So the lengthy technical discussions of this study are designed to provide evidence for this degree of agreement. There can be little doubt that improvements in measurement *will* be made in this area of research in the future, but until they are made the utility of the results of the exercise must be stressed. At the city-region scale, for example, the variations in 193 communities over 28 variables have been reduced to 5 dimensions of variation and 9 community types. Few would deny that it is impossible to simultaneously comprehend the variations in the original large data set in such a way as to reliably, yet subjectively, scale any *one* area against *all* the others. The multivariate measurements have completed this particular task. In doing so they have *complemented* our intuitive understanding of the areal differences of the region. More to the point, however, they can achieve this without the necessity for personal experience of life in the area. But, in addition, they have extended our knowledge of the settlements studied here by simply providing measurements of the degree of differences between the places.

Undoubtedly something of the flavour or character of the individual places is lost because of the procedures adopted. This is inevitable. It is the thesis of this study that all observations, measurements or experiences involve a certain degree of abstraction. So any description must be complemented by other methodologies if a balanced picture is to be attained. Such a pluralist attitude will not, of course, satisfy those who refer to the 'inhumanity' of the scientific approach (Harvey, 1973), or exponents of the idea that social scientific activity is performed 'on' rather than 'in' society (Gregory, 1978). For such workers 'society' not 'spatial character' or 'areal differentiation' is the key to their analysis and, in this focus on society as a whole, particular ideologies are the basic sources of variations. Such approaches, however, frequently have a commitment to a particular change and imply there is a single key to understanding. As Bottomore (1976, p. 169) has pointed out in the case of Marxist theory:

> the most obvious feature of its method is that it aims to locate all social phenomena in a specific historical context.

In other words, it is a particular or specific brand of evolutionary theory. This contemporary emphasis on society as the mainspring of social differentiation may represent a useful counterweight to decades of neglect of the relevance of social theory in human geography. However, the new degree of commitment to society surely take one beyond the confines of a distinctively geographical view; one becomes a social scientist in general, rather than one dealing with the particular, and still distinctively geographical problem of identifying and measuring the differentiation of places. In any case the results at different scales have shown that society alone is not the only factor at work. Moreover, it is worth quoting Bottomore (1976) once more:

> The principal contribution of recent structuralist doctrines has been . . . to re-assert the importance of structural analysis and of the development of structural models in the social sciences. Its influence on sociology . . . has not yet been very marked, but it may well lead us in the future to pay greater attention to the definition and classification of types of society and to the elucidation of the processes of change from one type to another as well as helping to introduce a greater rigour into such an analysis although we could have learned the lesson elsewhere.
>
> (Bottomore, 1976, p. 169.)

Such an opinion surely applies as much to the geographer as to the sociologist. Hence the task of this study has been to focus on the point about greater rigour in methodology and technique and to define the various types of society in an urban or social geographical context. Obviously the models and structures identified here have attempted to simplify the social relationships in order to provide the springboard for further study. Ideally, one should go beyond this interest in structures and models to deal with three related issues that would extend the focus of this study.

**(i)** Firstly, there is a need to identify the social and geographical processes that have created these structures. This would appear to involve the type of deep-seated approach that has been described as 'structuralism' in Chapter 2. In this context the discussion in the third part of this conclusion is important. It demonstrates that ecological or geographical forces should be as influential as others in this search for underlying causes. The spatial differentiation of places *cannot* be looked at only in terms of societal features; they provide the background, not the immediate cause of spatial differentiation. In the last thirty years the operation of specific planning policies have made important changes, although many of these changes are probably latent rather than manifest effects! Yet policy or causes have not been major objectives in this study. It has been enough to have identified a set of structures in terms of social dimensions and settlements, types than can be used as the elements to be explained by this theory.

**(ii)** Secondly, the work could proceed in the other direction, in the sense of using structural or contextual effects to determine the extent to which the communities and areas influence behaviour or attitudes. There is, after all, an acknowledgement, in literary terms (Smith, 1977), or in even caricature (Gren, 1979), of the distinctiveness of certain behavioural traits in the coalfield communities. Nevertheless, the fallacy of equating the ecological characteristics of places directly with individual behaviour or attitudes is well known and was emphasized in Chapter 2. Behaviour at an individual level relates to personal aspirations, values, and a multitude of other features not considered here, and these are not necessarily shared by *all* members of a community. But behaviour *does* take place in a context, and the characteristics of places may significantly affect these patterns. Such relationships are difficult to measure in the absence of experimental, control group, situations, and even when this has been attempted the influences that are relevant have rarely been clearly identified and separated out. In any case, such problems are more appropriately dealt with by sociologists or psychologists. What has been provided here that is of relevance to their work is a measurement of community differences, and, perhaps, a sampling frame for the choice of areas to study. Similarly, for planners, the identification of areal types and key indicators may ease their attempts to evaluate the effect of different types of policy on areas, although more subjective or attitudinal indicators would be valuable additions to the data set used here.

**(iii)** Thirdly, the study of the general characteristics of places needs to be complemented by views of the individuality of places; the place-particular features that represent the other side of the descriptive coin. Although it would be possible to separate the local peculiarities of places from the data set used in this study, in the last resort such quantitative features are probably less important than the subjectively derived views of places which may be more influential in behavioural terms. The first chapter of this study pointed out that such approaches demand a very different methodology or approach, and it is difficult to see how such community characterizations can be integrated with the type of study carried out in this monograph.

In this study, the search for the social dimensions and spatial patterns of a set of Welsh settlements has been placed in the context of alternative approaches to the study of urban differentiation, and has been developed within the generalizing methodology described as the Multivariate-Structural approach. Obviously other approaches exist, but it is always important to make the reason for any choice of objective and method explicit. This has been one of the primary concerns of this monograph. Yet the presence of so many alternatives represents part of the joy — yet also frustration — experienced by urban geographers. The multi-faceted character of places makes it impossible to accept only a single approach to the geographical study of places. Just as the geographers of old found new places to discover, so modern geographers have found new perspectives to apply to their studies. Yet as philosophers of science have constantly reminded us, the goal of complete understanding seems as elusive and unattainable as ever.

# REFERENCES

Abu-Lughod, J. (1969), 'Testing the Theory of Social Area Analysis', *American Sociological Review,* 34, pp. 198-212.

Adams, J. S. (1976) (ed.), *Contemporary Metropolitan America: Twenty Geographical Vignettes* (Cambridge, U.S.A., Ballinger).

Ames, H. B. (1898), *The City Under the Hill* (Reprinted, University of Toronto Press, 1973).

Alford, R. R. (1972), 'Critical Evaluation of the Principles of City Classification', in B. J. L. Berry (ed.), *City Classification Handbook* (J. Wiley, N. York), pp. 331-58.

Alihan, M. A. (1938), *Social Ecology* (New York).

Arnold, D. S. (1972), 'Classification as Part of Urban Management', in B. J. L. Berry (ed.), *City Classification Handbook* (J. Wiley, N. York), pp. 361-77.

Atkin, R. H. (1975), 'An Approach to Structure in Architectural and Urban Design', *Environment and Planning,* B, 2 pp. 21-57.

Banham, R. (1973), *Los Angeles: The Architecture of the Four Ecologies* (Pelican, London).

Ballard, P. H. and Jones, E. (eds) (1975), *The Valleys Call* (Jones, Publishers, Ferndale, Rhondda).

Barker, D. (1978), 'A Conceptual Approach to the Description and Analysis of an Historical Urban System', *Regional Studies,* 12, pp. 1-10.

Black, W. (1973), 'Towards a Factorial Ecology of Flows', *Economic Geography,* 49, pp. 59-67.

Bell, C. R. (1968), *Middle Class Families* (Routledge and Kegan Paul, London).

Bell, Daniel (1974), *The Coming of Post-Industrial Society* (Heinemann, London).

Bell, Wendell and Force, Maryanne (1956), 'Urban Neighbourhood Types and Participation in Formal Associations', *American Sociological Review,* 21, pp. 23-33.

Bell, W. and Moskos, C. C. Jnr. (1964), 'A Comment on Udry's Increasing Scale and Spatial Differentiation', *Social Forces,* 42, pp. 414-17.

Berry, B. J. L. (1969), 'Relationships between Regional Economic Development and the Urban System: The Case of Chile', *Tijdschrift voor Econ. Soc. Geografie,* 60, pp. 283-307.

Berry, B. J. L. and Rees, P. (1969), 'Factorial Ecology of Calcutta', *American Journal of Sociology,* 74, pp. 445-91.

Berry, B. J. L. (1971), 'Introduction. The Logic and Limitations of Comparative Factorial Ecology', *Economic Geography,* 47 (June Supplement), pp. 209-19.

Berry, B. J. L. (1972), *The City Classification Handbook* (J. Wiley, New York).

Berry, B. J. L. and Kasada, J. (1977), *Contemporary Urban Ecology* (Collier-Macmillan, New York).

Blanchard, R. (1935), *Grenoble: Etude de Geographie Urbaine* (2nd edition, Grenoble, France).

Blau, P. M. (1974), 'Parameters of Social Structure', *American Sociological Review,* 39, pp. 615-35.

Blau, P. M. (1976), *Approaches to the Study of Social Structure* (Open Books, London).

Booth, C. (1893), 'Life and Labour of the People in London', Presidential Address, *Journal of the Royal Statistical Society,* 55(4), pp. 557-91.

Booth, Charles (1902-3), *Life and Labour of the People of London,* (Reprinted 1969; A. Kelley, N. York).

Bottomore, T. (1976), 'Structure and History', in P. M. Blau (ed.), op. cit., 1976, pp. 159-71.

Bourne, L. S. and Murdie, R. A. (1972), 'Interrelationships of Social and Physical Space in the City', *Canadian Geographer,* 16, pp. 211-29.

Bowen, E. G. and Carter, H. (1974), 'Preliminary Observations on the Distribution of the Welsh Language at the 1971 Census', *Geographical Journal,* 140(3), pp. 432-40.

Burgess, E. W. (1925), 'The Growth of the City', in Park, R. E. *et al.* (1925), *The City* (University of Chicago Press; Reprinted 1965), pp. 37-44.

Burt, C. L. (1950), 'Tests of Significance in Factor Analysis', *British Journal of Psychol. Statistics,* 5, pp. 109-33.

Castells, M. (1977), *The Urban Question: A Marxist Approach* (Ed. Arnold, London, 2nd edition).

Cattell, R. B. (1966), 'Scree Test for the Number of Factors', *Multivariate Behavioural Research,* 1, pp. 245-76.

Cattell, R. B. (1968), 'Higher Order Factor Structures', in C. Banks and P. L. Broadhurst (eds.), *Studies in Psychology* (University of London Press), pp. 223-66.

Cattell, R. B. (1978), *The Scientific Use of Factor Analysis* (Plenum Press, N. York).

Carter, F. (1972), *Dubrovnik: A Classic City State* (Academic Press, London).

Carter, H. (1957), 'The Vale of Glamorgan' in E. G. Bowen (ed.), *Wales* (Methuen, London), pp. 401-30.
Carter, H. (1965), *The Towns of Wales* (University of Wales Press, Cardiff).

Carter, H. (1973), *The Study of Urban Geography* (Arnold, London).

Carter, H. (1974), 'Scale and the Dimensions of Socio-Economic Spatial Variation', *Geoforum,* 19, pp. 467-74.

Clark, D. (1973), 'The Formal and Functional Structure of Wales', *Annals, Association of American Geographers,* 63(1), pp. 71-84.

Clark, D. (1973), 'Normality, Transformation and the Principal Component Solution', *Area,* 5, pp. 110-13.

Clark, D., Davies, W. K. D., and Johnston, R. J. (1974), 'The Application of Factor Analysis in Human Geography', *The Statistician,* 23, pp. 327-57.

Childe, V. G. (1950), 'The Urban Revolution', *Town Planning Review,* 21, pp.3-21.

Cliff, A. D. and Ord, J. K. (1973), *Spatial Autcorrelation* (Pion, London).

Clifton-Taylor, A. (1980), *Six English Towns: A Pattern of Building* (B.B.C. Publications, London).

Cobb, R. (1975), *A Sense of Place* (Duckworth, London).

Coser, L. A. (1976), 'Structure and Conflict', in Blau (ed.), op. cit., p. 210-19.

Cox, K. R. (1969), 'Voting in the London Suburbs: A Factor Analysis and Causal Model' in M. Dogan and S. Rokkan (eds.) *Quantitative Ecological Analysis in the Social Sciences* (Cambridge, M.I.T. Press), pp. 343-69.

Davie, M. R. (1938), 'The Pattern of Urban Growth' in G. P. Murdock (ed.), *Studies in the Science of Society* (New Haven, U.S.A.). Reprinted in G. A. Theodorson (ed.), *Studies in Human Ecology* (Evanston, Illinois, 1961), pp. 71-92.

Davies, W. K. D. (1970), 'Introduction to the Study of Urban Geography', in H. Carter, W. K. D. Davies (eds.), *Urban Essays: Studies in the Geography of Wales* (Longmans, U.K.).

Davies, W. K. D. (1972), 'Data Analysis in Urban Geography', *Geography,* 57, pp. 196-206.

Davies, W. K. D. (1972), 'Conurbation and City Region in an Administrative Borderland: A Study of Greater Swansea', *Regional Studies,* 6, pp. 217-36.

Davies, W. K. D. (1975), 'Variance Allocation and the Dimensions of British Cities', *Tijdschrift v. Econ. en Sociale Geografie,* 66, pp. 358-72.

Davies, W. K. D. (1975), 'A Multivariate Description of Calgary's Community Areas' in B. Barr (ed.), *Calgary,* Western Geographical Series, No. 11 (University of Victoria, B.C.), pp. 231-69.

177

Davies, W. K. D. (1975), 'Variance Allocation and the Dimensions of British Towns', *Tijdschrift v. Econ. en Soc. Geografie*, 66, pp. 358-72.

Davies, W. K. D. (1977), 'Towns and Villages of Wales', Chapter 7 in D. Thomas (ed.), *Wales: A New Study* (David and Charles, Newton Abbot), pp. 191-225.

Davies, W. K. D. and Musson, T. C. (1978), 'Spatial Patterns of Commuting in South Wales: 1951-71', *Regional Studies*, 12, pp. 353-66.

Davies, W. K. D. (1978), 'Charles Booth and the Measurement of Urban Social Structure', *Area*, pp. 290-6.

Davies, W. K. D. (1978), 'The Social Taxonomy of Edmonton's Community Areas in 1971'' in P. Smith (ed.), *Edmonton*, Western Geographical Series (University of Victoria, B.C.), pp. 161-97.

Davies, W. K. D. (1978), 'Alternative Factorial Solutions and Urban Social Structure', *Canadian Geographer*, 22, pp. 273-97.

Davies, W. K. D. (1980), 'Higher Order Factor Analysis and Functional Regionalization', *Environment and Planning*, A (12), pp. 685-701.

Davies, W. K. D. and Barrow, G. (1973), 'A Comparative Factorial Ecology of Three Canadian Prairie Cities', *Canadian Geographer*, 17 (4), pp. 327-57.

Davies, W. K. D. and Lewis, G. J. (1973), 'The Urban Dimensions of Leicester, England', in B. Clark and B. Gleave (eds.), *'Social Patterns in Cities'*, Institute of British Geographers Special Publication No. 5, pp. 71-86.

Davies, W. K. D. and Lewis, G. J. (1974), 'The Social Patterning of a British City, Leicester, England', *Tijdschrift v. Econ. en Soc. Geografie*, 65, pp. 95-107.

Davies, W. K. D. and Welling, S. L. (1977), 'The Socio-Economic Differentiation of Alberta Towns in 1971', in B. M. Barr (ed.), *Research Studies by Western Canadian Geographers: The Edmonton Papers* (Tantalus Press, Vancouver), pp. 77-97.

Davies, W. K. D. and Tapper, S. (1979), 'Urban Dimensionality of the Major American S.M.S.A. System, 1970', Unpublished paper presented to Annual Meeting, Western Division of Canadian Association of Geographers, Calgary, 1979.

Davies, W. K. D. and Thompson, R. R. (1980), 'The Structure of Inter-Urban Connectivity: A Dyadic Factor Analysis of Prairie Commodity Flows', *Regional Studies*, 14(4), pp. 297-312.

Dent, O. and Sakoda, J. M. (1973), 'Potential Sources of Spuriousness in Factor Ecology Studies', Institute of British Geographers: Quantitative Methods Study Group Working Paper No. 1, Birmingham Meeting, Jan., 1973, pp. 37-44.

Davis, K. (1972), *The City: Essays from Scientific American* (W. Freeman, San Francisco).

Dubos, Rene (1968), *So Human an Animal* (Chas Scribner, N. York).

Engels, F. (1845), *Die Lage der arbei, tenden Klasse in England*. (Translated into English for London edition (1892) as *The Conditions of the Working Class in England in 1844)*. Reprinted 1962.

Eisenstadt, S. N. (1973), *Tradition, Change and Modernity* (J. Wiley, N. York).

Evans, D. J. (1973), 'Urban Social Structures in South Wales' in B. Clark and B. Gleave (eds.), *Social Patterns in Cities*, Institute of British Geographers, Special Publication No. 5, pp. 87-102.

Feyman, R. (1965) *The Character of Physical Law* (Cox and Wyman, London).

Fortes, M. (ed.) (1949), *Social Structure: Studies Presented to A. R. Radcliffe-Brown* (Clarendon Press, Oxford).

Fischer, C. S. (1974), 'Toward a Subcultural Theory of Urbanism', *American Journal of Sociology*, 80(6), pp. 1319-41.

Friedmann, J. (1972), 'A General Theory of Polarized Development', in N. M. Hansen (ed.), *Growth Centres in Regional Economic Development* (Free Press, N. York), pp. 82-107.

Fredericks, M. W. (1965), 'Towns and Houses' in J. P. V. D. Balsdon (ed.), *Roman-Civilisation* (Pelican), pp. 151-69.

Gans, H. (1962), 'Urbanism and Suburbanism as a Way of Life' in A. Rose (ed.), *Human Behaviour and Social Processes* (Macmillan, N. York), pp. 625-48.

Giggs, J. and Mather, P. (1975), 'Factorial Ecology and Factorial Invariance', *Economic Geography,* 51(4), pp. 366-82.

Giggs, J. A. (1970), 'Socially Disorganized Areas in Barry: A Multivariate Analysis' in H. Carter and W. K. D. Davies (eds.), *Urban Essays: Studies in the Geography of Wales* (Longmans, U.K.), pp. 101-43.

Giggs, J. A. (1973), 'The Distribution of Schizophrenics in Nottingham', *Transactions of the Institute of British Geographers,* 59, pp. 55-76.

Gittus, Elizabeth (1964), 'The Structure of Urban Areas', *Town Planning Review,* 35, pp. 5-20.

Gould, P. R. (1980), 'Q Analysis', *International Journal of Man-Machine Studies.*

Gregory, D. (1978), *Ideology, Science and Human Geography* (Hutchinson, London).

Gren (1979), *Ponty and Pop: The Aberflyarf Story* (Funfare Press, Cardiff).

Hagood, M. J. (1943), 'Statistical Methods for Delineation of Regions Applied to Data on Agriculture and Population', *Social Forces,* 21, pp. 287-97.

Hall, P. (1968), *The World Cities* (Weidenfeld and Nicolson, London).

Hardy, Thomas (1886), *The Mayor of Casterbridge,* Reprinted in J. Moynaham (ed.), *The Portable Thomas Hardy* (Penguin Inc. 1977).

Harman, H. H. (1976), *Modern Factor Analysis* (University of Chicago Press, Revised Edition).

Harris, C. and Ullman, E. (1945), 'The Nature of Cities', *Annals. American Academy of Political and Social Science,* 142, pp. 7-17.

Harvey, D. (1973), *Social Justice and the City* (Ed. Arnold, London).

Herbert, D. T. (1970), 'Principal Components Analysis and Urban Social Structure: A Study of Cardiff and Swansea' in Carter, H. and Davies, W. K. D. (eds.), *Urban Essays: Studies in Geography of Wales* (Longmans, U.K.), pp. 79-100.

Herbert, D. T. (1977), 'An Areal and Ecological Analysis of Delinquency Residence: Cardiff 1966 and 1971', *Tijdschrift v. E. S. Geografie,* 68, pp. 83-99.

Herbert, D. T. and Evans, D. J. (1973), 'Urban Environment and Juvenile Delinquency', Report for U.K. Home Office Research Unit (Geography Dept., University, College, Swansea).

Hitt, W. D. (1968), 'Two Models of Man', *American Psychologist,* 24, pp. 651-8.

Hodge, G. (1968), 'Urban Structure and Regional Development', *Papers and Proceedings of the Regional Science Association,* 21, pp. 101-23.

Homans, G. C. (1976), 'What do we mean by 'Social Structure'?' in P. M. Blau (ed.), *Approaches to the Study of Social Structure* (Open Books Publishing Ltd., London), pp. 53-65.

Hoselitz, B. (1955), 'Generative and Parasitic Cities', *Economic Development and Cultural Change,* 3, pp. 278-94.

Hoyt, H. (1939), *The Structure and Growth of Residential Neighbourhoods in American Cities* (F. H. A. Washington, D.C.).

Hughes, J. A. and Carey, G. W. (1972), 'Factorial Ecology: Oblique and Orthogonal Solutions', *Environment and Planning,* 4, pp. 147-62.

Humphrys, G. (1972), *South Wales* (David and Charles, Newton Abbot).

Hunter, A. A. (1972), 'Factorial Ecology: A Critique and Some Suggestions', *Demography*, 9, pp. 107-18.

Hunter, A. A. and Latif, A. H. (1973), 'Stability and Change in the Ecological Structure of Winnipeg', *Revue of Canadian Sociology and Anthropology*, 6, pp. 167-78.

Hunter, A. A. (1974), *Symbolic Communities* (University of Chicago Press).

Jackson, J. N. (1972), *The Urban Future* (Allen and Unwin, London).

Johnston, R. J. (1968), 'Choice in Classification: The Subjectivity of Objective Methods', *Annals, Association of American Geographers*, 58, pp. 575-89.

Johnston, R. J. (1971), *Urban Residential Patterns* (Bell, London).

Johnston, R. J. (1972), 'Towards a General Model of Intra-Urban Residential Patterns', in C. Board, P. Haggett, et al., *Progress in Geography*, 4, pp. 83-115.

Johnston, R. J. (1978), 'Residential Area Characteristics: Research Methods for Identifying Urban Sub-Areas', in D. T. Herbert and R. J. Johnston (eds.), *Social Areas in Cities: Processes, Patterns and Problems* (J. Wiley, London, N. York), pp. 193-236.

Johnston, R. J. (1979), 'On the Characterization of Urban Social Areas', *Tijdschrift voor Economische en Sociale Geografie*, 70(4), pp. 232-8.

Johnston, R. J. (1977), 'Regarding Urban Origins, Urbanization and Urban Patterns', *Geography*, 62, pp. 1-8.

Jones, P. N. (1978), 'The Distribution of Coloured Immigrants in the U.K.', *Transactions of Institute of British Geographers*, 3(4), pp. 515-92.

King, L. J. (1969), *Statistical Analysis in Geography* (Prentice Hall, Englewood Cliffs, N.J.).

Knox, P. L. and MacLaran, P. (1978), 'Values and Perceptions in Descriptive Approaches to Urban Social Geography', in D. T. Herbert and R. J. Johnston (eds.), *Geography and the Urban Environment: Progress in Research and Applications, I.* (J. Wiley, London), pp. 197-248.

Lapidus, M. (ed.) (1969), *Middle Eastern Cities* (University of California Press).

Levi-Strauss, C. (1952), 'Social Structure' in A. L. Kroeber (ed.), *Anthropology Today* (University of Chicago Press), pp. 321-90.

Liu, B-C. (1977), *Quality of Life Indicators in U.S. Metropolitan Areas: A Statistical Analysis* (Praeger, N. York).

Lovejoy, A. O. (1953), 'The Meanings of Emergence and its Modes', in P. P. Weiner (ed.), *Readings in the Philosophy of Science* (Scribner's, N. York), pp. 119-47.

Lovejoy, A. O. (1929), *The Revolt Against Dualism* (Open Court Publishing Company, La Salle, Indiana; Reprinted 1955).

Lynch, K. (1960), *The Image of the City* (M.I.T. Press).

Manners, G. (1965), *South Wales in the Sixties* (Pergamon Press, Oxford).

Mayhew, H. (1862), *London Labour and London Poor*, 1-4, 1862 (Griffin and Bohn, London; Reprinted, Dover Publications, London, 1968).

McElrath, D. C. (1968), 'Societal Scale and Social Differentiation, Accra, Ghana', in S. Greer, et al. (eds.), *The New Urbanization* (St. Martin's Press, N. York), pp. 33-52.

Marx, K. (1936), *Selected Works* (Reprinted by International Publishers, New York).

Marx, K. (1967), *Capital* (Three Volumes, International Publishers, New York, 1967 Edition).

McDonald, R. P. (1967), *Non Linear Factor Analysis*, Psychometrics Monograph 15.

McGee, T. (1967), *The South East Asian City* (Bell, London).

Mann, P. M. (1965), *An Approach to Urban Sociology* (Routledge and Kegan Paul, London).

Merton, R. K. (1976), 'Structural Analysis in Sociology', in P. M. Blau (1976) (ed.) op. cit., pp. 21-52.

Meyer, D. (1971), 'Factor Analysis Versus Correlation Analysis: Are Substantive Interpretations Congruent' in B. J. L. Berry (ed.), *Comparative Factorial Ecology, Economic Geography,* June 1971 (Supplement), pp. 336-43.

Meyers, W., Dorwart, R., and Kline, D. (1977), 'Social Ecology and Citizen Boards: A Problem for Planners', *American Institute of Planners Journal,* pp. 169-76.

Mid Glamorgan Planning Office, *Mid Glamorgan Structure Plan, 1978* (County Hall, Cardiff).

Morris, James (1960), *Venice* (Faber and Faber, London).

Morris, James (1963), *Cities* (Faber and Faber, London).

Moser, C. A. and Scott, W. (1961), *British Towns: A Statistical Study of their Social and Economic Differences* (Oliver and Boyd, Edinburgh).

Mumford, L. (1961), *The City in History* (Secker and Warburg, London).

Murdie, R. A. (1968), *Factorial Ecology of Metropolitan Toronto 1951-1961,* Department of Geography, University of Chicago Research Paper No. 116.

Murphey, R. (1954), 'The City as a Centre of Change', *Annals, Assoc. American Geographers,* 43, pp. 349-62.

Muth, R. F. (1969), *Cities and Housing* (University of Chicago Press).

Nie, N., Hall, C. H., Jenkins, J. G., Steinbrenner, K., Bent, D. H. (1975), *Statistical Package for the Social Sciences* (McGraw Hill, N. York; Revised Edition, 1975).

Nisbet, R. A. (1969), *Social Change and History* (Oxford University Press).

Newton, P. W. and Johnston, R. J. (1976), ''Residential Area Characteristics and Residential Area Homogeneity', *Environment and Planning,* A, 5, pp. 543-52.

Palm, R. (1973), 'Factorial Ecology and the Community of Outlook', *Annals, Association of American Geographers,* 63, pp. 341-6.

Park, R. E. (1925), 'The City as a Social Laboratory', p. 46 in T. V. Smith and L. White (eds.), *Chicago: An Experiment in Social Science Research* (University of Chicago Press), pp. 46-63.

Parsons, Talcot (1960), *Structure and Process in Modern Societies* (Free Press, N. York).

Parsons, Talcot (1964), 'A Functional Theory of Change' in A. and E. Etzioni (eds.), *Social Change* (Basic Books, N. York), pp. 83-97.

Peach, Ceri (ed.) (1975), *Urban Social Segregation* (Longman, U.K.).

Pearson, K. (1893), 'Contributions to the Mathematical Theory of Evolution', *Journal of the Royal Statistical Society,* 55(4), pp. 675-9.

Pennal, R. (1972), 'Routinely Compatible Confidence Intervals for Factor Loadings Using the Jack Knife', *British Journal of Mathematical Statistical Psychology,* 25, pp. 107-14.

Perle, E. D. (1977), 'Scale Changes and Impacts on Factorial Ecology Structures', *Environment and Planning,* A, pp. 549-58.

Piaget, J. (1970), *Structuralism* (Basic Books, N. York).

Poor, D. D. S. and Wherry, R. J. (1976), 'The Invariance of Multidimensional Configurations', *British Journal of Mathematical and Statistical Psychology,* 29, pp. 114-25.

Price, D. O. (1942), 'Factor Analysis in the Study of Metropolitan Centres', *Social Forces,* 20, pp. 449-55.

Przeworski, A. and G. and Soares, G. A. D. (1971), 'Theories in Search of a Curve: A Contextual Interpretation of Left Vote', *American Political Science Review,* 65, pp. 51-68.

Przeworski, A. (1974), 'Contextual Models of Political Behaviour', *Political Methodology*, 1, pp. 27-60.

Radcliffe-Brown, A. R. (1940), 'On Social Structure', *Journal Royal Anthropological Institute*, 61, pp. 1-19.

Rees, P. H. (1970), 'The Factorial Ecology of Metropolitan Chicago' in B. J. L. Berry and F. L. Horton (eds.), *Geographic Perspectives on Urban Systems* (Prentice-Hall, N. Jersey), pp. 319-365.

Rees, P. H. (1972), 'Problems of Classifying Sub-Areas Within Cities', in Berry, op. cit. (1972), pp. 265-330.

Robinson, W. S. (1950), 'Ecological Correlations and the Behaviour of Individuals', *American Sociological Review*, 15, pp. 351-7.

Robson, B. T. (1969), *Urban Analysis* (Cambridge University Press).

Robson, B. T. (1973), 'A View on the Human Scene' in M. Chisholm and B. Rodger (ed.), *Studies in Human Geography* (Heinemann, London), pp. 203-41.

Robson, B. T. (1975), *Urban Social Areas* (Oxford University Press, London).

Romsa, G., Hoffman, W., and Brozowski (1972), 'A Test of the Influence of Scale in Factorial Ecology on Windsor, Ontario', *Ontario Geographer* (7), pp. 87-92.

Rummel, R. J. (1971), *Applied Factor Analysis* (North Western University Press).

Rumley, D. (1979), 'The Study of Structural Effects in Human Geography', in *Tijdschrift voor Economische en Sociale Geografie*, 70(6), pp. 350-60.

Schwirian, K. P. and Smith, R. K. (1974), 'Primary, Modernization and Urban Structure' in K. P. Schwirian, *Comparative Urban Structure* (D. C. Heath), pp. 324-37.

Shaw, C. R., Zorbaugh, F. M., McKay, H. D. and Lottrell, L. (1929), *Delinquency Areas* (Chicago).

Shevky, E. and Bell, W. (1955), *Social Area Analysis* (Stanford University Press).

Shevky, E. and Williams, M., *The Social Areas of Los Angeles* (Berkeley, 1949).

Simmey, T. S. (1969), 'Charles Booth' in T. Raison (ed.), *The Founding of Social Science* (Penguin), pp. 92-9.

Sjorberg, G. (1962), *The Pre-Industrial City* (Free Press, Glencoe).

Smith, D. M. (1972), *The Geography of Social Well Being* (McGraw-Hill, N. York).

Smith, David (1976), 'Myth and Meaning in the Literature of the South Wales Coalfield: The 1930s', *Anglo-Welsh Review*, 25, pp. 21-42.

Smith, R. H. T. (1965), 'Method and Purpose in Functional Town Classification', *Annals, American Geographers*, Vol. 55(3), pp. 539-48.

Sneath, P. H. A. and Sokal, R. R. (1973), *Numerical Taxonomy* (W. H. Freeman, San Francisco).

Spearman, C. (1904), 'General Intelligence, Objectively Determined and Measured', *American Journal of Psychology*, 15, pp. 201-93.

Sweetser, F. L. (1965), 'Factorial Ecology: Helsinki 1960', *Demography*, 2, pp. 372-86.

Sweetser, F. L. (1965), 'Factor Structure as Ecological Structure in Helsinki and Boston', *Acta Sociologica*, 8, pp. 205-25.

Suttles, G. D. (1972), *The Social Construction of Communities* (University of Chicago Press).

Suttles, G. D. (1968), *The Social Order of the Slum* (University of Chicago Press).

Thomas, Dylan (1943), 'Reminiscences of Childhood', BBC Welsh Home Service Broadcast, Feb. 15th, 1943. (Reprinted in *Quite Early One Morning*, J. M. Dent & Sons; Reprinted 1971, p. 1).

Timms, D. (1971), *The Urban Mosaic*, Cambridge University Press.

Tyron, R. C. (1955), *Identification of Social Areas by Cluster Analysis* (University of California Press, Berkeley).

Tuan, Y. F. (1974), *Topophilia* (Prentice Hall, N.J.).

Udry, J. R. (1964), 'Increasing Scale and Spatial Differentiation: New Tests of Theories from Shevky and Bell', *Social Forces,* 42, pp. 403-13.

Van Arsdol, M., Camillieri, S. F. and Schmid, C. F. (1958), 'The Generality of Urban Social Area Indices', *American Sociological Review,* 23, pp. 277-84.

Vance, J. E. (1964), *Geography and Urban Evolution in the San Francisco Bay Area* (Institute of Government Studies, Berkeley, Calif.).

Vance, J. E. (1977), *This Scene of Man* (Harper's College Press, U.S.A.).

Velicer, W. F. (1977), 'An Empirical Comparison of the Similarity of Principal Components, Image and Factor Patterns', *Journal of Multivariate Behavioural Research,* 12, pp. 3-22.

Ward, J. H. (1963), 'Hierarchical Grouping to Optimize an Objective Function', *Journal of the American Statistical Association,* 58, pp. 236-43.

Webber, M. M. (1964), 'The Urban Place and Non-Place Urban Realms' in M. Webber et al. (eds.), *Explorations in Urban Structure* (University of Pennsylvania Press), pp. 79-153.

Webber, R. J. (1977), *The National Classification of Residential Neighbourhoods,* Planning Research Applications Group, Paper No. 23, Centre for Environmental Studies, London.

Weber, M. (1921), *The City* (Reprinted, Free Press Glencoe, 1958).

Welsh Office (1969), *Welsh Housing Condition Survey* (H.M.S.O., Cardiff).

Wheatley, R. (1974), *Pivot of the Four Quarters* (Aldine Press, U.S.A.).

Wilson, G. and Wilson, M. (1945), *The Analysis of Social Change* (Cambridge, U.K.).

Wirth, L. (1938), 'Urbanism as a Way of Life', *American Journal of Sociology,* 44, pp. 1-24.

Wishart, D. (1975), *CLUSTAN IC* (Package Program Manual, University of London Computing Centre, U.K.).

Woodsworth, J. S. (1911), *My Neighbour* (Reprinted by University of Toronto Press, 1972).

Yeats, W. B. (1938), *A Vision* (Macmillan).

Yeates, M. H. and Garner, B. J. (1976), *The North American City* (Harper and Row, N. York).

Young, D. (1965), *Edinburgh in the Age of Walter Scott* (University of Oklahoma Press).

Zorbaugh, H. W. (1926), 'The Natural Areas of the City', *Publications of American Sociological Society,* 20, pp. 128-97.